Logic of the Collection

LOGIC OF THE COLLECTION

BORIS GROYS

Sternberg Press

CONTENTS

PREFACE

COLLECTION AND REPRESENTATION

This book consists of two parts: the first is a translation of a collection of essays from the 1990s originally published in German, and the second compiles essays written two decades later. Each chapter reflects an interest in the fate of collections in the contemporary world. The renewed theoretical interest in the museum and other traditional collections over the last decades is related to the growing importance of the internet. Here questions emerge concerning the role of museums and art collections as institutions of memory and the ability of the internet to preserve images from the past and present. The comparison between collecting as an analog practice and the digital memory of the internet demonstrates that the criteria of selection in each field are different. And it is precisely these selection criteria by which collections that I discuss in the essays in this book.

Writings on collecting often depict the collector's position, describing a particular collection as reflecting the collector's personal taste and the tastes of the milieu in which they lived. This approach is, of course, totally legitimate, but the psychology and sociology of collecting is not what primarily interests me here. I am interested in the question of what collections have in common much more than in their differences. It seems obvious that every collection is defined by an interplay between the identical and the different. For example, if we decide to collect butterflies, we need to identify them to distinguish between them and all other insects. But we probably wouldn't collect only the same kind of butterflies. To create a collection of identical butterflies would be an interesting artistic project but not a collection in the usual sense of the word. Thus, a collection is always a collection of differences among the similar. A collection is representative if it contains every variation within a certain species or class of objects. To continue with the example, every collection of butterflies is not expected to be completely representative and include at least one specimen of every kind of butterfly known to science. But the sum of all collections of butterflies is expected to do just that. And if something is missing in the universal collection of butterflies, there will always be a collector who will notice and fill the gap. The goal of universal representation dictates the logic of collecting, which is understood not as a personal but rather as a collective, even anonymous practice.

Since the number of kinds of butterflies is finite, the goal of creating a collection or a set of collections that would be representative and include all kinds of butterflies is achievable. But what about art collections? One could argue that butterflies are not interested in having their corpses preserved in somebody's collection. But artists are interested in their artworks being collected and preserved—also after their death. The logic of collecting makes the promise that an individual artist can find a place in a collection and, at the same time, undermines this promise.

Art collections are expected to cover everything that we call art. Already at the beginning of the twentieth century, it became clear that everything previously considered nonart could now be identified as art. The production of identity became easy—but the production of differences remained a problem. And indeed there are different kinds of art—different media, styles, and so on. Standard art collections include only selected examples of different kinds of art. Collections of traditional art include art that originates in different cultures and thus looks different. However, under the conditions of modernity, artists in the same culture grasped the logic of collecting and began to consciously produce art that looked different from the art produced by other modern artists. Collectors were thus confronted with the task of including examples from every changing artistic style. The history of modern art can be described as a competition between the production of differences and the collection of differences. It first seemed that the production of differences would win the competition and the museum system would collapse. But the opposite was the case. The variety of art forms was quickly exhausted, and modern art was collected and musealized. It seemed that nothing new was possible anymore.

But this post-historical depression did not last long, and the problem of the production of difference was soon solved. In our times, to be different an artwork does not need to look different.

It is enough to show that the artwork was produced in a different cultural context or reflects a different cultural identity. A new competition has started between the production of differences and the collection of differences. And it seems that the museum system is losing the competition again. Indeed, museums are able to collect artworks but not their contexts, because they don't have the space or means to do so. Walter Benjamin recognized this when he spoke about the loss of aura that the practices of collecting and exhibiting produce—and by aura he meant the original cultural context of the artwork. However, the original context can be reconstructed—at least partially—by means of documentation. And contemporary museums and exhibitions are full of such documentation, the numbers of which seem potentially infinite. And so the finite space of art collections is in danger of being surpassed by the attempts to document and re-create as many of the original art contexts as possible.

We are only at the beginning of this new competition, but it is already clear that it is moving increasingly from the space of the traditional collection into digital space. The volume of digital memory seems almost infinite—at least compared to the traditional, analogue collection spaces. And digitalization promises an easy way to document the particular cultural contexts, including individual contexts—for instance, media platforms like Facebook or Instagram. However, digital hardware is also finite. And after a while we might come to the conclusion that the differences among cultural contexts are also finite in number. In this case, the trajectory of this new competition would repeat the previous one. The logic of collecting remains the same, even if the field of its application changes. And it is this permanence of the logic of the collection, and not the historical shifts and changes of the collecting practice, that is thematized in this book first and foremost.

PART 1

THE MUSEUM IN THE MEDIA AGE

Art today seems ready to follow the temptations of the media age and move out of the museum, with the goal of being spread through new channels. However, the value of art in the media context is hardly identical to its relevance in the art context. Decisions that are relevant for the art milieu—that is, purely formal, artistic decisions—leave the public cold. The times are over when the museum's presentation of hitherto "alternative" art forms was considered a media event. Different avant-gardes of the twentieth century benefited greatly from the press's attention to new art forms. The media nowadays is mainly interested in names that are already known to the public, and when the artistically new is discussed in the media it is only for reasons that are not specifically artistic.

The willingness of art to enter the media, public space, or politics—in other words, the space outside the museum—is quite understandable. In this way, art can reach and seduce a larger audience, and money can be earned that previously had to be solicited from the state or private sponsors—which gives artists a new sense of power, social relevance, and presence. This reason for leaving the museum, along with many others, is legitimate. And this book does not want to mourn, glorify, or transfigure the museum as an eternal, exclusive place of art, or call for stopping the course of time and preserving the museum as a privileged art context. The demand to preserve the museum would be paradoxical anyway, because the museum is a place of storage, and there can be no other place where the storage can itself be stored.

Rather, it is interesting to ask what the museum is today, and thereby benefit from the museum's new, questionable status. The museum is often understood as a place of memory, collecting and storing only what has been proved to be historically relevant, valuable, and important. Historical museums recall important historical events, automobile museums cars that are no longer manufactured, aircraft museums planes that no longer fly. Such museums have always existed, they continue to exist, and they always will exist. Thus, such museums are not the subject of this essay collection.

The subject of this essay collection is the art museum. The question is: What does it mean to collect art? The following chapters would like to answer this question.

At first glance, it seems that collecting art is no different from collecting cars or planes. One has to find works of art that have been proved to be historically relevant, important, meaningful, seductive—and collect them. The first difficulties begin to emerge, however, when one asks: How, and in what function, have the things we call works of art acquired historical significance? At least for the period prior to the creation of the modern art museum, these objects fulfilled certain pragmatic functions and could be collected under this aspect. In this way, paintings and sculptures of the past can be collected in a museum that documents the lifestyle and design of past epochs, or in a museum that reconstructs the religious rites of the past. The fact that certain items enter an art museum does not mean that these items used to function as art. On the contrary, these objects begin to function as art only after they are included in an art museum. All museums, except art museums, are cemeteries of things: what is collected is deprived of its vital function—that is, it is dead. The life of the artwork, on the other hand, only begins in the museum: it is, from the outset, life after death. The modern art museum is not a place of memory, because the objects collected in it were not considered artworks before their musealization. Rather, the memory of the earlier, pre-museum life of the artworks is erased by their inclusion in the art museum. This loss of memory is the prerequisite for objects of practical life to acquire a new function and begin a new life as artworks.

The modern art museum is thus not a cemetery but, if you will, a church for things. These things experience their repentance, their new birth, their second coming. They receive their baptism—or their portion of vampiric blood—which awakens them to new, eternal life. In modernity, such newborn things are called works of art. The museum replaced the church after humans conceived of themselves as things as a result of secularization. Being reduced to things, humans, as always happens in such cases, began to sacralize things. Therefore, even in modernity, only the things that initially display themselves as "nonart" have a chance to be included in the museum. On the contrary, art that displays itself from the outset as art and is reminiscent of artworks that can be found in the museum is rejected as kitsch. One has to first live a sinful, "real" life in order to be converted and saved. Those who reveal themselves to be too pious from the beginning are exposed as hypocrites and condemned. Certainly this is the concept of art as it first developed in modernity—that is, in the time of museums—but this concept is still valid for the present. Modern art has drawn all sorts of consequences from this concept, the readymade method being the most consistent one. And in fact, if musealization turns a thing into a work of art, anything can become a work of art—the only decision needed is taken by an artistic subjectivity regarding a certain object. The modern museum is therefore the place where modern subjectivity as such manifests itself directly—beyond labor, work, self-objectification, or alienation. Modern artistic subjectivity does not produce the work of art but creates it through a pure decision of will, through the act of pure contemplation—not in time, but in the moment. It can of course be said that such a pure manifestation of subjectivity is in fact never achieved. But here we speak of the regulative idea of the modern art museum, which, although it cannot be realized with ultimate radicalism, still determines the internal dynamics of art in the modern age.

Certainly today works of art are produced that do not find their place in the museum but are nevertheless perceived as works of art. However, they are only perceived this way because they are imaginatively placed in the museum context. Thus, one can consider any object in the context of "ordinary life" a work of art without explicitly including this object in the museum as a readymade, but the ability to see things as artworks is given to us by the museum, by familiarizing ourselves with the function of the readymade process in the museum. Free subjectivity can only be manifested as free because it is relieved of the work of art production by the museum, as the museum assumes this work. The difference between art and nonart is itself artificial. This difference cannot be revealed, discovered, or ordered, it can only be produced: the museum is the place where the difference between art and nonart is produced.

Each work of art is produced through a combination of repetition and deviation: through repetition the work of art is legitimized as a work of art, and deviation shows the originality of the particular work, which refers to the individuality of its creator. Placing the work of art in the museum, however, largely relieves it of the task of repeating artistic tradition, for this task is now taken over by the museum context. Thus, the museum-based work of art can exclusively demonstrate the deviation from tradition—that is, the pure individuality of the artist. The collective work of storage invested in the museum thus serves to relieve the individual of the task of performing an individual work of repetition. This collective work is enormous, because the construction, equipping, and maintenance of the museum costs society, which is mostly unappreciative of modern art, a great deal of money and effort. This cost is imposed on society by modern, enlightened governments. The museum's staging of free artistic subjectivity takes place according to an ideological mandate of the modern state, which feels obliged to protect the individuality of its citizens. If this staging diminishes or is no longer socially attractive, it means that one's individuality has lost its symbolic meaning and no longer represents a great social value.

The statement that the free subjectivity of the individual is staged in the museum only through collective work does not indicate contempt of subjectivity: only under certain—and problematic—metaphysical presuppositions can one come to the conclusion that staged subjectivity in some sense is worse or more deficient than "true" subjectivity. Subjectivity is produced; it is even the actual art product. But despite being produced, it is no less "real" than other products of civilization. The decision not to produce free subjectivity would therefore be a relatively momentous decision. And it would be made if museums were abandoned, because museums are the most effective production sites of subjectivity in modernity.

Subjectivity was and is produced through asceticism, prohibition, and renunciation. In this sense, too, the modern museum is the successor of the church and the monastery. The modern museum is a closed and bright space that clearly separates itself from the outside world, which it leaves in the dark. The museum excludes "the other" in at least two ways: first, all objects outside the museum are excluded from the viewer's field of vision; second, the museum itself is hidden from view in its materiality, practice, and institutionality. Thus a visitor feels imprisoned inside the museum—and wants to break away from its embrace. Subjectivity arises through this desire. It is therefore the primary function of the museum to create the illusion of a free space outside its walls that can function as the field of free subjectivity. If the museum is dismantled, the free space hidden behind it disappears. And again, the illusion of free space is no different from "real" space. When the illusion of free space disappears, the reality of subjectivity disappears with it.

The free space outside the museum is so-called reality or life—but understood as the profane space of potential museum collecting or, in other words, the artistic mission. Viewed from the well-lit narrowness of the museum's interior spaces, reality presents itself as the sum of everything that has "not yet" been collected, exposed, illuminated, perceived, and experienced as art—and that therefore remains hidden in the dark. The subjectivity imprisoned in the museum thus experiences reality "aesthetically"—that is, as a potential object of enlightenment, of pure contemplation in the light of the museum. The things of the outside world are to be converted, saved, resuscitated, brought to light; they are in need, and artistic subjectivity feels summoned to free them from their misery and transport them into the interior of the museum to preserve them for eternity. Out of this missionary spirit emerged the avant-gardes of the twentieth century, who repeatedly protested that "other" things are still not recognized, exhibited, enlightened, or saved by the museum. The internal logic of the museum collection manifests itself in the fact that the mere assertion that the other is the other—and thus new to the museum collection—is enough to give value to this other in the museum. Whenever a politically, aesthetically, or otherwise motivated demand is made to include the other, the repressed, or the excluded in the museum, this demand is actually completely superfluous, because it follows the internal logic of the museum collection itself.

Therefore, the eventual abandoning of the museum system should not be situated in the tradition of the struggle against the museum led by modern art in the twentieth century. Those who today scorn the museum and borrow their arguments from the artistic avant-gardes forget that the avant-garde commitment to life always seeks the artistic—that is, ultimately museum-inspired—transformation and salvation of life. The artistic avant-gardes sought to enter the free space created by the museum itself. At the same time, artistic asceticism, prohibition, and renunciation were tightened. Every avant-garde is first and foremost reductionist: it always forbids what was done earlier, it practices an ever-stricter asceticism, it removes more and more possibilities from the artist until nothing more remains than the pure gaze into dark, empty space (i.e., Malevich's *Black Square*). The art of the avant-garde, therefore, has its sole place in the museum, which stores and exposes all it has collected in life, and thus interprets life itself as nothing but the empty space of imagination. The abolition of the museum would therefore mean not that the free space beyond the museum space opened up, but that this space disappeared.

However, the abolition of the museum is not the only danger threatening it. Inherent in the museum is the danger of totalizing its view and conceiving of the whole world as a museum, with the line between the museum and its external space disappearing. The museum then becomes an ideology—and the many ideologies of modernity can be interpreted as different ways to expand the museum's gaze onto the whole world. In a sense, it can even be said that such an expansion is an ideological operation par excellence, constituting an ideology as such. Every ideology excludes the possibility of an external space: it is essentially the claim to an all-enlightening overview, to complete clarity. Of course, the internal dynamics of the museum collection have such total clarity as their telos—and this telos is completely legitimate. Ideology arises, however, where one tries to skip the path of laborious collecting, a process that is always unfinished, and jump to the final overview.

The essays in this book show and discuss the relationship between the logic of the museum collection and various modern ideologies of the collected world. Individual examples demonstrate how the logic of the collection produces or sabotages different ideologies. The cosmic, social, and political world presents itself to the museum-trained observer as juxtapositions of forms that can be compared, described, and archived, but that do not form a hierarchical or organic whole, thus opening a neutral, homogeneous space of contemplation. This space of contemplation is controllable as long as it remains the finite space of the real museum, but it begins to evade control as soon as the whole world is imagined as a museum—and the institution of the museum suggests, as mentioned above, such a total museal gaze.

The totalitarianisms of the twentieth century are a version of this total gaze. The Soviet culture of the Stalin era positioned itself at the end of history; it wanted to overlook its whole cultural heritage and only select what it considered the best parts. This attempt failed, but the museum's gaze was not discouraged. Today, in a similar manner, one tries to politically codify particular cultural identities and defend them against the destructive work of time and mass media. Thus, in a gentle way, fashionable multiculturalism wants to achieve worldwide cultural stabilization and museum preservation in the name of defending disadvantaged cultural forms. In a more aggressive form, the same demand is made by different cultural fundamentalisms. A certain kind of cultural-ecological reasoning, conservative in the strict sense of the word, is connected to a certain understanding of the museum. Here, the whole world, following Hegelian historicism, is understood as a museum—that is, as a place where the cultural-ecologically minded Absolute Spirit can contemplate all cultural identities that have arisen throughout world history. A new creation of identities is thereby excluded, because under the assumptions of Hegelian historicism no longer has an external space. Only the loss of cultural identities remains possible, and this loss is therefore perceived as final and regrettable.

The identification between the museum and the world, the totalization of the museal gaze, is contrasted with the model of the museum as a flow, constantly losing and regaining form—and never coming to a conclusion, to an end of history. To rest when a work has succeeded does not mean the end of every movement. The end of history is also presupposed by a certain model of political engagement: one must choose between existing political positions—there is no other way out. The art-immanent demand for the new cannot be reconciled with political engagement. Searching for fixed identities by means of photography is equally in vain: photography's claim to truth fails because of its innovativeness.

Ideological discussions on art often operate by the opposition of reality and fiction. However, this opposition is more than problematic. Art certainly cannot be confined to reality if reality is understood as the sum of things that already exist, for art produces new things that cannot be found in reality as it already exists. On the other hand, art is not fiction, because as soon as a work of art is produced, it becomes a part of reality. Art is reality "in progress"—not to be confused with progress in a certain direction.

Incidentally, the outside of the museum is not only the extra-museum space from which the museum transports profane things into its interior. The museum exhibition itself also creates another "immanent interior space"—or, if you will, the unconscious of the museum. The interior of the museum is constituted by different prohibitions: to not touch the objects on display, to not turn them over, to not disassemble them, to not examine them internally. One is only allowed to look at the surface of things; their interior, their essence, their material, ontological, form-carrying core are removed from the gaze of the beholder. The museum is thus by no means a site of pure enlightenment. The things transported from profane reality into the museum are illuminated, but their inner core is made inaccessible to the visitor. In profane reality it is possible to destroy the form of things in order to reach their material core. In contrast, the museum artwork prohibits a destructive handling of its form that discovers and exposes the material from which it is made; the observer's gaze remains on the surface, which serves as a protective shield for the object itself.

In an attempt to overcome this self-produced coverage of the interior, the museum stages the symbolic destruction of the artwork. Such a staging of the suffering, the monstrous, and the disintegration of the artwork serves to make visible the inner, material nature of the artwork, to present its anatomy, which becomes inaccessible to the observer through the protection of the museum. Various strategies of such a mise-en-scène of destruction are described in a number of texts in the middle of this volume. The goal of these deconstructive strategies is to collect all possible forms of destruction of museum art inside the museum itself. This goal, of course, cannot be achieved. Just as the profane space cannot be completely emptied and the difference between museum and non-museum spaces is preserved, the immanent exterior space of the collection cannot be completely revealed. On the contrary, every new piece in the collection enlarges this immanent exterior space, for every work of art once again conceals its interior behind its surface.

The impossibility of demonstrating the interior of the museum's artworks is exemplified by the fake readymades produced by Peter Fischli and David Weiss. These readymades look like everyday objects exhibited in a museum. In reality, they are duplicates of such everyday objects carved from polyurethane and painted by the artists. In profane reality, the difference is easy to notice: the duplicates weigh much less than their prototypes. In the museum context, however, the difference is hardly noticeable, because the material of the work remains inaccessible. Duchamp's readymades inspire confidence in the material from which they are formed. Even if the readymades no longer designate anything in the external world, and are in this sense completely self-referential, they still refer to their material interior. As Fischli and Weiss demonstrate, this reference can also be falsified. Every museum artwork leaves a space open in which manipulation and deception are possible. The museum never reaches its own truth. It would, of course, be wrong to conclude that the world as a whole is the realm of total simulation whose reality hides itself and is deprived of all experience. Such a generalization, in turn, means that the world is viewed with a totalizing museal gaze—only this time it is no longer the gaze of total enlightenment but an already deconstructed gaze. Now beyond the museum there is always a chance to gain the experience that the viewer is denied inside the museum. And the world cannot be thought complete either: another experience is always possible in the world.

If the museum has certain limits, its borders do not seem insurmountable at first sight. Even if the exterior spaces cannot be fully occupied by the museum, the museum can freely collect the objects of the profane exterior as well as the images of destruction from the interior without encountering an object that by definition cannot be collected. Nevertheless, an object that cannot be collected is the museum itself. The museum cannot collect another museum without questioning its own order. This limit leads to a certain crisis of the museum. Large temporary exhibitions, large installations, and various private collections cannot easily be included in the museum collection because they are similar to museums and create their own orders and contexts that cannot be integrated into existing collections.

It is not only museums that cannot be integrated into other museums; certain other social phenomena that are structured as museums cannot be integrated either. Today's city is structured like a museum. Communism was also structured as a museum and therefore cannot be easily accommodated in existing collections. Even an individual—for example, a migrant—is structured like a museum by acting as a carrier of heterogeneous signs collected throughout their life. The museum multiplies. Much, much too much is becoming increasingly museum-like. And that's where the museum finds its actual limits. The museum is a finite space in which the difference between old and new can be controlled—as the museum grows and the number of museum-like structures moves toward infinity, this difference is gradually wiped out. Free and infinite multiplication leads to tautology. The infinite perspective confirms Nietzsche's insight into the eternal return of the same.

The infinite is represented in our culture not by the museum but by the media. And the world of the media is the world of work, because the relief once experienced in the museum no longer takes place there. The bigger the audience that art wants to reach, the more it feels compelled to repeat itself. In the media, art has to strive for tautology because it has to do all the work of self-identification as art. Art in the media is no longer compared to the artistic tradition, to the art context; rather, it is compared to the infinite profane space of everyday "reality." Thus, art must identify itself in the media by showing the unusual, the non-everyday, the non-profane. The unusual, however, is always tautological, for the unusual is identified as such by the fact that it continues the tradition of the unusual. The new is the banal, the trivial, the ordinary, when placed in the art context. In the media, on the other hand, it is impossible to just exhibit an ordinary urinal, as Duchamp did. If a urinal is made the subject of a film, then it has to come alive and castrate the user in order to be considered interesting and suitable for the media. But this makes the urinal tautological, because castration is a well-known mythological topic. Thus, artistic subjectivity disappears in the media, because it is no longer allowed to show its own banality and is condemned to reproduce only the traditionally unusual.

When the totalitarian art of the 1930s and 1940s discovered the media as an alternative space to the museum, it was initially enthusiastic and believed that it had realized the avant-garde dream of a free space beyond the museum. But it became apparent relatively quickly that under the conditions of the media, art must give up its avant-garde reductions and return to the work of tautology in order to assert itself against the background of everyday triviality. The possibility of artistically addressing this triviality was obstructed by the abolition of the modern concept of the museum inside the totalitarian cultural system. In totalitarian states, the expansion of art into the media condemned art to classicism. Even the possibility of thematizing the imagery of the media itself—as American Pop art did, for example—is the consequence of contextualizing this imagery in comparison with the museum. However, totalitarian art is incapable of showing itself because it excludes the possibility of such a comparison.

Today, of course, artists can demonstrate their artistic professionalism by demonstrating their technical skill in dealing with computers and other wonderful devices of the kind. From this perspective, the time of museums seems to be a short break between two epochs of artistic skill. Previously artists had to prove their skills in dealing with paint and marble; today they need to demonstrate their ability to use computers. But they achieve both through work, through the sweat of their brow. Both exclude the staging of free subjectivity. Moreover, it is questionable whether the artists of the media age would be able to renounce classicism completely, since they have no other way to distinguish themselves visibly from a media engineer who has a corresponding technical skill.

It is thus no surprise that the strongest media attention today is enjoyed by sports. The athlete embodies an ideal classicist body achieved through great effort and hard work. Sports are a continuation of the great European aesthetic tradition, which was betrayed by modern art in its search for subjectivity; sports were popular with totalitarian regimes because these regimes have classicist taste. In the media, art is replaced by sports—and can only survive as an art sport. Through the media, the museum's art models are transported from the museum interior to the outside world, where they are spread. The art dynamic thus changes its direction. For a media user, the criterion of novelty loses its relevance: everything that is known from the media is by definition new. On the other hand, a high level of artistic achievement that follows clear, comprehensible criteria is highly valued and "enjoyed" by the spectator. Thus it is precisely through the media that an art is finally established that is often erroneously called "museum-ready."

However, these considerations do not indicate "the end of art." When art leaves the museum, its concept will certainly change, but this change will not end art. On the contrary, one should expect an explosion of art if new financial opportunities and media markets open up. Traditional, artisanal art can survive through the medium of the art trade. But above all, museums will continue to be relevant, they will remain interesting for the media—and with them truly museum-ready—that is, innovative—art will also survive. The nature of this media interest, however, will change.

The logic of the museum collection, as described above, is no longer transparent if the museum is viewed from the outside rather than the inside. And that's what it's all about: the museum gaze from inside to outside is replaced by the media gaze from outside to inside. For the museum-educated subjectivity, the finite, manageable, bright space of the museum is the place of light, whereas the infinite, uncontrollable exterior appears dark and dangerous. For the media consciousness, on the other hand, only the infinite field of communication is bright and transparent, whereas the monastery, the museum, and other sites of subjectivity appear obscure, mysterious, and suspicious.

However, this does not indicate any devaluation of these sites, because in fact it is the hidden, dark, and opaque that is particularly interesting for the media. For the museum gaze, the museum's exterior is interesting. For the media, on the other hand, it is particularly appealing to bring light to the hidden and the closed, to enlighten the public about a dark secret, and to make an isolated, private interior accessible for external communication. If the museum is obscured by the media gaze, then for the media the logic of the collection also becomes dark; it becomes a hidden place of conspiracy, and thus an interesting source of information. A source of information or subject of reporting and news should be opaque—otherwise the information makes no sense. And modern art, as well as religion before it, presents such an opaque space to a media-educated gaze; it is of particular value to the media because it is an opaque space that never becomes totally enlightened. Most criminal cases come to an end after they are solved. The opaque space of subjectivity, on the other hand, can never be fully elucidated, so that one can never send the message "The subject is dead," because subjectivity, seen from the outside, is the suspicion of hypocrisy, of simulation, of dark manipulation, of the discrepancy between inside and outside—and such a suspicion can never be fully refuted.

Today's museum, as the site of subjectivity, is suspected of conspiracy, intrigue, and dark machinations. It is not by accident that Jean Baudrillard, media philosopher par excellence, accuses contemporary art of being a conspiracy. Thus for the media modern art becomes interesting again as news—as a spectacular fraud. On no account should any art lover be ashamed of or protest this verdict of the media. Rather, it should be seen as the expression of the last sacrifice, of the last asceticism: if the museum used to be the place of the sacrificial economy, it is now itself the victim. And as a result, the museum in its entirety becomes news for the media of the outside world. Under the irrefutable suspicion of being pure manipulation, subjectivity can also survive under the dominance of the media's external view.

It is thus quite characteristic that the museum has been darkened by the advent of new media art, and not only in the metaphorical sense. The more new media art is shown in the museum, the darker it becomes, because the distribution of light and darkness works differently in new media than in the traditional museum. In the past, the things that were brought into the museum were dark and had to be illuminated by the museum's light. The new media images—that is, from cinema, video, computer, and so forth—produce light by themselves, whereby the observer of these pictures sits in the dark and can no longer, or only poorly, see the immediate surroundings. The new media images are night images, like dreams or visions from the hereafter: they come from a dark source and are received in the darkness. Only the images themselves have light.

Therefore, new media art as it is brought into the museum, especially in the form of video installations, brings the big night with it. It demonstrates the last sacrifice: the museum space sacrifices its own light, darkens, and puts viewers in a nervous trance in which they are able to receive signals directly from the space beyond the museum. Thus, the museum shows itself to be what it has become in the media age—that is, a dark place of mystery, of conspiracy, of semi-visibility. Even the darkening itself, the entry of night into the museum, is barely registered. As the viewers of the past overlooked the museum's light because their attention was focused on the exhibits, so today one overlooks the museum's darkness as a condition for contemplating the new media art. So the talk shouldn't be of the death of the museum, but of the museum's night, of sleep, of dreaming in the museum and the dream of the museum. In order to be able to perceive this transition in the museum from day to night, or from the new to the news, one should therefore take a certain unfamiliar view of the museum from outside.

Such a view—from the inside and the outside at once—is attempted in this volume. The museum is still described here in its pre-medial, waking state, but this description presupposes the author's knowledge of the museum's darkening under the dominance of the media. A paradise of things has become indistinguishable from a vampire's crypt—and this turn corresponds to the general dynamics of modernity. In modern society, there are fewer and fewer places in which the possibility of pure contemplation is socially guaranteed, and there is also no socially recognized position that would be concerned exclusively with contemplation, as there used to be at all times and in every place. Museums as places of contemplation and the staging of subjectivity are today increasingly suspected of manipulation by the media, which seems to correspond to the general course of modernity. However, when the museum darkens, it becomes a special subject for media attention. It seems advisable to follow these media strategies and turn the modern museum, which has long been a privileged place of contemplation, into an object of contemplation.

LOGIC OF THE COLLECTION

In our present age, "serious" and "autonomous" art is primarily produced with the aim of being collected. It is no longer conceived as part of a temple, church, or palace, as it used to be, rather it is intended from the beginning for the isolated, "autonomous" space of public or private collections. As a result, today's art production differs significantly from all other modern forms of production. All other products are intended for consumption. Consumption likewise means destruction. A piece of bread is eaten—and does not exist after. A car is driven for a while—and then, considered technically or aesthetically outdated, it is scrapped. A newspaper article or scientific text is read, understood, and then forgotten in its original form; if one wants to reproduce the corresponding information, one does it "in one's own words." The text as an object is consumed, annulled, devoured the moment it is understood.

A work of art, on the other hand, is not consumed as an object, but kept: it may not be eaten, used, or completely understood. Well-established cultural conventions protect the artwork from material disappearance, from exhaustion through the act of communication, or from final dissolution through a diversity of interpretations. Every artwork is also a commodity—not a commodity for consumption but a commodity for collection—and is therefore subject to a different economy than the economy of the consumer market. This raises the central question of any theory of art: How does a particular artwork deserve the right to be collected and preserved if that right does not stem from its market value? In other words, which symbolic criteria must this artwork satisfy in order for it to obtain value for a collection?

There are as many answers to this question as there are theories of art. However, most of the answers have something in common: they seek the value criteria of the collection beyond the collection itself—that is, in an external reality, however it is understood. For example, it can be argued that a work of art should be valid in itself in order to earn its permanent place in a collection, embodying the beautiful, the good, the divine, the human, the formally and qualitatively perfect, the rational, the geometric, the passionate, the natural, the unconscious, the erotic, the linguistic, the socio-critical, the democratic, or even, for that matter, the deconstructivist. However, these answers are more than problematic: if an artwork as such embodies something valid, it seems superfluous to preserve it. The question of the reason for preservation is actually only avoided if it is answered by pointing out that the artwork itself is already significant and worth preserving.

It has been further asserted that, especially in modernity, the decision about the value of a work of art is free, arbitrary, subjective. What is collected and proclaimed as art is that which pleases someone who has emancipated him- or herself from all preconceived value criteria. In practice, however, collecting does not follow personal or social taste. We collect and value works of art that seem important, relevant, and meaningful, and not necessarily those we like. Most notably, the art of the avant-garde theoretically questioned and practically abolished the primacy of personal and social taste by demonstrating that a work of art can be particularly collectable and valuable when it pleases nobody.

Ultimately, one tries again and again to regard the art collection as a representational space in which different times, cultures, peoples, and all possible others are aesthetically represented. An art collection is thus transformed into an expanded version of a democratic parliament. The main difficulty with this theory, however, is that the politically or ethnically or sexually defined "other" does not necessarily produce a different, other art. The social, "real," extra-artistic difference by no means guarantees an inner-cultural, inner-artistic, aesthetic difference. In the context of the collection, a work of art derived from a "different" culture, cultural stratum, or social situation can appear completely banal, conventional, or aesthetically indistinguishable. And vice versa: within the same social milieu, extremely diverse artworks can emerge that are separated by insurmountable aesthetic distances. The plurality of art phenomena is not because of the plurality of social groups supposedly represented by them. With this realization, however, art loses its representational value.

The difficulties with these and other comparable answers have led to a certain state of perplexity regarding the criteria by which works of art are collected and the ways in which their value is created. It therefore seems reasonable to try to find a way out of this perplexity by no longer looking outside the collection for the value criteria for collecting and storing artworks, but looking within the collection and according to the immanent logic of collecting. A work of art is collected not when it has proved to be important and valuable in external reality, in this or that respect, but only when it meets the internal criteria of collecting itself. Just as a picture does not merely depict external reality, the art collection in its entirety does not depict external social contexts, it rather follows its own autonomous logic.

At first glance, such a statement contradicts the main intention of modern art development. In fact, modern artists constantly protest against the power of collections and collectors—and especially against the power of museums, which, in the pamphlets of the artistic avant-garde, are compared to cemeteries, the museum curators to gravediggers. In the context of the artistic avant-garde, the modern era's struggle against dead "museum" art conventions is understood as a struggle of life against death. The logic of the collection is accordingly understood as the logic of death, as deadly logic—which should be the paramount duty of every living art to resist. A truly living art allegedly asserts itself beyond any museum convention: it must be understood as the ultimate gift of life itself. Unfortunately, as long as life is not confronted with the cultural logic of death, it does not make much of an effort. What is alive is aesthetically banal. Life constantly repeats itself. An interesting form can only be expected from death. If the avant-garde had been actually guided by living impulses, it would never have produced anything original. Every culturally significant production arises in competition with the dead. And so art producers first have to comprehend themselves as dead in order to produce something valuable for the collection.

The premise for the avant-garde struggle against the museum collection was the conviction that museums only recognize and collect art that conforms to the traditional criteria of artistic design and quality. The museum was thus regarded as an institution that prevented the emergence of a free, original art through its cultural domination. In fact, exactly the opposite is the case. When there is no collection, it makes sense to remain faithful to the old, to follow tradition, to resist the destructive work of time. In the past, new artworks were created in traditional styles because old artworks were constantly destroyed. Only when the old is collected and preserved in a museum does such repetition become unnecessary and is no longer rewarded by its inclusion in the collection: one does not need to repeat texts or images if they are already in the collection.

The museums of the nineteenth century were from the start aesthetically very heterogeneous. They contained various examples of European, Chinese, Japanese, and Egyptian art. There was no longer any unified tradition to conform to: rather, the internal structure of the museum collection, in which each historical epoch was represented by a respective aesthetic style, demanded the production of new historical styles. The historicist logic of the museum collection called for a different, innovative, alternative art to expand these collections. The avant-garde was from the outset the answer to this demand, because an epigonic art that imitated tradition had no chance of claiming a place for itself in the museum collection: this art became superfluous through the museum's preservation of tradition.

Insofar as the avant-garde wanted to create a new historical style, it understood—despite its superficial, vitalistic rhetoric—its own present as an already dead, musealized past that was to take its special place in the comparison of all times and all styles in the museum. The attempt to aesthetically represent the present and even, as the Futurists wanted, the future, led to the emergence of a plurality of styles, none of which could claim exclusive representation. For the first time in the history of musealization, the aesthetic representation of an epoch was no longer defined retroactively, it was freely invented.

According to a central historicist prejudice, earlier, pre-museum historical styles formed spontaneously and unreflectively, so that the museum could only reflect the significance of these styles for an aesthetic representation of the historical. The art of the avant-garde, in contrast, was produced from the very beginning in view of its potential position in historical comparison. Instead of waiting for an actual social development in order to establish and musealize the aesthetic changes that it brought about, the avant-garde began its artistic activity in conscious opposition to the art of the past in order to aesthetically designate the present and the future. Thus, the comparison in the museum does not follow a "natural" aesthetic development but precedes it, both permitting it to form and determining the course of this development. Here a new art that is produced outside of the museum is not compared to the old art, rather the comparison itself takes place before the emergence of the new art—and produces this new art in the first place.

The art of the avant-garde is the product of such a museum comparison, and its forms are so diverse because the comparison can be made and interpreted in different ways. But this makes it clear in retrospect that the aesthetic representation of the past also only came about as a product of museum comparison, because from the mass of inherited art, the only examples selected were those that could define a certain historical epoch in an aesthetically persuasive way. Everything redundant and repetitive was effectively removed automatically from the viewer's field of vision.

In the museum only "examples" are shown. But examples of what? The "creative" minority that provides these examples is identified as such by presenting itself in always new and different ways over time. The majority of the population, however, is relieved of this obligation—and is allowed to repeat. The historically relevant art of an epoch is thus only representative of the logic of the museum and can only serve as an example of this logic—and not of the epoch itself, which is always determined more by repetition than innovation. Incidentally, this also applies to times that are dominated by rapid developments in technology, society, and so on. A rocket or computer can be displayed with the same artistic means as a rider on a horse. There is no necessary connection between technical and aesthetic innovation.

Artistic innovation emerges not as the expression of a vital artistic freedom that seeks to express the social relevance of its time, but under the pressure to be different and new imposed by the collection. The artist must produce the new in order to be included in the collection. This pressure is often masked by the rhetoric of artistic freedom, especially in the modern world. The connection between freedom and innovation is usually understood in a very naive way. The real freedom of the artist would actually consist in being allowed to produce both the old and the new. But such freedom never existed in modernity. The repetition of the old was rather referred to as epigonism, as kitsch, or, as it is called today, department-store art—and thus rejected by the museum.

In fact, the greatest artists of the avant-garde repeatedly demanded that everything should be allowed in art. Kandinsky said that any form that has an effect on the viewer is permissible. Tatlin claimed that he sought not the old or the new, but the useful. Duchamp understood his readymades as the ultimate abolition of the traditional boundaries of art. But against the prohibition of repetition, these statements have proved powerless. As proof that everything had become possible in art, the avant-garde artist was allowed to only present the new, the not-yet-exhibited. On the other hand, when these artists tried to return to the old, as Malevich did in his later years, they were immediately disqualified as renegades. The only conceivable excuse in this case is to present the old in the avant-garde context—so that this can be interpreted as an innovative gesture.

Therefore the art of the avant-garde can by no means be considered an expression of the personal freedom of an individual artist. Incidentally, every avant-garde artist often changed his or her style to become more "radical" than other artists, so there can be no question of "authenticity." Rather, the artists took a strategic approach in view of the general art context in order to better situate themselves and their art within this context. But if the new art cannot be regarded as an authentic expression of artistic individuality, it also should not be regarded as an expression of its time or its society. Rather, it is always alien to its time and its society because it situates itself in relationship to the collection of the dead art of the past, the knowledge of which requires experience. The art of the avant-garde is the art of an elitist minority because it emerges under a pressure that the others, the general public, are not under. The public consumes art—and it can equally consume both the old and the new. Anyone who wants to produce art, on the other hand, must submit to especially strict conditions.

The space of the museum collection is thus unhistorical although—or perhaps because—history is represented in it. It is not that the art forms created in "real" historical life are collected in the museum, but rather that art produced under the pressure of the collection is then disseminated, marketed, and consumed in a "reality" outside the museum. So we can liberate the concept of innovation from its connection to the linearity of historical time—and with that we also detach it from its connection with the notion of "progress." The critique of progress and the historical utopias of modernity is basically the critique of the philosophical construction of a linear time. If artistic innovation is no longer understood in terms of temporal linearity, it escapes such critique. And indeed, innovation happens not in time but on the border between the collection and the outside world. A Chinese statuette from the third millennium BC can be just as new—or equally not new—for the collection as any object from the present or the future. The boundaries of the collection fluctuate constantly and are open to different times and places. Individual innovations that entail absorption into—or removal from—the collection do not form a linear history, though they influence the whole makeup of the collection and alter the logic of later innovations. However, such changes and restructurings do not fit the model of linear time because they always redefine or even reinvent their own past.

Innovation should not be understood as creation. Humans cannot create out of nothing—that remains a divine privilege. Therefore, all theories of art that want to interpret art as production from nothing or as a revelation of the hidden are more than problematic. For an innovation, everything has always been free, unconcealed, accessible. The innovation consists in moving something that was not in the collection into the collection. Of course, this description of innovation refers first and foremost to the readymade process introduced into art by Duchamp, which today largely dominates art practice. However, the readymade process should not be misunderstood as a particular art trend among a variety of other methods. Rather, the readymade process demonstrates how art has always been produced.

Incidentally, neither a single artist nor an institution has the right to decide what is recognized as art or what enters the collection and what does not. The readymade process, which seems to empower the subjectivity of the artist to make decisions about what art is, actually follows the external logic of the collection. A decision such as "This object is a work of art" merely shifts the requirement of innovation from the object to the decision itself. The artist is then the one who makes innovative aesthetic decisions, whereas the public is granted the right to elevate everything to art that pleases it in terms of image consumption. But this right has no consequences for the logic of the collection—and therefore for the history of art. The growth of the collection only follows the law of innovation.

Art creation is identical to art collecting. Duchamp's readymade process made the inner identity between creating art and collecting obvious by the fact that the valorization of readymades does not change their form, or does so only minimally. Thus it is no longer possible to produce the false impression that this change—that is, the creative intervention of the artist—and not the logic of the collection forms the very basis for the appreciation of works of art. Nevertheless, such a creative, artistic intervention always takes place, and incidentally Duchamp's readymades are no real exception here. Therefore, the question arises as to what goal these artistic interventions have. When art is consumed by an audience that has certain ideas about what art is and should be, the artists intervene with the aim of adapting their material to the usual, traditional rules of art production. On the other hand, in the art created for the collection, the creative intervention serves to purify the selected profane object from all sorts of associations with traditional art—in other words, to make the object even more profane than it already is in profane reality.

When one hears that nonart instead of art is produced today, that is of course correct. But this does not mean that producing nonart is easy. It is not as though a small island of art is surrounded by nonart and the artist only needs to take a small step over the border of recognized art to get to the nonart. Profane reality is saturated with art products. The artistic design of the visual environment constantly adapts to prevailing artistic concepts. In addition, much of the profane realm has already been aestheticized and included in collections—which in turn means that it is difficult to find what is potentially new in profane reality in order to place it in the context of the collection. For this reason, in this "placing in context," the artist's intervention in the selected object emphasizes and illustrates everything that brings this object into opposition to the already existing prototypes of the collection. Through such an intervention, everything that is contrastive, other, strange, or alternative is exposed that goes unnoticed in the ordinary context. The deliberate stylizations of the images of maniacs, for example, look even more maniacal than their own images. And in the art context, technology looks even more technical, the spontaneous even more spontaneous, the ugly even uglier, the primitive even more primitive, and the exotic even more exotic than in profane reality.

We are dealing here with a phenomenon that can be defined as negative adaptation to traditional art rules. One adapts to these rules by breaking them. Incidentally, the process does not differ significantly from the positive adaptation to the rules of tradition, in which these rules are adhered to as strictly as possible. In both cases, knowledge of the rules is required, and reference to these rules plays a crucial role in the manufacturing of the work. In both cases, the result is not the representation of reality but a fiction. While in the first case it is the fiction of a positive adaptation in which life looks exactly like its traditional artistic model, in the second case life is stylized and presented in reverse as nonart, as a great alternative, as the other of this model. Avant-garde's nonart is just as artificial and manufactured according to certain rules as traditional art—and that is why both can be equally represented in the collection.

The difficulty of negative adaptation—that is, the production of nonart—is sometimes not underestimated but overestimated, especially in recent times. It is said again and again that nothing new can be found because all borders have been crossed and all taboos broken: the collection is allegedly no longer different from profane reality. However, this statement is not necessarily true. Of course it is true that art has now absorbed a great deal of what used to be profane, and it is also true that profane reality is styled and designed more and more according to the models of high art, gradually dissolving the difference between valuable collections and profane reality. At the same time, it should not be forgotten that objects of profane reality change as they enter collections—even if "materially" they remain the same. These objects are viewed in a different context and thus viewed differently.

Also the recourse to old art-historical styles in so-called postmodern art does not signify an exhaustion of the new. The postmodern artist inquires about the changes that the art styles of the past have experienced in the profane reality of modern mass societies and the media—and aestheticizes these changes. This process is often misunderstood: it is suggested that postmodern art merely quotes the past. But this reproach is not justified, because it is not the art of the past itself that is quoted but rather the profane mass distribution of this art in the present—that is, the art classics that have gone through the meat grinder of mass media and mass reception. Here, attention is shifted from the novelty of the artistic form to the novelty of the social, media, and linguistic handling of the artistic form—and this shift is completely legitimate.

But there is an even deeper reason why engaging with nonart does not lead to the disappearance of the line between art and life or between the collection and profane reality. Just as each individual work of modern art looks much more profane than profanity itself, the collection as a whole forms a space that is more profane than the lifeworld. Today's art especially art suggests the image of far advanced entropy: it seems arbitrary, nonbinding, boundlessly pluralistic, and thus no longer hierarchical. One should not be surprised if the question of the value of art is asked today with such intensity and all existing collections threatened with total devaluation.

The traditional and still common concept of art assumes that the art system creates orders and hierarchies that give value to art: the work of art is valuable because it is given a higher ranking than other objects—and it's higher because art creates hierarchical orders that are missing in life. This has changed little in modernity. In the rejection of traditional hierarchies, models, and conventions, one sees the self-assertion of human freedom, which creates new values. Thus the new art corresponds to a new hierarchy headed by the zero point of individual freedom. Even if art does not depict the outer image of life or express the inner life of the artist, it can be credited with a life-stimulating function, which Nietzsche already claimed to be the new legitimation of art. This gives art a new vocation: to be even more alive than life itself. The result is a demand on art that internally controls most modern art-theoretical texts: to deliver what life is incapable of delivering. Art is required to construct an impossible utopia, to manifest an impossible desire or the sublime, to achieve an unprecedented intensity, to indicate a paradoxical presence of absence, to reveal ultimate meaning or ultimate meaninglessness, to create absolute order or absolute chaos—or to deconstruct all these oppositions. And if none of this can be done, art is at least required to criticize the institution within the institution and to reflect itself by its own means.

But even though artistic subjectivity is no longer in the center—having been displaced by different theories of the unconscious—it does not mean that all hierarchies are thereby abolished. Theories of the unconscious also create their own hierarchies: in the center is now the pure materiality of the artwork. Accordingly, the autonomy of art is no longer understood to be an expression of human autonomy, for meanwhile the individual, the author, and the subject, as we know, have been declared dead. Rather, the center of art is occupied by the artwork that most explicitly manifests its own materiality as transcending any artistic intention. Such an artwork should not be the image of human unconscious but it should make its own unconscious visible. Malevich's *Black Square* is a well-known example of the numerous attempts to reach the zero point of painting and reveal the unconscious of the image. Just when the work of art is purified of everything human, all too human, it gains the highest value.

The crisis of all legitimations of art, which is felt so keenly today, arises from skepticism about the theories of subjectivity and the unconscious and their legitimizing power. It seems that humans today no longer have an unconscious because everything has become accessible and permissible for them: the unconscious has been definitively taken over by the "system." Autonomous, non-referential works of art that reveal their own materiality are also already being collected. And if one has collected enough such works, one looks for something different. The unconscious of the image thus manifests itself as one form among many others, just as the manifestation of free artistic will has always been shown as one form among others.

If today there is something that can function as art's zero point, and thus its center, then it is the museum itself, which was grasped in the art of the last decades as the "white cube," pure emptiness. One can imagine the museum as an empty space without works of art—and in some installations of Minimalism or Yves Klein this vision has also been realized. It is obvious that the emptiness of the museum space internally structures museum collections. The rejection of the linear model of progress means that present-day museum exhibitions are gathered around this void. Any observer of the development of art today will find that its dynamics arise from the fact that every movement in one direction leads almost immediately to a movement in an opposite direction: when an ascetic, conceptual art is produced in large quantities, a movement toward colorful, expressionist painting emerges, and so on.

All these contrasting style movements, no longer historically separated, are practiced simultaneously. Taken together, these movements yield a zero sum, the state of homeostasis, an entropic void. Here we are no longer confronted with the concept of fashion anymore, which still suggests temporal linearity. Rather we are confronted with museal emptiness, in which the collection, by representing the whole palette of opposing artistic positions, amounts to zero as the sum of these positions—a zero point that reproduces the emptiness of the museum space itself. The museum collection is the articulation of zero in the void. Each collection strives for the ideal of comprehensive representativeness. A comprehensive representation of art that includes all imaginable positions produces in total a zero point. It is precisely this zero as the sum and center of a paradigmatic art collection that gives the art system its relative formal unity, which cannot be called into question by referring to the dependence of the museum space on external, political reality. Art that reflects such dependence, when added together with an art that does not reflect this dependence, yields the same zero sum. If this zero sum in the center of the art system is overlooked, art becomes merely a subsystem of the social whole, as Niklas Luhmann's systems theory suggests—art becomes communication; a statement is ascribed to it that is not a zero statement but still cannot be clearly defined, so that the whole thing acquires an abstruse if somewhat attractive mystical dimension.

Despite modern art's repeated and explicit rejection of the mimetic function and subjection to so-called reality, including communication, most people still find it difficult to accept—if need be, this rejection itself is interpreted as an expression of freedom, the unconscious, utopia, and so on. But, as I have tried to show, the hypothesis of human freedom is as superfluous in explaining the dynamics of modern art as the theories of the unconscious. These dynamics can be explained sufficiently from the internal logic of the collection without having to rely on the action of external forces. Works of art do not represent "real" or "living" orders. The growth of the collection exclusively follows the inner logic of collecting.

The question about the meaning of art ultimately leads to the answer that it does not have any meaning—if what is meant by the term "meaning" is an extra-cultural, extra-artistic reality to which art could or should refer. On the other hand, art is certainly in close complicity with the reality outside the museum's walls—above all with political reality. The deeper relationship of art to politics is overlooked, however, if it is understood as a matter of personal artistic-political engagement. Namely, an artist cannot freely decide whether their own work is politically relevant or not. Artists do not have the criteria to assess the political relevance of their own art. An art critic also has no criterion for distinguishing between different works of art in terms of their political meaning and function. Rather, the collection, whose logic art follows, is itself a determining figure of the political.

Politics takes place in the assembly of people; it is part of the design of the collective. And people are assembled the same way artworks are collected. The type of collection first gives the social space a form in which politics can unfold. The collection forms the frame for the assembly or the collective. The logic of the collection shapes and at the same time makes visible the space and the time in which the political takes place. Art therefore gives the overall context of political events a specific form. To reduce the meaning of art to concrete political influence within this context means to misunderstand its much deeper political role.

To explain this, I would like to refer to the three historical forms of the collection that I mentioned at the beginning: the church, the palace, and the modern collection. In the church or palace, with all their obvious differences, artworks are presented according to strict hierarchical orders. The importance of each particular artwork is determined by its place in these hierarchies. Thus, assemblies of people are structured according to these given hierarchies. And one can say that every single work of art in these collections repeats its general hierarchical structure in itself: it is structured and inwardly hierarchized in the same way as the space of the ecclesiastical or aristocratic collection as a whole. The prerequisite for such a hierarchical organization, however, is that all its elements can be substituted by others: in a church, an old icon or fresco can be easily removed, destroyed, and replaced by new icons or frescoes if these new works of art convey relatively the same meaning and are situated at the same hierarchical-spiritual level. The fact that new artworks in their outward appearance—that is, from the purely aesthetic perspective—might look different does not affect their hierarchical position and therefore their meaning or value.

The modern collection, on the other hand, is based on the principle of the preservation of the old, so that images that are different formally and aesthetically cannot be substituted for one another. For the modern museum, it is not enough that different images have the same "spiritual meaning" in order to regard them as identical and substitutable. Decisive are the external, aesthetic, formal differences. And two different works of art can never be completely identical in form. That's why old works of art are preserved in a museum: not only their message, which can also be expressed in other ways, but above all their form, which is unrepeatable in all its details, make up their identity. The destruction of this form thus cannot be compensated by the reformulation of the content. Hence, old and new forms are recognized as equally worthy of preservation and display, even if, on the level of their message, they are tautological when judged by the criteria of the pre-aesthetic age.

Accordingly, the new finds its place in the collection not as a substitution of the old, but alongside the old. This results in an impossibility of structuring and hierarchization that produces the entropic space of the modern museum. Thus the space of the collection, in which the new is situated on the same level as the old, loses its former hierarchical character: it is neutralized, deconstructed, homogenized, and accordingly made unqualifiable, indescribable. Incidentally, the modern work of art reflects this new space of the collection in itself in the same way that church or palace art used to. The modern artwork is increasingly decentered, dehierarchized, deconstructed, neutralized, also in itself. Namely, modern art tries again and again to internalize the indefinable, neutral, and therefore unrepresentable space of the collection and manifest it inside the individual work of art. But this never succeeds completely, because each new piece of art gets its own place in the space of the collection that it can no longer reflect in itself. The actual space of modern art is the space of the collection—that is, the space between the works of art and not within the works of art.

A modern political assembly is formed in a similar way. In the modern world, humans are understood predominantly from an aesthetic point of view: one sees two people as different if they look different even if they think the same, fulfill the same social function, have the same financial status, and so on. That is why the description of the human plays such a big role in modern democracies (consider photos and descriptions of human bodies like height, eye color, etc., on ID cards). Insofar as every human being is seen as a pure form—that is, purely aesthetically, as a work of art—he or she evades substitution (hence the fear of human cloning, which represents the real danger to the modern understanding of human beings, and has been fought against on a symbolic level by the musealization of reproduction since the invention of Pop art).

Thus humanity, under the museum-educated gaze, appears as a collection of different human forms to be assembled and represented through democratic political institutions. However, each democratic representation must also be experienced as deficient and provisional because it suppresses many aesthetic differences among individuals: each representation, including the democratic one, constructs a meaning that makes it possible to understand different human forms in terms of content, that is, identically. In every society there are only a relatively small number of political parties or interest groups. No political system, including a democratic one, can represent a person who only paints squares and triangles or a person who makes sculptures from fat. The modern artist creates a form that has no meaning so that it does not allow any kind of representation. Thus the artist expands the space of the collection of humans beyond any possibility of their political representation.

The social space of democracy is designed as a museum space of the collection. However, the space of a museum art collection in its neutrality, deconstructiveness, and entropy is much more radical and much wider than the space of political representation, which is still rather narrow and hierarchically organized. The person who will go from the museum into politics is just looking for more comfort and clarity. However, the radicalism of the art space should be interpreted as a challenge to politics to further approach the art space. And what's even more important, in art the human form is only one form among many. The collection of human forms that makes up modern humanity is but a fragment of a much greater number of inhuman or superhuman forms among which the modern museum also establishes a democratic relationship of equality. Just as in the Middle Ages human hierarchies were legitimated by their inscription in the cosmic and heavenly hierarchies, the equality of democratic humanity is inscribed in the zero sum of all forms represented in the museum. The modern museum thus offers both the legitimacy of the prevailing democratic political order and the possibility for its criticism—just as the church used to both legitimize and question the hierarchical order of secular powers.

The shortest definition of a space of the modern collection as well as one of modern political power would thus be: it is the space of entropy. This entropy of the collection, however, is as artificial as the traditional hierarchical order. The term "entropy" usually has a negative connotation, because one believes that life requires order, and that by destroying all order entropy threatens to destroy every life. But this very threat—that is, the presence of death in the midst of life—is the fascination of entropy, since the collection is a site of death as well as the site in which one tries to overcome death. The church was also such a site of death in which one felt threatened by a higher order—and at the same time hoped for salvation. In the past, death was understood as subsummation under a higher hierarchical order. Today, death is understood as pure dissolution in horizontal infinity—in a neutral space of entropy. The space of the collection therefore embodies the attempt to survive in entropy and through entropy—to overcome entropic death through itself. This dream of survival in entropy also generates the fascination for modern art as a whole. Any attempt to impose on this art a new, allegedly life-fostering order does not succeed, because such an attempt overlooks the real problem, and thus proves to be naive.

In fact, entropy goes deeper than any opposition such as chaos/order, ecstasy/normality, originality/imitation, speaking/writing, crime/morality, and so on, with which theories operate to give art a particular content. Through the process of collecting, all these theories are juxtaposed and thus situated on the same level of entropy. Different contemporary movements of thought and style form an irreducible plurality and seem to contradict one another, thereby provoking participation in a struggle or an election. In its entirety, however, this plurality forms the state of entropy in which the space of the collection unfolds. At the same time it guarantees neutrality, the indefinability and irrepresentability of the space, which cannot be occupied by any single work of art or any single theory. The unoccupied zero point of this plurality is therefore open to everyone—without struggles or elections.

The entropic space of the collection is the largest and, if you will, the only modern work of art. The design of this space is carried out through the collective work of expanding and changing the collection in which artists, curators, private collectors, gallery owners, and critics alike participate. For far too long, the attention of art historians has been focused on the individual achievements of modern artists. The role of the individual was grossly overestimated. Perhaps only now can we see that in modernity a vast collective work was accomplished and that the heterogeneity of individual contributions served in the end the expansion of the single impersonal space of the museum collection, which shapes and defines the present in its entirety, just like how church or palace spaces shaped and defined the past. In the museum space, different forms of life gather around the zero point of death that these forms carry within themselves, because in their totality they result in an entropic zero sum. Thus, the space of the collection depicts the initial big bang of an explosive unfolding of all forms from the black hole of matter as well as the eventual implosion of these forms at the end of time—that is, the whole cosmological myth of modernity.

COLLECT AND BE COLLECTED

The state where I am from originally, the Soviet Union, disbanded relatively recently. However, the Soviet Union understood itself not as a nation-state among other nation-states, but as the bearer of a universalist, internationalist communist idea. The national identities and interests of the large number of different peoples who lived within its borders were therefore subordinate to this ultimate goal: the emergence of a united, communist humanity that was to eventually make the Soviet Union itself superfluous.

But instead of this radiant future, the dissolution of the Soviet Union merely led to the emergence of individual nation-states on its former territory. And only as a result of this development could the question be asked about the national cultural identities of these new states and how these identities should be represented in different cultural archives, including museums. It seems to me that in the twentieth century we were watching not so much the collapse of nation-states as the dissolution of different universalist ideologies and imperial powers that wanted to legitimize themselves through these ideologies. The Soviet ideology was probably the last universalist ideology of this kind and the Soviet Union the last state with a universalist claim. Both ended up on the trash heap of history.

No matter how this event may be judged politically, it opened up a new opportunity for the museum, since the trash heap of history is the main source for museum collections. The transfer of artifacts from reality into museum collections can only begin after the collapse of the old social order, when symbols of power and signs of worship, of ideology, and of everyday life lose their former function and turn into historical trash. The museum has taken its modern shape as a result of the French Revolution and subsequent revolutions and wars; it was created by the modern nation-state to save the remnants of the ancien régime from final destruction. Symbolic heir to the old transnational orders based on religion and tradition, the modern museum is constructed as a system of universal representation within a national cultural context or as a kind of symbolic empire in the midst of the nation-state. Even in the context of modernity, the museum collects everything that falls out of fashion and out of use, as well as everything foreign, exotic, other. The modern museum is thus a symbolic space of the heterogeneous in the relatively homogenous context of the modern nation-state.

And likewise, the museum is the place where the cultural identity of the nation-state can be defined, because there is no other way to define one's identity than to compare it to other identities. The nation-state needs this space of heterogeneity to formulate its own identity. And at the same time the museum poses a constant threat to this cultural identity, because the museum presents all sorts of cultural forms that do not fit this identity. This ambivalent, paradoxical position of the modern museum vis-à-vis the modern state nourishes a permanent opposition between the two institutions, but at the same time it creates a close complicity. This situation is actually well known and defines the museum as a public institution.

In a sense, the museum is the most characteristic institution of modernity. Collecting has always been practiced, but it was only in modernity that the museum—that is, the state collection—was able to attain the central cultural position it holds today. With the advance of the Enlightenment and secularization, it became increasingly difficult to rely on God's eternal memory or the eternal laws of reason and nature to secure identity, including cultural identity. This is the reason why in modern times an artificial memory, a cultural archive, or a museum was created to preserve memories in physical form as books, images, or artifacts. Modern subjectivity can only be defined through collecting.

Since in modernity a metaphysical, preordained order of things is no longer believed, this order must be artificially produced through collecting. Susan Sontag once wrote that Karl Marx was only partially right: the world can in fact no longer be understood, but the world can also no longer be changed. The only thing one can do is to collect the world. The basic metaphysical, religious, or ideological question—namely, the question "What remains?"—has become a technical problem of museum collecting and preserving. We are what we collect.

But this redefinition of identity leads to some unpleasant entanglements and traps in practical, and especially financial, respect. God's memory was not only omnipresent and eternal, it was above all accessible at no expense. Access to this memory was granted by good deeds or rightful thoughts—and not primarily by financial investments. But museum collections cost money—and there's never enough money. So we are confronted with an economic or perhaps ecological question rather than a metaphysical one: What should be transported into the museum space from the ever-growing trash heap of history? Where does all the cultural trash go?

Today we are indeed confronted with a cultural-ecological crisis: the media and culture industries produce an abundance of cultural artifacts, which unfortunately are not destroyed fast enough by the power of nature and time. When asked "What remains?" there is only one answer: too much. Thus, today's museums become places of cultural-ecological censorship: their function is less to save the artifacts of the past condemned to disappear than to make a meaningful selection out of the mass of accumulated cultural waste. Meaningful—but in what way? Museums are places where cultural-historical waste is processed into cultural identities. Thus, museums are cultural-ecological reprocessing plants, recycling machines that "present" the artifacts of the past—that is, transform them into the signs of the present. This cultural-ecological process also determines the criteria of selection.

What are these criteria? The answer depends on how we define the end product—that is, cultural identity. The work of museums is definitely vital for the functioning of today's culture—like any other ecological work. Cultural identities, as they are produced by museums, are later used by politics, and also in the context of global media culture; for its part, the media today produces something like a virtual world museum. As a guide in an extremely heterogeneous reality, the media creates something like a cultural map of the world in which certain cultural regions are marked with easily recognizable symbols: the pyramids for Egypt, Coca-Cola for America, Lenin's mausoleum for Russia. These symbols first had to be aesthetically recycled in museums so that they could play their media role convincingly: pyramids and mummies would never have achieved their present-day universality without the Louvre or the British Museum, and Coca-Cola or Lenin's mausoleum would never have been culturally relevant without their aesthetic recycling by Andy Warhol and the Russian Sots art movement. On the other hand, the media's virtual world museum influences the design and functioning of the traditional hardware of museums, as these museums inevitably tend to inscribe themselves in the virtual universal museum, which happens mainly in two different ways. In the first case, a museum is created that replicates the structure of the media's virtual world museum in a small format and according to its means, financial and otherwise, with mummies next to Warhol's Coca-Cola or remnants of faded communism—just like everywhere in the world. In the second case, the museum specializes in a particular regional theme, and thus is understood not as a model but as part of the media's world-spanning museum. As a rule, however, both strategies are pursued at the same time, so that today's museum, whereby I primarily mean the art museum, represents regional interests as well as international art movements.

But this homogenization succeeds only partially. Modern museums are basically collections of heterogeneous objects in a homogeneous space. Even if these objects hang or stand side by side, they still do not form an organic unity, as used to be the case in the church or the aristocratic palace. This absence of inner organic unity, this irreducible inner heterogeneity, characterizes not only the modern museum but also modern subjectivity as such. But precisely this observation leads to a question that is often overlooked when one speaks about the relationship of the museum to the cultural identity represented within it, including national cultural identity. The question is this one: When we talk about the cultural identity represented in the museum, do we mean the subjectivity of the collector or the subjectivity of the collected? This is a difference that one tries to erase again and again, pretending to be able to collect oneself, one's own history, and thus transform the museum collecting into a self-reflexive practice. But this attempt never succeeds—or at least not completely or permanently.

What do the Louvre, the British Museum, and all museums that have come after them represent? Do these museums manifest the subjectivity and cultural identity of collectors—in this case, the states of France and England during a particular epoch of their existence? To assert this, however, is to deny the claim of these museums to a neutral, objective representation of world history—without this claim these museums are not relevant or interesting at all. However, according to this claim, the museum collectors themselves paradoxically have no fixed identity at all. Incidentally, Hegel, the father of modern historicism, also saw it this way: historical consciousness, which manifests itself in the institution of the museum, reflects history without itself being historical. The Hegelian vision of the Absolute Spirit as an identity-free curator of its historical memories still lives today in the virtual worldwide museum of the media, which is perceived as a museum without an author, without an individual curator, beyond any specific cultural identity. Only those who are represented in this museum by certain symbols and artifacts—that is, virtually collected and represented—are supposed to have an identity. In view of this inner division of museum practice, we must ask ourselves what we really want: Do we want to collect or to be collected? Do we want to become curators or museum objects?

Admittedly, the whole cultural-political impact of this question can only be appreciated if we realize that the overwhelming majority of newly created nation-states and regional cultural entities on the territory of old empires, as well as many of the old nation-states of Europe clearly chose the option of being collected. Today, we hear demands for the representation of national or regional cultural identities from all sides. Anyone who seeks such a cultural representation tries to distinguish oneself as clearly as possible from all the other items in the virtual museum collection so that one's own cultural identity becomes visible and distinct. One's identity is thus defined as a specific cultural form in the context of other cultural forms. And that in turn means nothing other than that cultural identity is seen through the eyes of a virtual visitor who can view this virtual museum that contains all cultural forms. The cultural plurality and the struggle for representation therefore still presuppose an identity-free, museal perspective, as thematized by Hegel.

And this recourse to the nineteenth century or even earlier is not accidental. With the goal of the production of cultural identities, artifacts, signs, and documents are presented that refer to the time periods preceding imperialist conquests and the emergence of communism or national socialism—in other words, to the times before these identities were subjected to different traumas in the course of imperialist, universalist projects of the nineteenth and twentieth centuries. Here the attempt is undertaken to skip and forget the times in which these cultural identities were subjected to violence that suppressed, damaged, or even wiped out such identities. It seems to be forgotten, however, that the characteristic symbols of these supposedly original cultural identities were ultimately taken from museum collections, which in turn owe their emergence to the universalist projects of the last two centuries. Here the universalist obligation for uniformity is merely replaced by the no-less-universalist gaze of the museum. The damaged, decayed cultural identity, degraded to historical trash, is recycled and repaired through the museum and then delivered home as a finished product. Thus, here one universalism, one imperialism, is merely exchanged for another.

Of course, we welcome it when signs of the past are saved from oblivion, collected, and made accessible. The recourse to premodern identities must not, however, lead to a defensive attitude toward modern art, which, associated with the defeat of one's own cultural identity in modernity, is often regarded as a sign of Western cultural imperialism. This defensive attitude can be perceived in many new nations, but a certain anti-modernist ressentiment is also characteristic of the West. Indeed, modern art manifests the dissolution of ancient cultural identities and threatens their alleged historical uniqueness, originality, and authenticity. The guardians of national cultural identity don't like it, but the international visitors of the virtual museum of cultural identities also don't like it, because they do not wish to be confused.

Therefore, a certain unpleasant complicity arises between fundamentalist national or regional cultural censorship and the international cultural tourism that today recruits visitors for the worldwide museum of cultural identities. The postmodern, global, identity-less flaneur, who places all cultural signs on the same level, is certainly extremely skeptical of any claim to universal truth. But it is precisely this fundamental skepticism that allows for the acceptance of any cultural standpoint as soon as it sees itself as regional and not valid universally. And so, this postmodern tourist readily accepts cultural fundamentalism, which seeks to establish absolute truth only regionally. The very fact that today the traditional connection between truth and universality is being dissolved demonstrates that the contemporary world has completely transformed itself into a virtual art museum in which we have already become accustomed to experiencing the drama of the absolute claims, which however only extend to a few square meters of canvas and are immediately negated in the eyes of the visitor by the white wall behind this canvas.

The postmodern tourists look at this drama with a tired, skeptical smile, but at the same time they are not ready to completely reject the claims being made, because, as stated above, from the outset they regard the whole world as a museum. And every museum is constructed in such a way that the cultural forms presented in it are distinguished by means of certain externally identifiable formal characteristics. The conservation work of the museum curator includes stabilizing and securing these formal differences. In this regard, museum curators may be too rigorous or overzealous, but they remain sympathetic because their exaggerated enthusiasm ultimately serves the noble purpose of preserving the cultural identities entrusted to them. For the museum's trained gaze, a local fundamentalist dictator who imposes a stable cultural identity on his subjects comes across like a somewhat overzealous but somehow sympathetic curator—because if he moderates his zeal, the identity he cares about will dissolve—and the world will become boring, shabby, and monotonous, not as appealing, colorful, and entertaining as before. The local fundamentalist identity seeker and the international tourist in search of cultural differences are therefore internally connected by the same museum-informed gaze. National cultural identity will therefore sell well on the international tourist market, which has been understood meanwhile not only by the cultural bureaucracy of the Third World, but by some Western European intellectuals as well.

Since the universalism of modern ideologies has been replaced by the universalism of the modern media, the ideal of universal truth has been replaced by the reality of universal accessibility. Meanwhile, the universalist, museum-informed gaze leads to a kind of negative universalism. This creates an inner complicity between the museum's perspective and the repressive politics of identity, which seeks to purify itself of all external influences, interferences, and distortions. It would after all be naive to argue against this restrictive policy of national identity from the position of universalist humanism.

On the contrary: a museum's gaze is guided by the thoroughly humanistic desire to be collected and represented. However, modern subjectivity cannot content itself with being collected and contemplated—it wants to collect itself. And collecting has its own laws. The most important of these laws is that every functioning collection wants to expand and continuously include the other, the foreign. Collecting, almost by definition, is the collecting of the other that was not in the collection; what is tautological, redundant, and already known are no longer of interest to the collection. The central position of the museum in modern culture thus explains the preference for the new and the other in modernity—and above all in modern art. By preserving the artifacts of the past, the museum has created the need to discover and collect what is new and different, and to incorporate it into existing collections. Museum collecting is the real motor of cultural, and especially artistic, innovation in the modern age, because collecting constantly generates a demand for new cultural products.

At the beginning of the twentieth century, the artists of the historical avant-garde vigorously protested against museums and their art. And even today, museums are criticized in the name of fair representation of the other, the oppressed, and the excluded. But the real protest of the artists of the avant-garde was directed not against the institution of the museum as such but rather against the exclusive right of museum curators to select, collect, and present art objects. The artists of the avant-garde did not just want to be collected—they wanted to collect themselves. One can interpret the emergence of modern art as a change of perspective from collection object to collecting: the artists of the avant-garde internalized both the curator's gaze and the collector's gaze. Thus they began to act as agents of the expansion of museum collections by bringing into the museum all that had not previously been collected. Marcel Duchamp's *Fountain*, the urinal, was just one outstanding example among many others. Soon museums filled up with the trash of modern life, unloaded by the artists of the avant-garde. The art of the avant-garde thus became an integral part of the museum landscape because it served primarily to expand the museum system. The artists of the avant-garde were indeed the better curators—and it soon became apparent that the production of art similar to the art already collected by the museum was the safest way to avoid acceptance by the museum, for this art was already sufficiently represented in museum collections and was no longer needed.

Now it becomes clear why cultural-identity politics inevitably leads to a conflict with modern art. The advocates of cultural identity, including national cultural identity, do not want to abandon the perspective of being collected. They perceive themselves not as collectors who are always ready to sacrifice their fixed identity in order to collect the new, the other, and the foreign, but as objects of contemplation that always remain the same for the foreign gaze. By contrast, collectors and artists are constantly changing: their identity flows.

The opposition between collecting and being collected that constitutes the modern museum thus makes it possible to better define the relationship between museum and nation-state. Historically, the modern nation-state, represented by museum curators, collected. Everything and everyone were collected. But this clear distribution of roles is now a thing of the past. Ever since the days of the historical avant-garde we are increasingly living in a situation in which we can collect as well as be collected—that is, a divided situation. The state and its representatives are no longer the sole subjects of the collection—if they don't resort to direct violence in order to prevent the modern strategies of collecting. These strategies are mainly based on the possibilities of the modern media. Personal computers, video recorders, sound recorders, and online services give the individual the ability to build not just an imaginary museum of which André Malraux spoke, but a real, actual, individual museum that uses new data carriers to store and preserve the collected images, texts, and pieces of music. These new possibilities of media collecting are constantly expanding.

But with all these wonderful new ways of collecting, why is the talk about national cultural identity not stopping, but rather getting louder? Why does one still want to be collected instead of do the collecting? Perhaps the answer is that the collecting subjectivity is confronted with the frightening question of how to manifest and preserve itself in a museum when it has lost its own fixed identity through the constant expansion of its collections. Hegel wanted to remove the collecting subjectivity's fear of self-loss by relegating the emergence of historical consciousness and the formation of the museum to the end of history. For Hegel, the modern nation-state comes after the end of history. And because the nation-state is no longer immersed in history, it can see the whole history as its own history and see itself represented in the other, because this other is merely a precursor to its own genesis. Thus, collecting and being collected become two sides of a nation-state's self-representation.

After the avant-garde proved that history progresses by privatizing itself, thus allowing private subjectivity to act like a state—in this case, to collect—the split between collecting and being collected opened again. Now I would like to show that this split determines today's museum practice.

Among other things, the attempts to musealize "real communism" illustrate the dilemma of today's museum system: these attempts lead to almost insurmountable difficulties arising from the nature of the modern museum. On the surface, these difficulties are created because the art of the former communist countries appears to the museum's gaze as trivial, not innovative, not different, not exotic enough, and thus it cannot find a place in museum collections. I still remember quite well how the collapse of the communist regime—especially in Russia—created expectations in the art world of discovering a completely new, exotic, authentic art that originated in isolation from the West and could therefore offer a real opportunity for Western art collections. The disappointment was even greater as it turned out that the official and unofficial art of the former communist countries did not differ significantly from Western art on an aesthetic level. The hopes of discovery of something radically new, as in the case of Japanese or African art at the beginning of the twentieth century, were dashed, creating a certain bitterness in the Western art milieu. This disappointment, however, is enlightening. For communist civilization is the most recent civilization to die, and it is reasonable to suppose that every modern civilization will end like the communist one. It is thus significant that the communist civilization left no monuments of its own that are comparable to premodern models: nothing to compare to the Egyptian pyramids or Greek temples. But it is also not surprising, because in modernity cultural forms and things are produced no longer by hand but by mass industry and the culture industry as readymades to be individually used. Modern subjectivity manifests not through the production of things but through their use. This also applies to the Soviet Union. It was not that things were different there—their use, however, was very specific.

But how can the museum show the use of things—instead of the things themselves? Modern subjectivity disappears when it dies: the collections that it has collected are dissolved, the items from these collections are used differently in different contexts—there is no body left, no pyramid, no temple, nothing that would have permanence, but rather just a trash heap that needs to be disposed of. Incidentally, the Soviet Union understood itself as a kind of world museum. Soviet communism claimed to use the greatest achievements of human history as readymades for its purposes. That is why after the dissolution of communism nothing was left—like after the dissolution of an immaterial ghost. And indeed, in accordance with the famous first words of Engels and Marx's *Communist Manifesto*, communism was from the beginning nothing but a specter that scared European humanity. The demand for the creation of a particular, proletarian, socialist, formally and aesthetically alternative culture, which the Russian postrevolutionary avant-garde continued to formulate with the aim of giving a body to this ghost, was, as is well known, rejected by Soviet power. The Soviet Union of the Stalin era did not want to be collected, rather it wanted to become a collector—at the end of history, which was understood as the history of victorious communism. It is no coincidence that only the "proletarian" Russian art of the earlier years is often shown in Western museums: How can one actually show a museum in a museum? However, this question is of central importance to today's museum, for it is precisely the fear of complete self-dissolution in death that leads one to prefer being collected to collecting. Nietzsche already said that it would be better to be a work of art than an artist because a work of art has a certain fixed identity that can be stored.

We are dealing here with the basic paradox of the museum: museum collections serve to store things, but these collections themselves are extremely unstable. Having no identity of their own and being in constant flux, they are at risk of vanishing without a trace. In this sense, collecting is an event in time par excellence, although museum collections are designed to outlive time. It was one of the illusions of the nineteenth century that museum collections can be permanent—an illusion linked, among other things, to a belief in the permanence and omnipotence of the nation-state. And it is obvious that the eventfulness of the collection is now reflected in the museum practice itself, whereby I'm certainly thinking of art museums in particular.

Indeed, the museum is increasingly changing its function: from being the location of the permanent collection to a stage for temporary large-scale exhibitions, which, like theater spectacles, are performed only for a certain period of time and then dismantled and dissolved. As a rule, these large-scale exhibitions are organized by internationally known curators who have no clear government mandate and act largely autonomously as stars of the international art scene. In addition, individual artists have begun to stage large installations that are only shown for a certain period of time and thus, unlike the traditional artwork, do not retain their identity, but are dissolved. Large temporary exhibitions as well as major art installations are basically temporary museums; they are collections of heterogeneous objects in a homogeneous space and convey a certain historical perspective that does not necessarily correspond to a state-certified history, but presupposes a subjective view of the historical process. In fact, today's artists and curators are mostly migrants who move from one place to another to demonstrate their individual way of dealing with things, paying little heed to national boundaries. When exhibits or installations are dismantled, only a catalogue or video recording may be left over. Thus transience is demonstrated not only as historical, but also as infecting our representation of history. History itself becomes historicized. As a result, the claim made again and again by a minority—cultural, national, or other—for the inclusion of a certain cultural identity in a preexisting system of cultural representation loses all meaning, for this system of representation itself begins to flow, becomes transitory, loses its general binding nature, and proves to be dependent on the respective subjective decisions of a curator or an artist. There is no longer a binding universal system of representation, and fighting for a place in this system seems to be no longer relevant.

Museums were originally conceived as places of tranquility and permanence—in the midst of ever-changing and fast-flowing urban everyday life. Today, when we arrive in a city as tourists and ask what's new in this city, we mainly expect the answer to be that there is a new big exhibition. Today, time in the museum flows faster than beyond its walls—in the city itself usually nothing special happens. Thus, the contemporary museum is experienced as a privileged place of cultural change, events, or innovation. People gather at a major vernissage as people gathered earlier at a major theater or opera premiere. However, while the same operas are still being performed today, the exhibitions are very different. The theatricalization of today's museums is often experienced and lamented as their degradation. In fact, this theatricalization is a concession to the entertainment industry and the power of the media. But the theatricality of the museum has a different origin: the performance art of the 1960s. Today, however, we are confronted not merely with a specific art movement among many others, but with a shift in the system of museum representation itself. The theatricality that is manifested in today's exhibition practice is a reflection of the historical transience of the collection as a collection. We are confronted today with a flowing museum, a fluid cultural archive that undercuts all identities and makes them unsafe. In this flux, all cultural identities need to be constantly redefined.

This new situation of the museum might be frustrating for some—I see it as a great opportunity for modern subjectivity. Any politics of cultural identity, including national cultural identity, whether it be left wing or right wing, is doomed to fail in this flowing museum, because it is futile and hopeless to fix an identity in a context that itself flows. In any case, the nation-state can no longer stabilize this context: it lacks not only the money but also the will. Museum practice is increasingly left to the initiative of individuals, especially individual curators—namely, their ability to find sponsors, to arouse the interest of the media, and to propose innovative, original, attractive perspectives of art.

The temporary exhibition or the large-scale installation closely corresponds to the basic paradox of the museum. Each of them is a collection that shows itself—that is, each is an attempt to reconcile the practices of collecting and being collected, to bridge the gap between them. This succeeds again and again—but it succeeds only temporarily, as an event in time. Then the gap reappears, the exhibition or installation dissolves—and another exhibition is staged. An ultimate reconciliation, an ultimate identity between collecting and being collected—which Hegel sought and which was to be guaranteed through a permanent museum collection controlled by the nation-state—has proved impossible. One can of course still desire this impossibility and try to protect the state authority and canonical character of the museum's selection from the flow of time using terms such as "quality" or "tradition" or even "cultural identity"—but I do not believe that this ever works. Rather, one day the protecting power will be gone with the wind, as actually happened before our eyes with real existing socialism.

FUNDAMENTALISM AS A MIDDLE GROUND BETWEEN HIGH AND MASS CULTURE

The phenomenon of modern fundamentalism—or, one can say, populism—is certainly too complex to be treated in a single essay. So I will focus on one aspect. I would like to ask what attraction modern fundamentalism exerts on intellectuals and artists today. At least I find it evident that there is such an attraction. Many contemporary artists and intellectuals—despite their morally motivated rejection of fundamentalism—have a vague feeling that fundamentalism offers a certain, if perhaps wrong answer to a question that is important to them. And my question is the question about this question: Where does the need for fundamentalism come from in today's culture? In other words, I want to show that fundamentalism is a thoroughly modern phenomenon, born of the inner problems of modernity, and not just a relapse into premodern times that can be overcome by even more radical modernization.

I would suggest that the longing that nourishes fundamentalism arises from the split of modern culture into high culture and mass culture. This division is not only characteristic but also constitutive of modernity; in a sense, the modern is nothing else than this division. At the same time, this split provokes acute frustration on both sides. Serious authors that belong to high culture feel disconnected from the masses and thus are marginalized by this split. The idols of mass culture, on the other hand, want to be taken seriously. So everyone is looking for the fundament of a new culture in which the serious could become popular and the popular serious. It is this search for such a hidden fundament that leads to modern fundamentalism.

The content of traditional art and culture was limited to certain themes: what was represented or reflected by traditional art dealt with the sacred, with the glory of power, with certain "high" feelings, "true" thoughts, "beautiful" objects, and so on. This division of life into two realms—one that was allowed to be treated philosophically and artistically and one that was not—was increasingly perceived to be an arbitrary convention in the course of modern times, a purely external limitation that one tried to overcome. And indeed, over time, all relevant taboos were broken and all boundaries overcome: hence the contemporary feeling that "anything goes," that everything can be made the subject of a theoretical discussion or the object of art.

There is perhaps only one small thing left that still needs to be overcome: the split not of the content but of the form of culture into high and low, or avant-garde and kitsch, or pure art and commercial art—there are different ways of characterizing this split. But this task, as far as it is purely formal, does not seem to require as much heroic effort as the historical struggles of modernity for the appropriate content. It seems that a certain postmodern irony is sufficient to relativize the excessively high ambitions of high culture, to discover an empire of desire in mass culture, and thus to create a worldwide, homogeneous cultural space that knows no divisions and impossibilities, and in which on the level of content as well as on the level of form the individual is completely free to move in all directions.

Here, however, postmodernism makes a promise that it cannot fulfill and awakens a hope that must be disappointed. And fundamentalism of any kind is an attempt to fulfill this promise by force rather than irony. In order to make this clear, I would first like to address the question of how the division into high culture and mass culture works, how it came into being, and why this division seems so central. At the same time, I would like to show how the fundamental as it was conceived in early modernity differs from what we today, in times of postmodernism, call fundamentalism. And also to show to what extent, on the other hand, contemporary fundamentalism stands in the wake of the modernist search for the fundamental.

Now let us recall a relatively short text that first described the splitting of modern culture in a way that is still unsurpassed. I am referring here to Clement Greenberg's essay "Avant-Garde and Kitsch" from 1939. Greenberg introduces this text by stating that today's culture produces two distinct types of artifacts that cannot be subsumed under the term "art." His first examples include a painting by Georges Braque and a cover of the *Saturday Evening*

Post, both of which respond to the state of modern art, but in different ways. After art aestheticized the whole world, it reached its limits, and divided itself internally. According to Greenberg, the avant-garde takes the work of art itself as its subject: it renounces any external, "real" content and deals with the materiality of the artwork itself, with its own technical-material nature. For the work of art is not merely a picture of things, it is rather a thing among other things—and the avant-garde reveals the technical processes by which artworks, like other technical things, are made. Greenberg says that the avant-garde imitates art that imitates nature—and the avant-garde is able to imitate art because art is also part of nature.

Kitsch, on the other hand, does not analyze the work of art but strategically implements its effect, and this effect is known in advance: the work of art in modernity is a well-tested instrument of social influence. This means that in the context of kitsch—as in the context of the avant-garde—the work of art is conceived as a technical thing. In this regard, avant-garde and kitsch are identical and both belong to modernity. And so Greenberg summarizes his analysis through the now-famous formula: "If the avant-garde imitates the processes of art, kitsch, we now see, imitates its effects." In the midst of modern culture, there is a gap that cannot be bridged: either one makes avant-garde art or one makes kitsch. According to Greenberg, simultaneously practicing avant-garde art and kitsch is structurally impossible: if the work of art is analyzed, its effect is suspended. Kitsch directly serves the desire of the audience; its goal is a symbolic fulfillment of the audience's wishes. The avant-garde, on the other hand, is ascetic, reflective, analytic—and ineffective.

Greenberg's analysis is certainly reminiscent of the writings of Theodor W. Adorno—but the drama that characterizes Adorno's understanding of art is completely foreign to Greenberg. Art that demonstrates the drama of the modern soul and its utopian aspirations is for Adorno the art of the avant-garde, but for Greenberg that art remains in the realm of kitsch. The criterion of distinction does not lie in whether art wants to demonstrate harmony and an affirmative attitude or disharmony and a critical attitude. For Greenberg, if art wants to demonstrate anything, to express anything, it belongs in the realm of kitsch.

Although Greenberg's analysis sounds theoretical and neutral, making both avant-garde art and kitsch legitimate activities after the end of traditional art, he obviously prefers the avant-garde—and not so much for aesthetic reasons as for moral ones. The avant-garde is pure in the moral sense: self-sufficient and autonomous. Kitsch, on the other hand, is manipulative and interested only in appearances. However, this moral choice reveals its true meaning when Greenberg abandons the familiar sphere of Western civilization divided by class and turns to the analysis of the totalitarian cultures of National Socialist Germany and the Soviet Union, with Soviet art clearly at the center of his argument.

For Greenberg, the analysis of totalitarian, and especially Soviet art is of paramount importance for the question of the distinction between avant-garde and kitsch—it is not a case among many others, rather it is a test case for his theory. As is well known, Greenberg proclaims all totalitarian art, including Soviet art, to be kitsch, since this art is designed to achieve certain propagandistic effects. This seems to be immediately obvious, and in a certain sense it is also correct. However, avant-garde and kitsch are defined by Greenberg as products of the split through the middle of modern culture. It is a dualism that only has meaning as a dualism. But if it is said that the entire culture of totalitarianism is *only* kitsch, then the word kitsch immediately loses its theoretical relevance and becomes the instrument of a moral judgment that only means that totalitarian art is morally bad. But this judgment does not grasp or reflect the search of totalitarian culture for totality. For totalitarianism consists precisely in the attempt to overcome the division of modern art into avant-garde and kitsch, to remove the corresponding divisions, and to create a homogeneous—and therefore total—cultural space.

In fact, the project of overcoming the division of modern culture was originally formulated in the context of the avant-garde itself. From the beginning, the artists and theorists of the avant-garde saw the emergence of this division—and from the beginning they experienced this division as a new and unreasonable limitation of their creativity that substituted old taboos and boundaries. The formal structuring of the work of art was never an end in itself for the artists of the avant-garde, it was rather a precursor to the discovery of a universal formal-technical nature of art beyond all its historical, national, regional, stylistic, and other particular characteristics. Kazimir Malevich's *Black Square*, for example, is one of the results of this analysis—the transcendental scheme of every possible picture, so to speak—but *Black Square* was also conceived by Malevich as the starting point for a new art that should not only analyze but also eventually replace old art. It reveals the technical fundament of traditional art, which used to be masked by a variety of traditional forms, so that in the future one could build a new unified culture on this fundament. The avant-garde is not only analytic and universal, as Greenberg says—it also wants to be fundamental. Its analytic discoveries are intended to form the unified fundament of a new culture that should not have any room for kitsch. Greenberg overlooks this fundamentalist claim of the avant-garde in his analysis. Malevich would never accept Greenberg's duality of avant-garde and kitsch, which suggests their equality. For Malevich, kitsch should simply disappear to make space for a new art that should be analytic and, at the same time, as a result of previous analytic work, exceptionally effective in determining the conditions of art's production and reception. Malevich is just one example among many. The Bauhaus, de Stijl, and all the other schools of the radical avant-garde wanted to reshape the human habitat in its totality and radically increase the effectiveness of art through direct manipulation of the human unconscious.

Soviet communism was also an attempt to shape the totality of life and change individual unconscious by placing the population in a new, completely different life context. At the same time, Soviet ideology thought of communism as the manifestation of the universal, fundamental conditions of social life that were previously hidden under all possible historical particularisms. To a certain extent, the same applied to the ideology of National Socialism, whereby class struggle was replaced by racial struggle. The Aryan race was conceived as a race among many others, but at the same time a universal race—just as the proletariat in Marxism is conceived as a class among many others and at the same time as the embodiment of all humanity. The concept of the proletariat, as well as the concept of the Aryan race, exemplifies the fundamental paradox of avant-garde universalism: something particular is declared universal at the same time, just as Malevich's *Black Square* functions as a single image among many but should represent the universal image at the same time, the transcendental image as such.

Ultimately, the totalitarian, universalistic ideologies of this era could neither dissolve nor endure the abovementioned paradox—and they broke. Incidentally, the products of this break confirm that Greenberg was wrong in defining totalitarian culture as kitsch. Totalitarian culture is certainly not high culture, but it is not kitsch either—if only because it is boring and therefore does not have the entertaining effect that one expects and demands of kitsch. Totalitarian culture does not fulfill one's desire. The person who doesn't have the chance to enjoy a striptease is certainly ready to at least watch a military parade, but remains unsatisfied. Totalitarian culture was able to work because it made its real theme the external, political compulsion to consume this culture. As this compulsion disappeared, so did the immediate attractiveness of this culture. Today's mass audiences want to see the *Terminator* films, listen to hard rock or techno—but not be ideologically schooled. The eradication of the boundary between high culture and mass culture, attempted by the different totalitarian regimes of modernity, could not succeed. It is not possible to find a strategy that would combine wish fulfillment and asceticism, enthusiasm and analysis. The same cultural products can easily be used in both the realm of high culture and the realm of mass culture, as Pop art demonstrated. But these different uses do not abolish the corresponding boundary—rather, they confirm it.

Therein lies the very cause of all the bitter complaints that are heard today after the collapse of Soviet communism—not only in Russia but worldwide. The disappearance of communism reinforces the boundary between the intellectuals and the artists on the one side and the masses on the other, which prevents a mass impact of art. Not only the left-leaning, pro-communist intelligentsia suffer from this, so do the right-wing anti-communists of all stripes who have derived their claim to social impact from the same communist claim, albeit in a negative form. The Russian intelligentsia suffers from it especially, because they lived by this claim for a long while. During the Soviet era, the Russian intelligentsia wanted freedom, to overcome the border that separated them from the outside world, from the world of Western modernity. Now this border has disappeared, but the old border, the old and deeper gap between high culture and mass culture, is back. And only now does one remember why in the past totalitarianism was practiced: to overcome this gap.

A Russian writer today is full of concern for the tragic fate of his country. He suffers, he sacrifices his time, his money—because he doesn't earn anything with his work—and his whole life to be useful to his country. He is full of deep feelings and thoughts; he is authentic, sincere, and deeply shocked to see what has happened to his country—and wants to convey this shock to his fellow citizens, strengthen them spiritually, provide spiritual nutrition to help them overcome this tragic period of national history with dignity, and thus do something important and meaningful. These are all lofty goals, which the writer may suspect are shared by most others. Now, this writer writes a novel—and finds that nobody wants to read it. Neither the Russian audience nor the international public want to read it. The representatives of high culture say, "This novel is trivial, banal. It does not reflect the process of writing, textuality, or intertextuality. Obviously its author has not heard of Barthes, Blanchot, or Derrida." The novel is searched in vain for the problem of the body, desire, and the other. Also the end of literature is never mentioned. Thus: it doesn't have a chance.

But the same happens with the popular reception, because the mass audience finds the book too boring, too instructive, too complicated, not entertaining enough, not exciting enough—and rather buys, as everywhere across the world, a new book by Stephen King, John Grisham, or Michael Crichton. Our good author has thus found himself in the gap between high culture and mass culture—in a cultural emptiness in which only a downward free fall is possible. All of his noble feelings disappear into this emptiness—and find their grave in its shallows. For they don't belong to kitsch or high culture, to entertainment or an analysis of the writing process. But our writer does not want emptiness: he wants a fundament on which to stand. On the other hand, the writer no longer believes in the universal fundament of the totalitarian era: he knows that this fundament cannot be found anywhere in this emptiness. All pertinent constructions have failed before his eyes—and the white bones of their engineers can still be seen in the gap. Our writer has experienced the free fall of the Russian avant-garde, totalitarian Soviet culture, and the "universal human values" of Gorbachev's era—and has drawn his conclusions.

So our writer faces the following problem: he desperately needs a fundament because he cannot produce either avant-garde or kitsch—his education and personal history simply did not prepare him for that. But he knows that there is no fundament. And so our writer becomes a fundamentalist. I would call someone a fundamentalist who seeks a fundament even though he knows for sure that there is none. The insight that there is no fundament opens the postmodern perspective—fundamentalism belongs to postmodernity. The insight that there is no fundament can cause two different reactions: one can be satisfied with this insight or one can counter this insight with the project of building a fundament precisely because there is none. Here lies the central difference between modern totalitarianism and postmodern fundamentalism. Totalitarianism believed that it had discovered the universal and fundamental (as class, race, etc.) and wanted to enforce its discovery by political means. Fundamentalism, on the other hand, has to first create the fundament. This results in different cultural and political strategies that can be characterized in this way: instead of a global universal power, an alliance is sought between local fundamentalism and global pluralism. This alliance is possible because postmodernism itself, as mentioned, seeks to overcome the boundary between high culture and mass culture.

Thus, kitschy images or kitschy texts of American mass culture had their immediate effect neutralized within the framework of early Pop art by their transfer to the context of high culture. In the museum, an image from advertising becomes ineffective, even in Greenberg's sense. In the museum, a poster of Marilyn Monroe looks like Malevich's *Black Square*: self-referential, autonomous, a pure form that only demonstrates the process of its own production. Over time, a greater and greater number of kitschy forms or kitschy forms of tradition or even kitschy forms of the avant-garde had their immediate effect neutralized in this way, and thus became the avant-garde in Greenberg's sense.

On the other hand, Greenberg's formulation of the autonomy of art was heavily criticized. The art of the avant-garde was increasingly interpreted as an expression of desire or placed inpolitical, social, and linguistic contexts to demonstrate its dependence on these contexts. In the era of postmodernism we can thus observe a twofold and seemingly paradoxical interpretative move: kitsch is interpreted as avant-garde and avant-garde as kitsch. However, these two seemingly opposite interpretive strategies have the same goal: a gradual leveling of the avant-garde and mass culture, and thus a soft, nontotalitarian closing of the gap between them, or the fulfillment of the totalitarian program with democratic, liberal, pluralistic, soft methods.

However, this did not overcome the boundary between avant-garde and kitsch but merely transferred it to the interior of every cultural sign, for every sign received an autonomous, elitist, high-cultural, avant-garde, and at the same time "kitschy," mass-cultural, heteronomous interpretation. Every cultural sign today is divided in itself. The modern split between avant-garde and kitsch, between pure form and its external effect, no longer functions as a split in the entire field of signs, so that we, like Greenberg in the modern age, could decide whether a sign belongs to the avant-garde or kitsch. Today, however, it is not the field of signs but the field of interpretation that is split. Every sign today is both avant-garde and kitsch at once. The field of interpretation of every sign is thus split—and we cannot choose between these two interpretations. This is the undecidability of interpretation that Paul de Man speaks of.

And above all, we ourselves are such divided signs. For in postmodernity, personality, individuality, and subjectivity are thought of as a sign or mask that means nothing, has no referent. So we are inwardly divided between the ability to play freely with all sorts of cultural masks, identities, and qualities and the fact that we always wear a mask that fixes our cultural identity. And we cannot escape this external image that society makes of us and imposes on us, as was possible in modernity. We can no longer aspire to discover our true, hidden, inner, universal identity and break the outer, false, particular identity, because as an alternative to our external identity we find only the general game of signs in which our cultural mask has a particular significance. So we cannot throw away our mask to expose our hidden, true face—and we cannot "reveal" the other by tearing away their mask to show their true face. The mask is the face—behind it, nothing is hidden. But on the other hand, all masks can swap places and create a carnival, which Mikhail Bakhtin spoke of as part of his theory of the "carnivalization" of culture.

Postmodernism has thus not fulfilled its promise to bridge the gap that defined modernity, it only shifted this gap into the interior of each sign, hollowed out each sign, and staged a constant exchange of signs that involves each sign equally. However, this constant exchange of signs makes one uneasy. And so the desire arises to simply stop it. This desire is the desire for fundamentalism. It is no longer about revealing oneself as proletarian or Aryan, or perhaps revealing, unmasking, others as bourgeois or Jewish, as was the case in classical modernity. Rather, one wants to proclaim the mask to be the face—knowing that it is a mask. This proclamation does not mean the discovery, overcoming, or transformation of what exists—nor the subjugation of pluralism to a universal principle. The only thing that happens is the interruption of the constant exchange of masks: the carnival comes to a standstill and becomes a motionless scene. The world becomes a museum exhibition. The signs of Germanness are no longer exchanged with the signs of Americanness, the signs of Russianness with the signs of the Westernness, the signs of the avant-garde with the signs of kitsch. However, it is an exhibition without an observer, because only God would be able to see it. Everything human becomes an image. And every image gets a fundament to which it is nailed so as not to be exchanged.

Incidentally, the nature of the fundament is always the same, even though the images are different. It is therefore possible to talk about fundamentalism as such without having to specify which fundamentalism is being discussed. The universalism of modernity was quite diverse. Different universalisms had to fight against one another to prove their universality. Class, race, the unconscious, the structure of language, and innumerable other universalisms were constantly at war with one another. Modern universalism was thus belligerent and pluralistic. By contrast, postmodern fundamentalism is extremely homogeneous in its theoretical assumptions and cultural-political strategies. The fundamentalist rhetoric of the absolute, the ultimate truth, the highest values, the sacred sacrifice, metaphysical danger, unconditional surrender, and responsibility are completely interchangeable—in this rhetoric any sign can be used without the rhetoric needing any correction. This rhetoric of the fundamental, the ultimate, the highest, the absolute, and so on, unfolds in the void created by postmodernism. This rhetoric only commands the postmodern movement of signs to stop—no matter if the signs are beautiful or not. In fact, all that is needed is a fundament on which to attach all cultural signs—and not a multitude of fundaments, as in modernity, so that we are indeed entitled to speak about fundamentalism as a unitary phenomenon.

Today literally everything has the same opportunity to become a fortified, fundamentalist sign, and thus acquire the highest value. Seals that are endangered or old customs that are being forgotten—they all address the unconditional demand of absolute sacrifice, which we can no longer ward off. It used to be said that such demands were justified, but that there was something more important, something deeper, even higher, such as God or reason, culture, love of the arts, or charity. Today we can no longer argue this way, because all hierarchies and emphases have been dismantled by postmodernism. All signs are constantly interchanging, all stand side by side on the same fundament. In this situation, every sign has the same claim to the highest value and fundamental meaning. The fundamental was democratized in postmodernism. Fundamentalism is the guiding ideology and, at the same time, the rhetorical practice of this democratization of the fundamental, the ultimate truth, the absolute moral obligation. Today, absolutely everything can become absolutely important—because everything is equally unimportant.

But the most important thing is the separation between the highest value and the universal claim of today's fundamentalism. Previously they were inseparable. Only the universal was allowed to be the highest value; just as particular concepts must be logically subordinated to the more general concept, particular values must also be subordinated to the highest, universal value. This inner connection between logic and ethics is deeply rooted in our tradition of thought. It does not apply anymore. After post-structuralist theorizing replaced logic with rhetoric, one can no longer assert that one concept is logically subordinate to another. Rather, every word can be put into a rhetorical context with every other word. And every cultural sign can become a sign of the highest value through its rhetorical anchoring in the fundamental, without having to designate a universal concept.

Thus, above all, national values and customs are declared particularly valuable without the compulsion to prove their general validity. If National Socialism still needed a connection to the universal—the name itself really means nothing else than this connection of the particular (nationalism) with the universal (socialism)—today every particular nationalism can assert its absolute value without even questioning the universality of this value. This new situation is particularly evident in the countries of Eastern Europe, which were formerly subject to the universalist ideology of communism.

Russia finds itself currently in a cultural situation that has no comparison in its long history. For the first time, the national question is posed—the question of the peculiarity of the Russian nation, its national interests, geographic boundaries, national values and goals. The Soviet Union never understood itself as a nation-state. Rather, the Soviet Union defined itself as a transition to the worldwide victory of communism—to a unified communist humanity in which the Soviet state, as a specific historical entity, would dissolve. The claim to power of the Soviet leadership sprang from this universal vision. The Communist Party legitimized its absolute power within the Soviet Union by the fact that this community of over one hundred different peoples was to be the model for all communist humanity, beyond all national, egoistic interests.

The national feelings of the Russians were repressed in the Soviet Union, as were the national feelings and interests of the other peoples. The writings of most Russian historians and philosophers, as well as much of the literature of the past, were banned in the Soviet period because of their alleged Russian-nationalist stance. All Russian history, including intellectual history, was officially described as leading to the emergence of the Russian Communist Party. The religion—Russian Orthodox Christianity—was persecuted and kept silent. Thus a large part of Russian national culture was excluded from official cultural life. To call something Russian in a positive way meant it was only part of a culture that has proved capable of receiving the good news of communism and helping it to victory.

In the West, people often speak of the "West-East conflict" when there is talk about the struggle, now historical, between Western capitalism and Eastern communism. People forget that the communist doctrine is of Western origin and is not "Eastern" but universalist. This doctrine found fertile ground in Russia because it promised Westernization—integration in the West beyond all traditional religious and national differences that separated Russia and the West for centuries. In the long civil war that preceded the establishment of Soviet power, one fought on the red, Soviet side for "the International" and on the white, anti-Soviet side for Russia. Russia lost this war. The International won it. Now it's time for revenge.

At the end of the Second World War, the collapse of National Socialism meant first and foremost the defeat of nationalism—not of socialism. The recent defeat of Soviet power means the defeat of internationalism and the worldwide victory of nationalism. People often wondered whether National Socialism and communism would differ significantly. No matter the answer, grave differences in the ideological repercussions of these regimes remain: they compromised different cultural attitudes, patterns of argumentation, and theoretical constructions, thereby having a lasting influence on later ideological decisions.

Communist universalism relieves the postcommunist countries of any historical guilt. The specter of communism of which the *Communist Manifesto* famously spoke is guilty of everything—but a ghost cannot be held liable. As far as people are concerned, they are in fact not communists but Russians, Ukrainians, Latvians, or Georgians, who as such were oppressed or persecuted under the ghostly communist regime. The universalism of communist ideology disburdened, just as the nationalism of National Socialist ideology was burdening. Therefore communism seems to perform better in comparison. But experience shows that many people suffer more from a postcommunist unbearable lightness of being than from the tragedy of national guilt. A national tragedy elevates—a child of perpetrators or a child of victims is born with tragedy in their chest, which distinguishes and elevates. So if a writer wants to be tragic without a big personal effort or inconvenience, the source of tragic feeling and its justification can always be found in a national tragedy. And which nation does not demonstrate tragedy?

Self-identification with the national past provides the individual intellectual or artist with the tragic seriousness that their everyday existence clearly lacks in the commercial, superficial, comfortable present. Any intellectual or artist wants to be taken seriously and stand at the height of a great and tragic cultural tradition. But everyone fears that this goal is particularly hard to reach today because the times are not up to it. It makes one seem a bit cheap and unserious—and one feels aggrieved.

Today's nationalist fundamentalism thrives on this demand for the serious, the tragic, and the ultimate, which nationalism best corresponds to because it is most likely to enable one to escape one's own time and relocate into a condition of timeless tragedy—to understand one's own life as part of a national whole and thus become the subject of historical tragedy. Therefore, as part of a nation, people believe to be experiencing something great that would otherwise be withheld from their modest lives. This gives pleasure and awakens pride. It is far from this postmodern style of nationalism to imagine one's nation as superior and chosen, because the claim of superiority still presupposes certain universal criteria and could be refuted. By contrast, a tragic nationalism of the postmodern kind does not claim to be universal at all. It is only about deep feelings and inner despair, which elevate people above the superficiality of their own present—but this kind of sublime, admittedly, is not measurable.

Thus, postmodernity and fundamentalism are equally concerned with the break between high culture and mass culture, between avant-garde and kitsch. But they use different strategies. Postmodernism opens the institutions of high, serious culture to mass culture and to the infinite exchange of all signs. This gives the impression that high culture has been hollowed out, has lost its seriousness, has dissolved in the flow of mass culture and entertainment, and thus has betrayed the great cultural tradition. So one tries the opposite approach: in the form of a national tradition one seeks to attach the signs of mass culture to the fundamental seriousness of the high, tragic attitude. Here high culture finally triumphs over mass culture: in fundamentalism, the border between avant-garde and kitsch is eliminated, as kitsch submits to the gravity of the autonomous, high avant-garde. This seems to stop the frivolous, irresponsible, postmodern game. Eliminating the border between high culture and mass culture means no longer surrendering to mass culture but finding a middle ground that allows the avoidance of both superficial entertainment and elitist inefficiency.

This strategy is certainly as understandable as it is justified. However, experience and theory have often shown that this border cannot be eliminated—at most, it can be displaced. Even fundamentalism, too, merely exchanges the fundaments.

THE CITY IN TRANSIT

Cities originally came about as projects for the future: people moved from the countryside to the city in order to escape the ancient forces of nature and build a new future that they could shape and control themselves. The entire course of human history has been defined by this movement from the countryside to the city—a dynamic to which history in fact owes its direction. Although life in the country has repeatedly been stylized as the golden era of harmony and "natural" contentment, such embellished memories of a life spent in nature have never prevented people from continuing on their originally chosen historical path. In this respect, the city as such possesses an intrinsically utopian dimension by virtue of being situated outside the natural order. The city is located in the *ou-topos.* City walls once delineated the place where a city was built, clearly designating its utopian character. Indeed, the more utopian a city was signaled to be, the harder it was to reach and enter, be it the Tibetan city of Lhasa or the heavenly city of Jerusalem. Traditionally, cities isolated themselves from the rest of the world in order to make their own way into the future. So a genuine city is not only utopian, it is also anti-tourist: it dissociates itself from space and moves through time.

Of course, the struggle with nature did not cease inside the city either. At the beginning of *Discourse on the Method*, Descartes observed that for a rational and perfect city to exist, historically evolved cities would in fact need to be completely demolished since they were not immune to the irrationality of the natural order. Later, Le Corbusier called for the demolition of all historical cities—including Paris—to make way for new, rational cities to be built in their place. Thus the utopian dream of total rationality, transparency, and controllability of an urban environment unleashed a historical dynamism that is manifested in the perpetual transformation of all realms of urban life. The quest for utopia forces the city into a permanent process of surpassing itself and destroying itself—which is why the city has become the natural venue for revolutions, upheavals, new beginnings, fleeting fashion, and incessantly changing lifestyles. Built as a secure haven, the city soon became the stage for criminality, instability, destruction, anarchy, and terrorism. Accordingly, the city presents itself as a blend of utopia and dystopia, whereby modernity undoubtedly cherishes and applauds the dystopian rather than the utopian aspects—decadence, danger, and eeriness.

This city of eternal temporariness has frequently been depicted in literature and staged in cinema. This is the city we know from *Blade Runner* or *Terminator*, for instance, where everything has the potential to be blown up or razed to the ground simply because people are always endeavoring to clear space for what's next, for the future. And over and over again the arrival of the future is impeded and delayed because the remains of what's already built can never be fully removed and the ongoing preparation phase never completed. If anything permanent ultimately exists in our cities, it is only this constant preparation for the creation of something permanent—the perpetual postponement of permanent solutions, never-ending adjustments, eternal repairs, and piecemeal adaptation to new constraints.

In modernity, the utopian impulse—the quest for an ideal city—has grown progressively weaker, and has been gradually supplanted by the fascination of tourism. Today, when we cease to be satisfied with the life that is offered to us in our own city, we no longer strive to change, revolutionize, or rebuild the city; instead, we simply move to a new city—temporarily or permanently—in search of what our home city lacked. Mobility between cities—in all shades of tourism and migration—has radically altered our relationship to the city. Globalization and mobility have fundamentally called the utopian character of the city into question by reinscribing the urban ou-topos into the topography of globalized space. It is no coincidence that in his reflections on this globalized world, Marshall McLuhan coined the term "global village" to describe the opposite of the global city. For the tourist and the migrant alike, the key issue has become the country in which the city is located.

It was primarily the first phase of modern tourism—which I will now term "romantic tourism"—that spawned a distinctly anti-utopian attitude toward the city. Romantic tourism, in its nineteenth-century guise, cast a certain paralysis over the city, which was commonly viewed as an aggregate of tourist attractions. Romantic tourists are not in search of universal utopian models, rather they seek cultural differences and local identities. Their gaze is not utopian but conservative—directed not at the future but at the past and origins. Romantic tourism is a machine designed to transform temporariness into permanence, fleetingness into timelessness, ephemerality into monumentality. When tourists move through a city, the place is exposed to their gaze as something eternal that lacks history, which amounts to a sum of edifices that have always been there and always will remain as they were at the very moment of the tourists' arrival, since tourists are unable to keep track of a city's historical transformation or perceive the utopian impulse propelling the city into the future. So it can be said that romantic tourism abolishes utopia precisely by having us see it as already accomplished. The touristic gaze romanticizes, monumentalizes, and eternalizes everything that comes within its range. In turn, the city adapts to this materialized utopia, to the medusan gaze of the romantic tourist. A city's monuments, after all, have not always been standing there simply waiting for tourists to see them; instead, it was tourism that created these monuments. It is tourism that monumentalizes a city: the gaze of the passing tourist transforms urban life—relentlessly fluid, incessantly changing—into a monumental image of eternity. The growing volume of tourism also speeds up the process of monumentalization.

We are now witnessing a sheer explosion of eternity, or to put it more succinctly, of eternalization in our cities. It is no longer only famed monuments such as the Eiffel Tower or the Cologne Cathedral that seem to cry out for preservation, but rather anything does that sparks a sense of familiarity in us to make us think, "Look things have always been this way and this is how they'll stay." Even, for example, a run-down or high-crime New York neighborhood is imbued with the dignified aura of monumentality for visitors. The first striking thing is the visitors' impression that this is how things have always been here and how they will stay—the street life, the picturesque city ruins, the lurking sense of danger. At a later date, reading in the papers that this district is being gentrified, the reaction is of shock and sadness, similar to how one feels upon hearing that the Cologne Cathedral or the Eiffel Tower were being demolished to make way for a department store. One thinks, "Here a slice of authentic, unique, and different life is going to be destroyed, here everything is going to be flattened and rendered banal, here what was monumental and eternal will be lost forever." But this grief is premature. Because on the next visit to the now gentrified area, one says, Everything here is incredibly insipid, ugly, and banal, it must have always been this insipid and will always stay this way. With this, the area is instantly re-monumentalized—because while traveling, the everyday and banal are experienced as being as monumental as that which is exceptional. Rather than being guided by some intrinsic quality of a monument, our sense of monumentality is derived from the relentless process of monumentalization, de-monumentalization, and re-monumentalization unleashed by the romantic tourist's gaze.

Incidentally, it was Kant—in his theory of the sublime in *Critique of Judgment*—who first philosophically assessed the figure of the globally roaming tourist in search of aesthetic experiences. He describes the romantic tourist as someone who perceives even their own demise as a possible travel destination and has the capacity to experience it as a sublime event. As examples of "the mathematically sublime," Kant cites mountains and oceans, phenomena that appear to dwarf normal human proportions. As instances of "the dynamically sublime," he quotes colossal natural events such as storms, volcanic eruptions, and other catastrophes whose overpowering force directly threatens our lives. Yet as destinations visited by the romantic tourist, these threats are not in themselves sublime—just as urban monuments are not intrinsically monumental either. According to Kant, sublimity does not lie in nature, rather it lies in the capacity we have within us to judge and enjoy without fear the very things that threaten us. Hence the subject of Kant's infinite ideas of reason is the tourist who repeatedly embarks on journeys in search of the extraordinary in enormity and danger in order to confirm their own superiority and sublimity in regard to nature. But in another section of the treatise, Kant also points out that "the simple-minded, and, for the most part, intelligent Savoyard peasant [...] unhesitatingly called all lovers of snow-mountains fools. And who can tell whether he would have been so wide of the mark."[1] Indeed, in Kant's time the romantic tourist's gaze still differed radically from that of the mountain dweller. But in the meantime, as we well know, the situation has again completely changed. Even though the inhabitants of any particular region might still regard internationally roaming tourists as fools, they nonetheless increasingly sense the need—no doubt for economic reasons—to absorb the globalized gaze and adjust their own way of life to the aesthetic predilections of their visitors, the travelers and tourists. Besides, mountain dwellers have also started to travel and become tourists.

The times in which we live are thus an era of post-romantic (i.e., comfortable) and total tourism, marking a new phase in the history of the relations between the urban ou-topos and the world's topography. This new phase is in fact not hard to characterize: rather than the individual romantic tourist, it is instead all manner of people, things, signs, and images drawn from all kinds of local cultures that are now leaving their places of origin and journeying around the world. The rigid distinction between romantic world travelers and a locally based, sedentary population is rapidly being erased. Cities are no longer waiting for the arrival of tourists, rather they are starting to join the global flow, to reproduce themselves on a world scale, and to expand in all directions. As they do so, their movement and proliferation are happening at a much faster pace than the individual romantic tourist was ever capable of. This fact now prompts the widespread outcry that all cities increasingly resemble one another and are beginning to homogenize, with the result that when tourists arrive in a new city they end up seeing the same things they encountered in all the other cities. This experience of similarity among all contemporary cities often misleads the observer to assume that the globalization process is erasing local cultural idiosyncrasies, identities, and differences. The truth is not that these distinctions have disappeared, but that they in turn have also embarked on a journey—they have started to reproduce themselves and expand.

For quite a while now we have been able to enjoy Chinese cuisine not only in China but also in New York, Paris, and Dortmund. On speculating in which cultural surroundings Chinese food tastes best, the answer is not necessarily "China." If we go to China today and the cities fail to seem exotic, this is by no means simply because these places have been strongly shaped by an international modern architecture of Western origin, but also because much of what one witnesses there as "authentically Chinese" has long been familiar to visitors from America or Europe, where such Chinese attributes can be found in any town or city. So, far from being endangered, local features have in fact become global. The differences between various cities have turned into differences within cities themselves. The result is a world city that has replaced the global village. This world city operates like a reproductive machine that multiplies, relatively swiftly, any local attribute of one particular city in all other cities around the world. Thus, over the course of time, quite dissimilar cities begin to resemble one another, without any particular city serving as a prototype for all the others. When a new variation of rap music emerges in a borough of New York it promptly begins to influence the acoustic environment of other cities—just as a new sect in India swiftly multiplies and spreads its ashrams throughout the entire world.

But above all, it is today's artists and intellectuals that are spending most of their time traveling—rushing from one exhibition to the next, from one project to another, from one lecture to the next, from one local cultural context to another. All active participants in today's cultural world are expected to offer their productive output to a global audience, to be constantly on the move from one venue to the next, and to present their work with equal conviction regardless of where they are. A life spent in transit like this is bound up with equal degrees of hope and fear. On the one hand, artists are now given the possibility of evading the pressure of prevailing local tastes in a relatively painless way. Thanks to modern means of communication, they can seek out like-minded associates from all over the world instead of having to adjust to the tastes and cultural orientation of their immediate surroundings. This, incidentally, also explains the somewhat depoliticized condition of contemporary art that is so frequently deplored. Formerly, artists compensated for the lack of response to their work among people of their own culture by projecting their aspirations largely onto the future, dreaming of political change that would one day spawn a new and future viewer of their work. Today the utopian impulse has shifted direction: acknowledgment is sought no longer in time but in space. Globalization has replaced the future as the site of utopia. So rather than practicing avant-garde politics based on the future, we now embrace the politics of travel, migration, and nomadic life, paradoxically rekindling the utopian dimension that ostensibly died out in the era of romantic tourism.

This means that as travelers we are now observers, not so much of various local settings as of our fellow travelers, all caught up in a permanent global journey that has become identical with life in the world city. Moreover, present-day urban architecture has begun to move faster than its viewers. This architecture is already there before the tourists arrive. In the race between tourists and architecture, it is now the tourists who lose. Although they are annoyed to encounter the same architecture everywhere they go, they are also amazed to see how successful a certain type of architecture has proved to be in a wide range of disparate cultural settings. We are now prepared to be attracted and persuaded particularly by artistic strategies capable of producing art that achieves the same degree of success regardless of the cultural context and conditions in which it is viewed. What fascinates us nowadays is not locally defined differences and cultural identities, but rather artistic forms that persistently assert their own specific identity and integrity wherever they are presented. Since we have all become tourists capable only of observing other tourists, what especially impresses us about all things, customs, and practices is their capacity for reproduction, dissemination, self-preservation, and survival under the most diverse of local conditions.

With this, the strategies of post-romantic total tourism are now supplanting the old strategies of utopia and enlightenment. Redundant architectural and artistic styles, political prejudices, religious myths, and traditional customs are no longer to be transcended in the name of universality, rather they are to be touristically reproduced and globally disseminated. Today's world city is homogenous without being universal. People used to believe that attaining universal ideas and creativity depended on the individual transcending one's own local traditions in the name of universal validity. Consequently, the utopia hailed by the radical avant-garde was reductive: one was first expected to aspire to a pure, elemental form stripped of all historical and local traits in order to claim its universal and global validity. This, too, was how classic modernist art proceeded—first reduce something to its essence and then spread it around the world. Today's art and architecture, by contrast, are globally disseminated without even first bothering with any such reduction to some universally valid essence.

The possibilities of global networking, mobility, reproduction, and distribution have rendered traditional calls for the universality of form or content utterly obsolete. Nowadays any cultural phenomenon can proliferate without being required to make claims for its own universality. Universal thinking is being supplanted by the media's universal dissemination of any kind of local ideas whatsoever. The universality of artistic form is being displaced by the global reproduction of any kind of local form. As a result, while today's viewers are constantly confronted with the same urban surroundings, it is impossible to say whether the formal character of these surroundings is in any sense "universal." In the postmodernist period, all architecture following in the footsteps of the Bauhaus was criticized for being monotonous and reductive—

as architecture that first leveled and then erased all local identities. But today the whole plethora of local styles is spreading at the same global pace as the International Style once did. As a consequence of total tourism, we are now witnessing the emergence of a homogeneity bereft of all universality, an utterly new and up-to-date development. Accordingly, in the context of total tourism we once more encounter a utopia, but one that radically differs from the static, immobile utopia of the city that demarcates itself from the surrounding topography and is segregated from the rest of the country. Thus we now all live in a world city where living and traveling have become synonymous, where there is no longer any perceptible difference between the city's residents and its visitors. The utopia of an eternal universal order has been replaced by the utopia of constant global mobility. In turn, the dystopian dimension of this utopia has also changed—terrorist cells and designer drugs now proliferate in cities all around the world at the same pace as, say, Prada boutiques.

Interestingly, as early as the beginning of the twentieth century several radical utopians in the Russian avant-garde put forward plans for future cities where all apartments and houses would be uniform in design and mobile. In an astonishing manner, their designs made the touristic journey synonymous with its destination. In a similar vein, the poet Velimir Khlebnikov proposed that all inhabitants of Russia be lodged inside glass cells mounted on wheels, allowing them to travel everywhere freely and see everything while also staying visible to others. Thus the tourist and the city dweller become identical—and all that the tourist is capable of seeing is other tourists. Incidentally, Malevich took Khlebnikov's project one step further when he suggested placing every single person inside an individual cosmic vessel to constantly float in space and fly from one planet to the next. His proposal irrevocably turns the human subject into an eternal tourist on a never-ending journey, whereby, insulated within their very own yet always identical cell, humans become monuments themselves. We encounter an analogous vision in the TV series *Star Trek*, where the starship *Enterprise* is a constantly moving, utopian, monumental space that never alters throughout the series' countless episodes, even though—or precisely because—it is always moving at the speed of light. In this instance, utopia pursues the strategy of transcending the antagonism between immobility and traveling—between sedentary and nomadic life, between comfort and danger, between the city and the countryside—as the creation of a total space in which the topography of the earth's surface becomes identical with the ou-topos of the eternal city.

In a striking fashion, such a utopian transcendence of nature was already being considered in the period of German Romanticism. Evidence of this can be found in a passage in *Aesthetics of Ugliness* (1853), written by Hegel disciple Karl Rosenkranz: "If you take, for instance, our planet Earth, in order for it to be beautiful as a mass, it ought to be a perfect sphere. But it is not. It flattens at the poles and bulges at the equator, and besides, its surface is of the greatest inequality of elevation. A profile of the Earth's crust, regarded only stereometrically, shows us the most casual disorder of elevations and depressions in erratic outlines. In the same way we cannot say of the surface of the moon with its confusion of highs and lows that it is beautiful."[2] At the time this was written, humanity was technologically still far removed from the possibility of space travel. Here, in the spirit of an avant-garde utopia or a sci-fi movie, the agent of global aesthetic contemplation is nonetheless depicted as an alien that has just arrived in a rocket from outer space and, observing from a comfortable distance, forms an aesthetic judgment of our galaxy's appearance. Of course, this alien is imputed to have distinctly classical tastes, which is why it fails to consider our planet and its immediate surroundings as especially beautiful. But regardless of the alien's final aesthetic judgment, one thing is clear: this is a first manifestation of the gaze of the consummate urban dweller who, constantly in motion in the ou-topos of black cosmic space, peers down at the topography of our world from a touristic, aesthetic distance.

1
Immanuel Kant, *Critique of Judgment*, trans. James Creed Meredith, ed. Nicholas Walker (Oxford: Oxford University Press, 2007), 95.

2
Karl Rosenkranz, *Aesthetics of Ugliness: A Critical Edition*, ed. and trans. Andrei Pop and Mechtild Widrich (London: Bloomsbury Academic, 2015), 37.

THE FUTURE BELONGS TO TAUTOLOGY

Modern methods of creating, storing, copying, and transmitting texts and images have given us the ability to produce more and more "culture" and "art" at ever-greater speeds. This excess of texts and images must somehow be limited so that we don't get lost in the textual and visual waste we produce. Thus the question arises of the criteria that would allow us to pick out and store certain texts and images—and to dispose of others. We need censorship to limit cultural production and avoid turning the world into a single cultural trash heap. Every civilization has such ecologically motivated censorship, which only in a few cases also functions as ideological or political censorship. Such political-ideological censorship often proves to be insufficient anyway, because it is not radical enough. For example, recently faded Soviet socialism, despite strict political censorship, produced vast amounts of texts and images. This shows how easy it is to adapt to such censorship, and how ineffective such censorship is when it comes to effectively limiting cultural waste.

In the past, corresponding cultural-ecological censorship usually operated—and very effectively at that—with the term "quality." Works of art, literary or philosophical texts, and other cultural artifacts were judged and selected according to their "quality." The works, which possessed this mysterious "quality," were carefully preserved, but their qualityless colleagues were pitilessly thrown away. The quality of a new cultural product resulted from comparison with a preestablished canon of masterpieces. If a certain "level" that supposedly distinguished these masterpieces was achieved by the new work, this new work could be accepted into the great tradition. How this level was determined remained deliberately unclear, because the explicit declaration of criteria of censorship would make it much easier to adapt new works to these criteria, and thus overstimulate cultural production. For science and philosophy, quality was defined as "truth"; for art, it was defined as "beauty."

In order for truth and beauty to be achieved, certain rules by which one produces them must be reproduced. In earlier, premodern times, the reproduction of these rules was difficult and required much effort on the part of the artist and the scientist. In the modern age, which developed new technical reproduction processes that function independently of individual human beings, cultural reproduction, and thus the achievement of the desired "quality," has been made much easier. The limiting effect of censorship as a defense of quality was drastically reduced, and cultural overproduction increased to a threatening extent. In the course of modernity, the number of "quality" cultural products grew immeasurably. Too many artists learned to paint well. Too many writers learned to write well. And too many philosophers and scholars began to produce too much truth according to all the rules of their art. Thus, quality censorship could no longer provide proper protection against the abundance of cultural artifacts.

This led to the need for a new foundation of cultural censorship. The new term that was introduced with this aim, and still legitimizes the prevailing censorship today, is called "innovation." It would be a great misunderstanding to believe that the valorization of the new in modernity favored a cultural dynamic, an unfolding of creative freedom, or an acceleration of cultural production. On the contrary, the concept of the new in modernity served to slow down and suppress text and image production accelerated by new technology. In modernity, the concept of the new took over the ecological censorship function that the concept of quality used to fulfill. If one used to be able to say, "Get rid of it, its quality is not high enough," today one may say, "Get rid of it, it's not innovative enough." The rejection of a work, be it a work of art or a scientific theory, is today generally justified if the product in question is not new, not innovative, not creative. "We've seen/heard/read this before," one hears again and again when a negative assessment is made.

At the same time, the term "innovation" remains as vague as the term "quality" used to be. If possessing "quality" is similar to being reminiscent of traditional models, being "innovative" or "creative" means producing something different from those models. However, similarities as well as differences essentially depend on how one compares the new with the old. What is similar in one respect turns out to be completely different in another. Thus all discussions of legitimacy today revolve around the question of how to compare the new with the old. Opinions are always divided. For example, some believe that postmodern art, from American Pop art to the present, embodies a regressive, non-innovative, anti-modern attitude because it depicts the things of the outside world from which abstract art had freed us. On the other hand, others believe that abstract art did not radically challenge the social status of the work of art, and that postmodern art is much more innovative than abstract art by doing just that. The comparison in this case appears to be on two different levels, blurring the meaning of the term innovation. And yet, censorship based on the criteria of innovation is not seriously questioned, because as soon as it can be proved with a certain degree of plausibility that a particular work is not innovative, the work is equated with trash, and thus is culturally disposed.

And so most of what is produced in modern times automatically becomes trash. As mentioned earlier, modern civilization is characterized above all by its ability to exactly reproduce what exists. Enough has been written about the technical reproduction of texts and images, at least since Walter Benjamin, but perhaps the most important institution of cultural reproduction is general education, which provides all children with the same knowledge. Modern media reproduces certain forms of everyday culture and entertainment, international hotel and restaurant chains serve the same food, and psychological counseling, in its differing variants, always reproduces the same patterns of inner life. Also, enough has been said and written about the homogenization of work processes in the modern age. Modern civilization primarily produces identities: the same cars, people who look and think the same, and so forth. It is obvious that in light of this, the demand for the new, for innovation, for creativity has primarily a repressive function. Indeed, most cultural products and the majority of people become culturally disqualified and labeled as irrelevant by this demand. The demand for the new has become the new legitimation for the formation of the elite at the historical moment at which the traditional criteria of the true, the beautiful, and the good have proved to be no longer functional—for the true, the beautiful, and the good have been devalued by their over(re)production.

The social valorization of innovation in modernity was often misunderstood as an expression of human freedom, mistakenly interpreted as license to do the new. But the valorization of the new is actually a ban on doing the old. The expression of genuine human freedom would be the opportunity to do both—the old and the new. But this possibility does not exist in modernity. Instead, the modern human is constantly confronted with manifold and complex prohibitions based on the ideology of innovation. First, it is forbidden to do all that had been done before. Second, innovation forbids itself, because as soon as something is already thought or done it is no longer new, and may therefore not be repeated. Thus, creators are condemned to constantly take distance to themselves and contradict themselves—they are forbidden from reproducing themselves. Above all, the artistic avant-garde of the twentieth century, which most radically embodied the principle of the new, was governed by the principle: it can't be done that way anymore. Under these conditions, any new innovation does not open up new fertile land but leaves behind a new desert, because, as I mentioned earlier, it forbids everything that was there, including itself. The artists of the avant-garde are therefore not explorers of new continents but hermits in the desert, where they are trying to survive.

Prohibition and repression also determine the inner structure of the modern artwork: the main processes of modern art are reduction, renunciation, and asceticism. It has often been noted that all elements of modern art can also be found in earlier eras—abstract painting, sound poetry, and so on can be identified as standard components of traditional artworks. What is new about these forms? The answer is: new is the reduction of the work to these specific components; new is the prohibition to use other components; new is the asceticism that defines the modern work of art; new is the fate of always painting only squares or making senseless noises.

Even postmodernism has not changed this fate, because it forces artists to paint borrowed images or repeat borrowed texts—and to renounce what is their own. The modern artist is like an early Christian ascetic or an Indian yogi who is pushed further and further into the desert, forcing the body into ever more unnatural, innovative, unbearable poses.

Recently a democratically motivated revolt against elite formation through the new has been increasingly stirring. In many different ways the new is thus theoretically and practically undermined. One declares one's joy of kitsch and mass culture. One pays tribute to triviality and pop culture. And above all, one questions the universal historical context in which the new is determined. Indeed, if we do not have the general cultural context or vision of universal history, we cannot say what is new and what isn't. The term innovation loses its prestige, so that for a partial context and in the course of a partial history something can be recognized as new that is by no means new to other partial contexts and histories. Under these conditions of radical plurality, everything can be considered new. There is always someone who has not yet heard about certain things that everyone else can't bear to hear about anymore.

However, such attempts at undermining the new have been only partially successful until now, because the place for the creation and identification of the new are not personal stories and memories but cultural archives such as museums, libraries, film archives, and so on. With the help of these archives it can be determined whether something is new or not, regardless of whether it seems new. Moreover, the discourses that want to contextualize, particularize, and thereby undermine the new are interesting for cultural archives only insofar as these discourses are themselves new. The postmodernist, populist critique of the concept of the new can therefore soften the censorship of the new in a culture that archives itself, but it cannot abolish this censorship, because this critique can legitimize itself only through the same concept of the new.

In modernity, the archive plays the same role in relation to the new as the traditional canon played in relation to quality in premodern times. The canon was the collection of relatively homogeneous models with which new works could be compared to establish similarities. The archive is a collection of heterogeneous innovations, of deviations and differences, that allows us to determine to what extent a new work is innovative—that is, to what extent this work represents a departure from all that already has been collected in the archive. The canon produces identity, the archive produces difference. As long as the archive exists, innovation will be both possible and necessary. The question is, however, for how long?

Over time, a deep crisis of the archive becomes ever more obvious. The new, on the other hand, is always produced faster and on a more massive scale, as used to be the case with the identical, because people are getting better at understanding what it means to be innovative. Moreover, today's technology not only allows originals to be reproduced identically, it also generates programmed deviations from these originals. Like identities, differences can now be produced technically and serially. In addition, through skillful reinterpretation, the cultural artifacts that used to be considered "identical" have been (re)discovered as being different. As a result, the archives become overcrowded, as was once the case with the collections of works considered canonical. Wherever you look today, you see differences. Thus, the concepts of the new and the other gradually become less suitable for containing cultural overproduction. Innovation censorship becomes just as ineffective as quality censorship once was. This raises the current question: What happens next? How will culture protect itself from its own waste if neither identity nor difference will provide this protection?

In fact, the abolition of innovation censorship would most likely mean the abolition of any censorship, because we have no other legitimizing concepts beyond identity and difference. So we have to reckon with the possibility that the cultural institutions that have the governmental or social mandate to decide what is good and what is bad will definitively lose their legitimacy. In these circumstances, when there is no criteria or independent authority to determine the cultural value of a work, there will be direct competition among the different cultural attitudes and works, as is already taking place in the realm of mass culture. And it is already clear which principle underlies this competition. It is the principle of tautology.

If both the canonical and the archival collections of cultural works no longer possess any normative power and the institutions that hold these collections no longer exercise effective censorship, texts and images become difficult for their recipients to understand, because understanding can only be achieved through comparison with what is already known. However, such a comparison is no longer possible in the sea of uncensored cultural production. When archives forfeit their normativity, the only place of comparison becomes the soul of the individual recipient. But no one knows what is going on in the other's soul when there is no tradition that is equally known and binding for all. This applies to both the producers and the recipients of culture. For example, suppose we see Malevich's *Black Square* for the first time. We can deem this work a revolution in painting if we compare it with the well-known works in the archive of painting. But if this comparison is missing, we can assume that all Russians have always painted black squares (for example, as part of a local ritual) and that, accordingly, *Black Square* cannot signify an artistic revolution.

The assessment of the cultural competence of the producer and the recipient thus becomes crucial for the understanding of the work. But today one hardly knows what other people read, see, or think. This new state of affairs manifests itself in everyday life through, for example, the increasing disappearance of humor as a primary form of cultural creativity. Since no one knows what the other person knows, humor has become impossible: when one hears a remark, one has no means of determining whether the remark was intended ironically or not, for in our pluralistic society we cannot classify any opinion a priori as "unserious." So one prefers to remain serious even when confronted with an obviously absurd remark so as not to offend the speaker if he or she meant it seriously. Only when the speaker assures that the remark was meant ironically does one force oneself to laugh—this time in order not to offend the speaker by one's serious facial expression.

This little example shows in a nutshell the problems contemporary cultural producers are confronted with. First, they must be able to guess what the people they are addressing already know. Second, they must explicitly repeat what they have researched, so that the audience knows that they know what the audience knows. In doing so, all forms of irony, shifts of meaning, and wordplay—that is, all forms of difference—are excluded, because if they occur, the audience will not be able to judge them as a deliberate strategy but only think that their producers, by virtue of their nature or cultural background, are "different." Under these conditions, the new or the different are no longer possible. On the other hand, the identical must always be determined anew because it is no longer fixed in advance, as was the case in traditional or totalitarian societies. Identity, banality, and tautology become a problem in a pluralistic society, and the search for the perfect tautology increasingly dominates today's mass culture.

In the context of mass culture in the United States, the search for the perfect tautology seems especially urgent because the country is very heterogeneous culturally. The production of tautology is not only the main practice but also the major topic of American mass culture. American films and television series always offer extremely heterogeneous cultural figures: their protagonists are different races, come from different social classes and historical times, or are often monsters, extraterrestrials, ghosts, animals, fantastic characters, computers gone crazy, talking cars or refrigerators. Over the course of a film or a television series, however, all these very heterogeneous heroes must come to realize that they ultimately have the same ideas and desires (family, social recognition, finding their own place in life, etc.). The search for this tautology determines the plot: it serves primarily to bring the heroes into an extreme situation, which forces them to reveal their innermost desires and thoughts and compare them with the desires and thoughts of others with the goal of eliminating all possible differences and misunderstandings. The plot doesn't end before all participants understand and explicitly formulate that they think and feel the same as everyone else. The achievement of the perfect tautology plays the same central role here as does catharsis in Aristotelian aesthetics. However, once achieved, the tautology does not last long and has to be staged again and again, just like classical catharsis. Incidentally, the film and TV heroes who do not participate in the tautology are eliminated over the course of the plot, but their death by no means implies that in principle they cannot participate in this tautology. So the first Terminator gains the necessary insight in the second installment of the film series, and one can well imagine that the second Terminator may gain the same insight in a third installment.

Thus, under the conditions of radical cultural diversity, dominant otherness, and mass-produced innovation, the production of perfect tautology becomes the main criterion of cultural achievement—especially because, as I mentioned earlier, this tautology is not guaranteed by any traditional cultural identity, and must therefore always be reestablished anew and on an ad hoc basis. It is obvious that the content of the established tautology must tend toward zero, toward nil, as permanently increasing cultural diversity allows for less and less overlap. Hence mass culture tends to be nihilistic, because in the search for the all-encompassing tautology, any concrete content or meaning must be negated. Even if the images and characters it uses are realistic they do not mean anything: these images have their own reality, in that they are recorded on a particular sign carrier. The less content these signs have, the more they become real, because their reality consists in their reproducibility. The signs whose content tends toward nil can most easily break through cultural immune systems and civilizational boundaries and proliferate indefinitely. They become cultural viruses that infect all souls equally.

Surely it is not easy to discover or breed such viruses—what infects people in Duisburg does not necessarily become viral in

Singapore. Therefore, Americans have the advantage of being able to quickly test these cultural viruses in their culturally pluralistic society. But also in the realm of so-called high culture some people have already produced such viruses: Freud with his psychoanalysis, Sartre with his existentialism, Picasso with his variations of old artworks, and Warhol with his invariants of mass taste. They have all practiced avant-garde reduction—but less with the aim of inscribing themselves into the archive of innovations than with the hope of discovering tautologies that were equally obvious to all. So readers of Freud or Sartre are amazed that their own relationship with mom Mom and Dad is also of great importance for philosophy. And viewers of a Warhol exhibition are delighted at the sight of the same Coca-Cola bottle that they just bought in the supermarket. Under such rapidly spreading tautologies, great competitive matches will be fought in the future. And the winner will automatically demote the loser to trash. Additional censorship will be superfluous. Instead of ideology comes tautology.

TROTSKY, OR METAMORPHOSES OF ENGAGEMENT

The discussion about politically engaged art tore apart the art world in the twentieth century, and still does today. The advocates of absolute artistic autonomy react to engaged artists in a quite confrontational mode, and vice versa. However, the idea of the autonomy of art is deeply connected to the project of artistic engagement. It is not particularly difficult to show that the radical autonomy of art can only be manifested through radical political engagement. And only the artist who is completely free and autonomous can become engaged.

The word "engagement" became famous especially through the writings of Jean-Paul Sartre. Sartre's existentialism defined itself as consistent humanism—that is, as an assertion of the radical autonomy of the human individual. The individual was thereby understood as pure nothing, as absolute freedom of choice, as an existence that is not predetermined by any essence. Humans, therefore, were allowed to choose their own nature, but at the same time they *had to* choose their nature, for if they were to linger in nothingness, this nothingness would become their nature. According to Sartre, humans are nothing other than their engagement: there is no "hidden" person beyond what the person does in the world.[1] Hence humans, following Sartre's existentialism, can assert their absolute freedom only by its ultimate radicalization—that is, by demonstrating their freedom through an engagement with a certain intra-worldly attitude—which at the same time should have exemplary significance for all of humanity so that this engagement acquires an "absolute character."[2] In Sartre's "commitment" one can thus easily recognize Kant's "aesthetic judgment." For Sartre, commitment is determined—as is aesthetic judgment for Kant—by the paradox that although it cannot be legitimized, it nevertheless claims universal validity. Thus, political commitment as an irreducible and universally valid decision of individual liberty cannot be interpreted as a subjugation of art under the conditions of politics. Rather, it can be interpreted as an extension of aesthetic judgment, with which Kant founded the modern autonomy of art, onto the totality of sociopolitical life.

The possibility of political engagement thus excludes, above all, any philosophical determinism that denies the engaged individuals their original freedom and interprets their sociopolitical behavior by the historical origin of the individuals and not as a consequence of their free choice. Thus, any engagement also indicates the possibility of betraying the cause to which one is committed, because any choice can be revoked. And even more, only by being revoked can a choice be manifested as a choice and not as an effect of causal determination. The possibility of betrayal is part of the nature of engagement. If engagement cannot be betrayed, it is not engagement but merely the expression of an external or internal necessity that one passively submits to without having control over one's own engagement.

So in order to become engaged, art first had to learn betrayal. Only by breaking with its own tradition does art gain the necessary freedom to become engaged. However, this break should not be understood as dictated by an inner need—for example, as Kandinsky understood it.[3] Rather, the break with tradition is to be understood as a pure act of betrayal that establishes the freedom of the artist and is rooted in pure nothingness. Only an art that is completely founded in nothingness and freed from all causal ties with reality can and must become engaged in order to gain a new access to the world. If art no longer represents or signifies anything, it has to become useful.

Historically, the determination of art as having its place in nothingness was stated most radically in the first decades of the twentieth century—especially by Russian Suprematism and German and French Dadaism. It is no coincidence that the question of the political engagement of art was posed with extreme radicalism in the wake of these currents. Only when one recognizes that art has no original relationship to reality does one want to produce this relationship artificially. Thus, art as art is completed because its relation to reality also becomes artificially chosen and made. Here artists engage themselves for something that they are not—and thus complete themselves as free artists. It is characteristic that Malevich, for example, who perhaps most radically asserted nothingness as the essence of art, was criticized by the artists of the next generation. The criticism was that he was still passively portraying this nothingness instead of engaging in the construction of the new, communist world, thereby manifesting his art as an act of nothingness. And at that same time, Tarabukin wrote that the modern society of communist production is in itself a work of nonrepresentational art because it serves no particular purpose—in the sense of consumption—and practices production only for the sake of production.[4]

But this also announces the difficulty that arises the moment aesthetic judgment is transferred to sociopolitical reality in the form of engagement. It is well known that while the choice of engagement in the pertinent theories was postulated as free, in reality it was mostly practiced in favor of the different variants of Marxist socialism, especially the Stalinist-style international communist movement. There are at least two key reasons for this. The first reason is that Marxism is a social theory that sees humans as beings completely defined by their social activity. For Marxism, a human is nothing beyond his or her life practice. And that can be interpreted as this nothingness that is claimed by modern subjectivity, and especially modern art, as freedom and a source of engagement.

Therefore Sartre, who also defined people by their intraworldly engagement, sympathized with Marxism, though he criticized the economic determinism of Marxist theory because this determinism threatened the autonomous freedom of choice.[5] Even Bataille, who seemed to hold an opposite position, spoke quite positively, in the context of his analysis of the Stalinist Soviet Union, about the reification of the human in Soviet communism, and found in the self-identification of the individual with the thing a certain form of self-chosen "sovereignty."[6] Heidegger sharply criticized Sartre's existentialism in his famous "Letter on Humanism" from 1947. This contributed significantly to the decline of Sartre's influence in France, even though or perhaps because Sartre often refers to Heidegger's existential analysis. However, in his letter Heidegger also praises Marxism for its vision of the alienating character of history: "What Marx recognized in an essential and significant sense, though derived from Hegel, as the estrangement of man has its roots in the homelessness of modern man. [...] Because Marx by experiencing estrangement attains an essential dimension of history, the Marxist view of history is superior to that of other historical accounts."[7] Here homelessness is the other word for freedom: only the history of alienation addressed in Marxism gives the homeless person the opportunity to become engaged in this history.

Radically autonomous artists, who see themselves and their art as a place of nothingness, and Marxism, which sends them into nothingness, seem at first glance to be made for each other. Because art in the twentieth century was understood as an autonomous practice, as the sum of technical devices and no longer as a spontaneous expression of the inner being of artists, it felt at once omnipotent and completely powerless: art can do everything, but it becomes an autonomous, purely technical object and receives its assignment from outside. In the context of bourgeois society, this is always a very limited assignment.[8] Only Marxist-socialist doctrine gives the artist an external assignment that is at the same time a total assignment. Marxism and modern art seem to complement each other perfectly. But twentieth-century history has shown us that this harmony has never materialized in practice, and that the relationship between Marxism and modern art was marked above all by mutual rejection, disappointment, and betrayal. So something did not work in the perfect calculation after all.

This disharmony is related to another important reason for modern art to engage in the Marxist-socialist project: the expectation that socialist society will be new. The new is understood here the same way in which modern art itself became new by creating artistic styles that stood in visible contrast to tradition, and thus testified to the break with this tradition in a manner obvious to everyone. By betraying tradition and engaging in new forms of art, modern art wanted not only to be free but also to demonstrate its freedom. This, however, set certain limits to the freedom of engagement, for absolute freedom as such does not distinguish between the old and the new.

If free engagement wants to show itself as such, this engagement becomes unfree through this wish alone, because only the new can become a potential object of engagement. In Sartre this difficulty becomes noticeable through his condemnation of "bad faith" (*mauvaise foi*), which reveals itself to Sartre in the choice of what already exists. At the same time, Sartre essentially assumes that all—old and new—engagements are equal. But Heidegger, to whom Sartre refers, wrote: "Thinking is not merely *l'engagement dans l'action* for and by beings, in the sense of the actuality of the present situation. Thinking is *l'engagement* by and for the truth of Being. The history of Being is never past but stands ever before."[9] In other words, Heidegger, who already had his own unfortunate experience of engagement behind him, demanded one to become engaged not in what is already there and present but, rather, in the absolutely new. And much later, Derrida did not sum up his Marxist engagement much differently when he defined Marxism as an apocalyptic waiting for the absolute other.[10] Novelty, unfamiliarity, and radical otherness are here the firm criteria of an authentic engagement. Now, however, this expectation of the new in relation to the communist society envisaged by Marxism has never been and cannot be fulfilled, for from the start this society understood itself both as a continuation of tradition and as a break with it. Marxism never defined itself as a new aesthetic-political style, for such a definition would contradict the Marxist dialectic, which seeks to undermine all such determinations.

On the side of artists, it has often been said that the reason for Marxism's sympathy for tradition was that Marxist officials did not understand the new, radical, revolutionary art. That may be so. The question remains as to why the artists who so often formulated this accusation so stubbornly cling to the new art forms they created. If art is only a sum of technical devices, if it does not "express" anything and is not dictated by any inner necessity, there is just as little reason to insist on the new as on the old. Every engagement must, as has been said, if it is truly free, also be revisable, whereby not the aesthetic consistency but only the usefulness of the artistic process should serve as a criterion. The communist leadership could therefore reasonably assume that for the artists associated with it, the demonstration of aesthetic freedom and innovative power was more important than real engagement—by freeing themselves from their own artistic style. Art wants to be visible—it wants to show itself. And if art wants to be free, it also wants to show that it is free. But in politics it is different: one is free precisely when one does not reveal one's own position. Modern art has in most cases proved incapable of appropriating this invisible and more radical freedom of aesthetic-political manipulation. Modern artists merely hoped that the mass influence of the Communist Party would replace the traditional public they had lost as a result of their artistic innovations. Of course, the communist leadership did not want to be exploited in this way.

Thus, artists and intellectuals repeatedly felt betrayed by the Communist Party, and they complained about this alleged betrayal. It was perceived as a betrayal that the party proved to be organized in a quite traditional manner: politically repressive, bureaucratic, aesthetically conservative, and economically greedy. However, this betrayal was certainly just imaginary. The Communist Party did not follow tradition but rather dealt with it in a purely manipulative way. The party's political struggle for power was also the struggle for power over tradition, over the past, over the existing archives of cultural forms. The abandonment of tradition preached by the avant-garde was perceived from the Communist Party perspective as an arbitrary limitation of the party's power—a limitation that was perceived as anti-communist. It was not the communist apparatchiks but the artistic avant-garde that remained deeply rooted in tradition: every aesthetic break with tradition is necessarily also the next step in the continuation of tradition. For tradition itself is nothing other than the history of changing cultural forms, as described for instance by Hegelian dialectics.

But Marxist ideology is an ideology after the end of history, after the conclusion of the Hegelian dialectic, when all opposites and dividing lines have already become conscious and manageable. In this situation, the border crossing that the artistic avant-garde practiced was not a step forward, which would remove old boundaries, but merely a betrayal. The post-Hegelian, Marxist-socialist self-understanding would discover not a new territory beyond all borders but only a hostile territory that already has been long occupied by enemy forces. The avant-garde artist pretended to be a Columbus who could still discover an unknown continent on the voyage into the unprecedented. But the Marxist ideologue knew that America had already been discovered and had become a citadel of the class enemy. In our world, where all borders are already marked and all territories are occupied, every border crossing is just an emigration, a defection to the enemy. Thus the avant-garde artists who considered themselves a vehicle of the spirit that breaks through the borders of the status quo could only cross the already-marked borders, sometimes in one direction and sometimes in the other. The border crosser became a border traveler—that is, a professional traitor or refugee, as exemplified by Charlie Chaplin in the film *The Pilgrim*, in which he runs along the US-Mexico border.

Marxist ideology is of course also a dialectic, but it is a *materialistic* dialectic. And that means that borders can no longer be eliminated in spirit but only in material practice. If, for example, the United States and Mexico were simultaneously destroyed by a nuclear strike, the border between them would also be eliminated. But as long as these nations exist materially, a purely imaginary, spiritual crossing of their border remains only a change of position in relation to the border, which leaves the border as such intact—that is, as mentioned earlier, the betrayal. The late Marxist dialectic, especially in its Stalinist form, is basically a theory of such a betrayal: the betrayal by people and things. For dialectical materialism, the dramaturgy of events develops by virtue of the negation of negation or by virtue of the betrayal of the traitors. Nothing remains in its familiar place. Everything is constantly repositioned. Friends and enemies are constantly redefined. People and things change their positions with regard to boundaries intentionally or unintentionally but in any case permanently. Every attitude constantly turns into its opposite. What was reactionary and damnable yesterday is progressive and welcome today—and maybe reactionary again tomorrow. But nothing can be neither progressive nor reactionary but merely different: a third way is impossible in a divided reality.

There is a well-established opinion that Soviet dialectical materialism influenced by Stalinism is a dogmatic, immovable doctrine that seeks to theoretically comprehend life in a complete and final way. Nothing is further from the truth. The core of dialectical materialism is the doctrine of reality as the unity and conflict of opposites: for dialectical materialism, life is a paradox that cannot be resolved theoretically, for every theory, if it wants to be consistent and move in a certain direction, sooner or later crosses an invisible border and becomes its opposite. Just as those who continuously move in one direction on the earth's surface will leave their country's territory and go over to the enemy. So in order to come back to themselves, they have to turn around and move in the opposite direction—but then one no longer knows if the people in question aren't launching an enemy attack on their own country. Here we are dealing with the paradox of a dialectic after the closure of the infinite historical perspective, whereby a new dialectic of the finite or a dialectic of reversibility is instituted. Every thought fails before this paradox, which cannot be overcome dialectically—precisely because it itself is the principle of every inversion. It is only possible to repeat this paradox monotonously in order to surrender before it and clear the way for the inner paradox of Soviet ideology—which Orwell parodied in slogans such as "peace is war." Similarly one can say "tradition is innovation," or "innovation is tradition." The paradox of official Soviet Marxism is deeper than the political engagement of the avant-garde.

Thus, an intellectual or artist gradually begins to understand that engaging in a certain position in the context of a post-Hegelian, post-historical dialectical teaching such as Marxism is at the same time an engagement to the opposite of this position. One commits oneself as a friend and is treated as an enemy. Or one engages as an enemy and is welcomed as a friend. The boundaries are always the same, but the positions are constantly rotating, as if the United States and Mexico constantly changed places. The difference between difference and identity cannot be stabilized. Thus the avant-garde artists who search for the other are seen as traitors, but at the same time they are betrayed if they persist in their belief in their own. Incidentally, it is naive to speak today about the demise or the end of Soviet Marxism. The Soviet Union, the empire of dialectical materialism, wasn't defeated by external enemies or an internal uprising. Rather, this empire changed its political positioning. The system betrayed itself in the person of Gorbachev as its highest representative, because from the beginning it was a system of betrayal. So this change of political positioning was nothing but another victory of the Marxist dialectic.

Thus, now it becomes clear why the Marxist-socialist engagement of intellectuals and artists has generally led to disappointment: this engagement presupposed a certain consistency, be it consistency in the constant search for the other or consistency in the fidelity to one's own choice. But it is exactly this consistency that has proved impossible in the materialistic-dialectical play of total reversibility. Engagement, as a visible choice between the positions, loses all its pathos when all positions become interchangeable. And the search for the other becomes treasonous when the supposedly unknown other proves to be the long-known enemy. And so the artist begins to search for someone who shows a certain irreversible consistency in the field of politics in order to engage oneself for this person. For example, one engages oneself for Trotsky after his break with the Stalinist Soviet Union.

Here one finally sees someone who has remained consistent, who wants a permanent revolution, and who rejects all that exists in every form. Trotsky, of course, did not cross new borders, he only crossed the already existing Russian border to the West, from which he had previously returned to Russia, which he had emigrated from even earlier. Thus Trotsky, although by his own fate, also demonstrated the reversibility of the late dialectic, and merely passed the same border in both directions several times. But at least he found refuge in Mexico—a country beyond the immediate East-West conflict—and there in the house of an artist.

In the person of Trotsky, politics asked for art's help. The reaction was easy to predict. Most artists and intellectuals rightly interpreted this request as a sign of weakness and rejected it. Because of its historical weakness, many authors, including Sartre and Bataille, saw Trotskyism not as a solution but merely as a Western intellectual current that was not worth the effort to commit to. This should not be overlooked: one wanted to commit to the historical winner and not to the historical loser. Trotsky's criticism of conditions in the former Soviet Union was known in the West. It definitely shaped the relationship of many Western artists and intellectuals to Stalinist Russia, and even if it did not fully immunize them against Stalinist propaganda it did raise some doubts. However, the image of the lonely representative of the world spirit who wanders throughout the world was too familiar to artists and intellectuals to evoke any special enthusiasm.

Perhaps the only prominent exception was Breton's Trotskyist engagement. But this exception confirms the rule, for Breton understood Surrealism not as a purely aesthetic style but, rather, as a study of the unconscious by artistic means. From the very beginning, Surrealist art had its own autonomous content and its own external task for Breton. As a result, more than political engagement—that is, voluntary submission to an effective political force that would allow formalistic art to find a new relation to reality—Breton sought a political ally who could support the goals of the Surrealist revolution of the unconscious. The refusal of Breton to see art as pure form and anchor it in nothingness has something old-fashioned about it: the Surrealism of Breton reminds us of nineteenth-century realism with its claim to its own truth and scientific nature—even though the Surrealists searched the truth of the unconscious. Thus, Breton committed himself to Trotsky because he did not seek a free engagement but simply followed his belief in the necessity of Surrealism.

Therefore, in the 1920s Breton was able to put his Surrealism *au service de la révolution* and at the same time demand the autonomy of the Surrealist work with the unconscious. Only when artists are completely modern—meaning that their art is grounded in nothingness—are they confronted with the alternative of completely abandoning reality or submitting to it. Otherwise, the artist is not free enough to become engaged but is always already determined. And it is this feeling of inner determination that frees the artist from submission to external powers. Here is the point at which Trotsky and Breton met in the 1930s, for Trotsky was a Marxist determinist, trusting in the political freedom of the arts. In *Manifesto for an Independent Revolutionary Art*, coauthored by Breton and Trotsky in 1938 but not signed by Trotsky for reasons of censorship, the authors insist on the political independence of art, even if they reject a reactionary—that is, anti-communist—art.[11] Incidentally, Trotsky's aesthetic views allowed him from the beginning to define the field of art as autonomous.

Trotsky's deterministic, traditionally Marxist conception of art had led him even earlier to deny the possibility of socialist or proletarian art under the conditions of his time. He considered the attitude of the Stalinist dialectic of free choice, which called artists to take up the standpoint of communist ideology, unrealistic. For Trotsky, the position of the artist was historically conditioned and could not be artificially changed by means of conscious engagement. Thus the choice between Stalinism and Trotskyism becomes, as it were, the choice between inner freedom, which leads to external political submission, and inner determinacy, which guarantees external political freedom.

In the Soviet Union, Trotsky was long considered the epitome of the traitor to the cause of Soviet communism. At the same time, Trotsky himself spoke of the "revolution betrayed," meaning that the revolution was betrayed by Stalinist leadership, whose victory for Trotsky meant a "Thermidor"—that is, the beginning of the counterrevolutionary process in Russia. This parallelism shows how far Trotsky distanced himself from Soviet ideology. The idea that a country or a party can betray a person is completely alien to Stalinist ideology, because it sees no compelling reason for the individual to refrain from adapting to prevailing circumstances. Every human being has the inner freedom and at the same time the duty to accept historical judgment. Incidentally, almost all the Bolsheviks condemned in the period of Stalin shared this view, and so they tried constantly, albeit in vain, to prove their loyalty. Trotsky, on the other hand, felt betrayed and insisted on an inner vision of the revolution that was compelling to him and could not be the subject of free choice or dialectical substitution. Sartre as a philosopher of engagement rejects the determinism of Marxist doctrine. Trotsky embodies this determinism, which is reminiscent of the Protestant doctrine of divine predestination. Stalin embodies the Catholic side of Marxism with its emphasis on free choice, which not by chance especially fascinated the post-Catholic French intelligentsia. Trotsky is a deterministic, Protestant soul who refuses to decide or let others decide freely about his inner truth. Thus, Trotsky remains attractively conservative—that is, nonstrategic.

This becomes particularly clear if one remembers his earlier polemic against postrevolutionary Russian Futurism, which called for an absolute break with the past and the creation of a proletarian culture in which the radically new avant-garde artistic form was supposed to unite with the equally radical communist content that was supposed to be obligatory in the new Russia. For Trotsky, the call for a break with the past merely shows that the Futurists still defined themselves in the context of bourgeois tradition, albeit negatively. Trotsky writes: "The Futurist break with the past is, after all, a tempest in the closed-in world of the intelligentsia [...]. The Futurists have done well to push away from them. But it is not necessary to make a universal law of development out of the act of pushing away."[12] The aesthetic separation from the past, according to Trotsky, did not mean a separation from the bourgeoisie. For him, the transition of the Futurists to the demand for proletarian culture was merely an effect of an event completely independent of the Futurists' activities, namely the October Revolution, which disempowered the bourgeois class and made it impossible for the Futurists to return to their traditional role. According to Trotsky, the Futurists are not free artists, freed from the burden of tradition, willing to engage themselves for the cause of the proletariat, but rather victims of a change in circumstances to which they, like all others, had to adapt.

Trotsky by no means blames the Futurists for their bourgeois tradition. Rather, he sees the superiority of his own position in recognizing his own determinacy through history: "We Marxists live in traditions, and we have not stopped being revolutionists on account of it. [...] We were educated, and we entered the struggle during an organic epoch, and we lived on revolutionary traditions."[13] The Futurists' unwillingness to accept that their aesthetic revolution also has a tradition tempts Futurism to demand a proletarian dictatorship in art. But according to Trotsky, proletarian—that is, socialist—art can only emerge within a historically established socialist order: the new art does not arise through an individual free decision but as the necessary consequence of a changed social determination.

Moreover, Trotsky denies the possibility of a proletarian culture even in the future, because unlike the bourgeoisie, the proletariat historically had no chance of forming itself culturally. The proletarian dictatorship cannot produce its own art because this dictatorship in essence represents only a transitional period to the future classless society: "This seems to lead to the conclusion that there is no proletarian culture and that there never will be any and in fact there is no reason to regret this. The proletariat acquires power for the purpose of doing away forever with class culture and to make way for human culture."[14] Here Trotsky basically disputes the usual interpretation of the "permanent revolution," a concept associated with his name and commonly understood as a call for the separation from tradition as the law of world evolution. Trotsky understood the permanent revolution merely as a transition from the bourgeois revolution to the proletarian revolution, which, however, was meant to introduce a new epoch without historical ruptures. For Trotsky, art represents, first, an autonomous domain of mastery, and second, a representation of reality whose character is decided by the artist's social determinacy and therefore cannot be dictated from outside: "The Marxian method affords an opportunity to estimate the development of the new art, to trace all its sources, to help the most progressive tendencies by a critical illumination of the road, but it does not do more than that. Art must make its own way and by its own means. The Marxian methods are not the same as the artistic. The Party leads the proletariat but not the historic processes of history."[15]

These formulations are certainly far removed from the demand for partisanship in arts as it was understood in the Stalinist era: art that is partisan or, if you will, engaged, should shape reality in its entirety rather than simply portray it. For Trotsky, on the other hand, art remains above all the subject of Marxist analysis and diagnosis, which only apply if art follows its own inner logic that necessarily connects it with the historical process, which can only be reflected upon but not directed. In the context of the polemic against Futurism, Trotsky writes: "Art, it is said, is not a mirror, but a hammer: it does not reflect, it shapes. [...] If one cannot get along without a mirror, even in shaving oneself, how can one reconstruct oneself or one's life, without seeing oneself in the 'mirror' of literature?"[16] This passage shows why Trotsky later so vehemently protested against the control of art and literature in the Stalinist Soviet Union: Stalinist cultural policy adopted and enforced the demand of the radical avant-garde for an art not to depict the world but rather to transform it—however, under its own direction and using other artistic means. Thus, art was robbed of its diagnostic value and could no longer serve as a mirror of life. For the Marxist Trotsky, only art that does not become engaged is good art, being an art suitable for Marxist analysis. On the other hand, a free art beyond any inner necessity becomes only an accomplice in political manipulation. Trotsky's insight has proved itself over time.

At the end of the twentieth century, the story of the engagement of new art to new politics reveals above all the problematic character of the claim to absolute freedom with which this new art emerged at the beginning of the century. If it wished to enforce its inner freedom consistently, it would have to step out of its own realm, deny its original relationship to reality, and commit itself to external ends—it had to, as Vladimir Mayakovsky said, "step on the throat of its own song." Art had to replace its own with the foreign and be ready to become insincere and unbelievable.

However, the new art was also under pressure to recognize the reversibility of all things typical of late dialectics and to renounce the identifiability of its own engagement. Anyone who decides for the world of politics decides for the whole of this world and submits to the constant exchange between friend and foe. The freedom of choice loses its meaning because the opposite of this choice is always chosen. But if the new art wanted to be aesthetically consistent, it had to give up the claim of absolute freedom and legitimize itself through a kind of necessity—be it the inner necessity of the unconscious or the external logic of the development of artistic form. However, such an aesthetically consistent art remained behind the expectations of its recipients, who in the twentieth century had long since learned to ignore every kind of inner necessity, and instead think and act in a purely strategic manner. Thus Trotsky remained alone with his deterministic analysis of Stalinist society, which likewise quickly learned to simulate every inner determination in a purely external way.

1
Jean-Paul Sartre, *L'existentialisme est un humanisme* (Paris: Éditions Nagel, 1970), 58.

2
Sartre, 71.

3
Wassily Kandinsky, *Concerning the Spiritual in Art*, trans. M. T. H. Sadler (New York: Dover Publications, 1977), 31ff.

4
Nikolaï Taraboukine, *Le dernier tableau* (Paris: Éditions Champ Libre, 1972), 69.

5
Sartre, *L'existentialisme est un humanisme*, 81.

6
Georges Bataille, *The Accursed Shared: An Essay on the General Economy*, vol. 1, trans. Robert Hurley (New York: Zone Books, 1991), 138ff.

7
Martin Heidegger, "Letter on Humanism," trans. Frank A. Capuzzi and J. Glenn Gray, in *Basic Writings*, ed. David Farrell Krell, rev. ed. (New York: HarperCollins, 1993), 243.

8
Peter Bürger, *Theory of the Avant-Garde*, trans. Michael Shaw (Minneapolis: University of University Press, 1984), 49ff.

9
Heidegger, "Letter on Humanism," 218.

10
Jacques Derrida, *Spectres of Marx: The State of the Debt, the Work of Mourning and the New International*, trans. Peggy Kamuf (New York: Routledge Classics, 2006).

11
Helena Lewis, *The Politics of Surrealism* (New York: Paragon House, 1988), 146–47.

12
Leon Trotsky, *Literature and Revolution*, ed. William Keach, trans. Rose Strunksy (Chicago: Haymarket Books, 2005), 138.

13
Trotsky, 138–39.

14
Trotsky, 184.

15
Trotsky, 217.

16
Trotsky, 143.

TRUTH IN PHOTOGRAPHY

When discussing the question of identity as it pertains to photography, another question inevitably poses itself first: whether this discussion of the personal, particular identity, individuality, or subjectivity of the photograph and the photographer is in any way justifiable; whether photography is at all able to reflect the truth of subjectivity, be it the subjectivity of the photographer or the particular identity of the photographed object. Obviously, photography is based on a mechanical process that is in itself impersonal, making no reference to subjectivity or individuality. In taking photographs, the photographer certainly selects themes and viewpoints, and in doing so only realizes the possibilities that are objectively and technically available—namely, it is imaginable that every object has already been photographed from all possible perspectives. Thus no individual photograph can comprise a substantial creation in itself, and the individuality of the person taking the photograph becomes completely exchangeable. In this case, the photographer's inner identity, whatever it may be, is not truly, authentically expressed, but remains concealed. It is here that photography differs from traditional painting, in which the individuality of the artist expresses itself in an irreducible personal style and represents the unique expression of a creative individual. No matter how critics and historians of photography have tried to establish photography as art in terms of traditional painting and analyze the artistic individualities of particular photographers, they have been unable to theoretically overcome the basic condition of photography—that its mechanical quality thwarts every claim to individual identity.

Yet this fundamental lack of individuality, subjectivity, and identity in photography, as one now knows, should not necessarily be understood as a shortcoming. In tracking the art history of the last decades, one observes that it has been the goal of almost all influential art movements of this period to avoid, dissolve, or transcend artistic individuality so as to get to the things themselves—that is, to an unconscious, automatic, quasi-mechanical, or machinelike art. Such art does not strive for the truth of subjectivity; it rather strives for a deeper truth of reality itself. Thus Surrealism strived for *l'écriture automatique*—automatic writing. The aesthetics of the readymade since Duchamp has challenged the irreducibility of artistic individuality. Different trends within Constructivism and Conceptualism also wanted to dissolve subjectivity. Expressionist painting of the twentieth century, on the other hand, tried to transcend the limits of conscious subjectivity and manifest the unconscious, impersonal, machinelike dimension of artistic practice. Instead of representing the world in a subjective, individual manner, artists now wanted the world to leave its traces directly through them. It is photography that stands at the end of this development—embodying, so to speak, the telos of modern art by seemingly overcoming the individual style of painting or the individual way of seeing as a distortion of reality, and producing an imprint of the world itself—beyond all subjective artistic intentions.

Photography explicitly gets rid of the illusion of the total creative power of artists over their work that governs traditional art—and modernist art is included here. In a photograph, there will always be something that in the end cannot have been planned. In photography, chance, the nonscheduled effect of reality itself, has to be calculated in the process. This corresponds to another important strategy of depriving individuality of its power, which art as a whole has long practiced—the attempt to give chance the right to create. Photography is once again able to make good on a promise that traditional art was never able to keep. The transition from traditional art to photography, already demanded by artists such as Aleksandr Rodchenko in the 1920s, thus seems to have been dictated by the inner logic of the development of art itself—by the logic of the constant transcendence of subjectivity and the deprivation of its power or, and this is the same thing, the increasing dissolution of all fixed identities in order to open the way for the other, the unconscious, the automatic, and the machinelike. But if this is the case, why are people now asking about identity, subjectivity, and originality in photography, which has apparently happily overcome all these specters? Here one can perhaps even diagnose a reactionary return to past values. Yet I do believe that there is a true problem at hand—a return of the repressed, so to speak—this time in the form of subjectivity itself.

The fulfillment of the wish for depersonalization and difference that photography has achieved shares its results with many other wish fulfillments of modernism. This fulfillment is of course primarily technically established and guaranteed. It is here that photography once again differs from traditional art. The artists of modernism wanted to turn themselves into mediums of the unconscious, of automatism, of the other—and they guaranteed this quality with their own authenticity. Such an artist was honest and ascetic, as were Mondrian or Breton—or seemingly the opposite, constantly drugged or drunk, as were many other artists. In any case, modernist artists wanted inner transcendence—their conduct, their whole inner attitude should be the guarantee that they have destroyed or relinquished their individuality, subjectivity, identity, and that they take the greatest risks, going even as far as self-annihilation to become an empty surface on which the world can leave its traces. Photographers, in contrast, have no need to make all these heroic efforts—for them, it is quite enough to operate their camera appropriately, which is from the start technically constructed in such a way that they can depict the world without any conscious artistic intervention. The existential drama is unnecessary. A moral or existential guarantee is replaced by a technical one—and in all respects unreliable consciousness is simply eliminated.

But is what appears in the photograph really "true"? Does the total elimination of individual and conscious control mean that things present themselves as they actually are and that the visual arts have for the first time finally become "true" and not merely beautiful? The answer to this question certainly depends on a person's general definition of truth. Since Plato, European philosophy has been convinced that nothing true can be said about the perpetual flow of reality, since this reality is constantly changing. Truth cannot be directly experienced, it can merely be thought, because truth must have a certain stability so that it can be comprehended and conveyed to others. Consequently, truth has to be invisible, since that which is visible is not stable and not identical with itself. For Plato, the aim of thought was to perceive this invisible, self-identical true reality. It was for this reason that Plato sharply condemned the fine arts of his times, because they merely portrayed outward appearances, hence untruths. Plato would have condemned photography all the more, for the traditional fine arts are still closer to his notion of truth. The traditional artist does not merely reproduce but creates a synthetic image of an object out of a variety of experiences and observations—beyond the object's constant alterations in reality. With this, the artist strives to arrive at the essence of this object, which is both revealed and concealed by its many manifestations. The photographer is incapable of capturing essence in this way. He can only capture appearances, and each of these appearances is equally far from the truth. From the Platonic point of view, photography as such seems to be condemned to untruths—and with it all of modern art, which renounces capturing the inner essence of things.

We have here an interesting constellation. For some, the truth is that which conceals itself behind appearances, remaining stable and self-identical—it is that which constitutes the essence of things. This essence of things is then to be the object of art that wants to be categorized as "serious." This quality is precisely the aspect that defines serious, high, true art—it concerns itself with that which is hidden, invisible, and which can only be made visible by art. It is from this position that a clear and unambiguous line is drawn between art and nonart, a line that is incidentally still upheld even when the essence of things is no longer believed in. For it is just as possible to claim that this hidden essence of the world is merely a product of the human imagination, a lie, an illusion, a romantic fantasy. Nevertheless, this lie remains, so to speak, a sublime lie—and hence justifies the art that concerns itself with it. Accordingly, photography is clearly defined as nonart, drowning in the endlessness and banality of mere appearances.

For others, however, essential stability and self-identity are not possible—neither as reality nor as illusion, for even illusions change constantly. For them, the only reality of the external world as well as inner life is the flow of appearances by which we are utterly caught and from which we cannot escape—whether we want to or not. The boundary between art and nonart then disappears completely—it is dissolved in this never-ending flow, which manifests itself in an endless multiplication of images. With respect to this flood of images, it is practically impossible to make any other differentiations—all images prove to be traces of reality and are of equal value, whereby photography has a paradigmatic role, for photographic images have above all the ability to proliferate themselves indefinitely, to extinguish all social, hierarchical, and cultural boundaries through this inundation, and to destroy all fixed identities.

For the moment, we will remain with this more modernist (or, if you will, more postmodernist) interpretation of truth, because it is exactly this interpretation that has aided photography in achieving its present triumphal march. And in this context a topical problem arises that also has to do with the problem of identity, namely the question: How do we make a meaningful selection of significant photographs from this flood of images if we no longer have criteria to differentiate among them according to their importance—that is, their proximity to what is essential? For photography, this question is particularly relevant, as in this case the equidistance of all photographic images from the reality—or, if you will, imagination—hidden behind them is particularly obvious. Just the same, one makes distinctions, justifies collections, and organizes exhibitions. But according to which criteria? And what is the relationship of these criteria to the question of the truth of photography, or, to be more exact, to the specific understanding of truth to which photography is inherently connected? Before I try to answer this question, I would like to first clarify this understanding of truth—and to do so with several texts that can be seen as important for the discussion on photography.

One of these texts is a relatively short article by Siegfried Kracauer from 1927 entitled "Photography." As an example, Kracauer takes a photograph of his grandmother—that is, a private photograph, a photograph of sentimental value—and observes that it does not bring back memories of his grandmother as it should, but blocks them. His grandmother as a person, as an individual, as an inner being is not disclosed, but instead only her outward appearance is visible, which however through the fashion of the times—that is, through clothes and makeup—seems impersonal and de-individualized. Kracauer writes: "Nothing of these [things] contains us, and the photograph gathers fragments around a nothing. When the grandmother stood in front of the lens, she was present for one second in the spatial continuum that presented itself to the lens. But it was this aspect and not the grandmother that was eternalized. [...] What appears in the photograph is not the person but the sum of what can be subtracted from him or her. The photograph annihilates the person by portraying him or her, and were person and portrayal to converge, the person would cease to exist."[1] Hence photography endangers not only the identity of the photographer but also the identity of the model, for this inner identity cannot be captured in external features. For Kracauer, every photograph is merely a general inventory of diverse fragments or details that, however, lacks an inner unity. Such a unity can only emerge on the level of meaning, sense, signification, and yet this sense and meaning by definition cannot be photographed. As a consequence, photography for Kracauer is mere refuse, a phantom and a sign of death: instead of vanquishing death, photography kills, for it captures only the body, the corpse, and negates the soul.

The disintegration of memory images in photography has a moral dimension for Kracauer. He writes: "The meaning of memory images is linked to their truth content. So long as they are embedded in the controlled life of the drives, they are inhabited by a demonic ambiguity."[2] It is exactly this demonic nature that Kracauer diagnoses in photography. Though he primarily connects his diagnosis with the spectral or, as he puts it, unredeemed character of the photographic representation, it can be claimed that the connection lies somewhat deeper, as I tried to show earlier. The life of the drives is primarily linked with a certain automatism, with the direct action of the unconscious mind. Photography serves this automatism in that it enables a direct, spontaneous gratification of desire, which is no longer prevented by any asceticism of the work, as was the case in traditional art. A simple click is now enough to create a picture. The camera is a machine of desire, of the unconscious, of the other, which transcends, fragments, and undermines all identities. This is also the somewhat hidden motive for Kracauer's condemnation of photography. It is therefore interesting to observe that Kracauer's strategy is repeated, in all of its essential tendencies, in a book that belongs to those texts that play a key role in today's discussions of documentary photography—Roland Barthes's *Camera Lucida* from 1980.

Barthes takes photographs of his deceased mother as an example, and tries to recognize her in these photographs—but he also does not succeed. The inner being, the true identity of his mother, once again escapes photographic representation. Instead of his mother, Barthes sees in these photographs—just as Kracauer had—merely impersonal fashions of former times. Barthes can recognize his mother in only one photograph, but it is one that shows her as a child—that is, at a time of which Barthes himself has no memories. Hence Barthes's analysis confirms Kracauer's negative line of reasoning—but with one important difference. For Barthes, photography definitely captures "that it was so." Photography has, according to Barthes, its own truth—it is the truth of the trace or the immediate effect of reality. Painting can create illusions, portray something that has never existed. Photography, however, always presents something that actually existed—no matter how slight and insignificant that which is presented might have been. Barthes's position is therefore divided. He does not know to which definition of truth he should give preference. He must admit that the truth of the hidden essence or the inner, subjective truth of imaginative power—that is, identity—is destroyed, extinguished in photography. He discovers, however, that another truth, the truth of the immediate trace, of the unconscious, of automatism, is completely secured by photography—and he insists over and over again that photography in this second sense cannot lie about reality, because the subject of the lie disappears in it.

It is at this point that the question of identity and all the problems related to it with regard to photography make themselves noticed again. For traditional art, the identity of the artist, their consciousness, morals, individuality, are the guarantee for the genuineness of their art. It is for this reason that the other, the unconscious, the mechanical, the instinctual are traditionally considered dangerous—as something that must be fought. It was also for this reason that the battle for the unconscious, for dissolving boundaries, for the other in art was led by the historical avant-garde in order to disrupt the traditional notion of identity. Malevich once said that he was fighting primarily against the honesty of the artist.

Now with photography the situation is exactly the opposite. Genuineness or truth has a mechanical, unconscious, or "different" guarantee here. In this situation, the conscious or the identical disappears—although not completely, as Kracauer or Barthes meant, but in that it becomes a threat for truth in photography, or, to be more exact, for photographic truth. For every technical guarantee is prone to conscious manipulation. Consciousness, therefore, functions no longer as a safeguard of tradition and truth but as a source of lies and delusion—so that it is necessary, above all, for photography to be on guard against identity, subjectivity, or individuality in order to assert its own peculiar, unconscious truth. Photography is always suspected of being manipulated and of being produced in such a way that the traces of reality found in it are merely simulated—a suspicion that neither Kracauer nor Barthes takes into consideration.[3] And again two strategies exist to attenuate this suspicion. One strategy is the vigorous claim of photographers that they do not manipulate their pictures, that they simply tune out their consciousness, their identity, and record life utterly spontaneously as it is. This is a defensive strategy of little benefit, for such a suspicion lies much deeper and cannot be attenuated by mere assurance.

The second strategy consists in offensively demonstrating the possibilities of manipulation and, in doing so, incorporating them into the canon of photography. This is the strategy of a certain photographic avant-garde, and although not unlike the traditional strategy of the artistic avant-garde, it leads, one could say, in the opposite direction. The classic avant-garde upgraded the unconscious, the mechanical, the other of subjectivity to offensively anticipate the suspicion that artistic tradition cannot retain its identity. Nowadays, reversely, an attempt is made to demonstrate the conscious manipulation, to anticipate the suspicion that photography's automatism does not represent a guarantee of its authenticity.

Illustrative of this approach is work by such Appropriationists as Sherrie Levine or Richard Prince.[4] Here it is not reality but another photographic image that is rephotographed. In this case, it is no longer possible to assert, as Barthes does, that photography portrays something that was definitely there, because now we have no criteria to determine what left the traces captured by the photograph—reality itself or an image of reality. Conscious manipulation intervenes here in such a manner that the conscious mind is no longer undermined by means of the unconscious, but instead the unconscious is undermined by means of the conscious. It is not accidental that this intervention has to be marked with the name of the photographer, for what is accomplished here is what may be called a negative escape from the anonymity of photography. It is the other of photography, the conscious and individual manipulation of its traces that becomes visible here.

On another level, Cindy Sherman manipulates the border between a photograph of herself and a staged photograph of someone else. The basic criticism of photography, as uttered by Kracauer or Barthes, is realized here by means of photography itself. The absence of the central identity of the body depicted by the photograph, the disintegration of this body into fragments that cannot be fitted together—all this is usually not evident to normal viewers because they discover a certain external resemblance in the different representations that allow them to ascribe these to one single object. By varying the staging of the externals of her own appearance in her photographs, Sherman makes even outward identification impossible—or at least highly problematic. As a result, the unreliability of the photographic image, which was already diagnosed earlier by its critics, becomes quite obvious. It is for this reason that these works are considered important. And they are important not because they come close to revealing a true identity, but because they reveal a threat of manipulation that might otherwise be hidden.

The same holds true for cultural identities related to differences in race, class, or gender. The fact that these identities are of such great interest these days is in no way self-evident. In this context, I must again mention that all art of the twentieth century has strived to free itself from these identities in order to reach the other, the unconscious, desire, and the automatic, all which unfold beyond consciously perceived differences. The struggle against the bourgeois small-mindedness that places all persons in social niches was the great theme of the classic avant-garde. When one repeatedly reads and hears today how artists, critics, and curators describe themselves and others in a way in which only diligent civil servants in immigration or social-welfare offices are otherwise prone to do, one gets the feeling that this struggle is lost for good.

The similarity of related practices can be seen at a glance. What is nowadays understood by identity is no longer the hidden identity of the soul, the spirit, reason, the self, subjectivity, or individuality, as it was formerly by Kracauer, Barthes, and others. These days, identity is understood as an "identification-card identity," established bureaucratically: location and date of birth, sex, profession, single or married and to whom, skin color, shape of nose, distinguishing marks, and so on. All these data are then specified and itemized, so that this process of differentiation, while potentially never-ending, remains on the same level. Today, when one looks for the other, it is according to this ID description. The other is no longer the unconscious in all its forms as it was until recently, and as it still is in the context of deconstruction, where the other functions as textuality or difference. Instead, the others are those who fill out their questionnaires in another way.

What is striking here is that every important questionnaire, and certainly every ID, is accompanied by a photograph. And this is no accident, as ID identity corresponds to the same understanding of truth that photography itself has—that is, this ID identity is a specific kind of photograph that is established with linguistic means. For ID identity is also a collection of fragmentary details of a person, an inventory of their external features, their appearance. A person disaggregates in an ID description just as they do in a photograph. Hence, Kracauer's or Barthes's interpretation of photography applies to ID identity as well: it is also a collection of the traces left by reality on paper. No stable identity results from it, for such an identity can only be guaranteed through the inner identity of mind and memory. Yet such an inner identity cannot be captured photographically or bureaucratically: the civil servant and the artist today both only concern themselves with external facts.

But why has this ID identity become so relevant? Again, it is the fear of conscious manipulation, which has the ability to raise doubts about the factual truth of photography—as well as other art forms, such as the readymade. Every photograph can be seen not only as a trace of reality but also as a combination of cultural codes, as a culturally coded simulacrum of reality. Barthes, among others, had pointed out this possibility in his earlier book *Mythologies* (1957). For indeed it is possible to claim that photography is always practiced in such a way that certain cultural clichés are merely confirmed and certain cultural viewpoints automatically repeated. Hence the facticity of what is real remains unattainable for photography as well, because the eye that practices it is from the very start culturally coded. The cultural coding of consciousness proves here to be a danger for the truth of photography. And it is ID identity that serves as the way to avoid this danger.

By reporting on the photographer's cultural identity, sex, and so on, one believes to localize the photographer's consciousness and give them a specific facticity. Doing so provides a simple explanation for the way the photographer works: the photographer works like this or that because the photographer is like this or that. This use of ID identification is believed to reestablish the photographer's credibility.

When we look at a photograph, we have two basic possibilities for interpreting it. One possibility is to simply read it as a trace of that which actually was—as Barthes suggests. The second possibility is to see the photograph as the presentation of certain cultural codes that remain concealed from us and, as a result, make the photograph unreadable, unrecognizable. In this case, ID identity helps—it offers a way back to reality by informing us, for instance, that these codes are the codes of a white heterosexual European man. When we hear this information we are reassured, for we finally recognize what this photograph actually is: if not reflecting or conveying an external reality, it at least reflects or conveys the reality of the photographer. In this way, the mystery of photography is supposed to be cleared up—and the corresponding dangers warded off.

In this context, it is quite typical that in many (at first glance) completely different cases the discussion about others seems almost identical—no matter if one is talking about women, indigenous peoples in the Amazons, or former East Germans. This observation gives reason to suspect that in all these various cases it is in fact a question of something else: the manipulative subjectivity that threatens contemporary art's belief in unconscious authenticity. The differences between diverse photographic works made by photographers with different ID identities are indeed difficult to recognize. On the other hand, it is immediately possible to recognize which works reflect this ID identity and which remain naive and unreflective in this respect.

By working with their ID identity, contemporary artists strategically and artistically use their own identity like a readymade.

Here one can speak of a logical continuation of Duchamp's work with readymades. Duchamp demonstrated that it is possible to work artistically with an object without giving it a new form, without altering it, which until then had been seen as an absolute prerequisite of artistic work. Consequently, artists today do not fight their bourgeois identity: they no longer want to transcend or transform it, rather they want to use it as an external readymade available to them within the context of art. Artists have become readymades for themselves. Yet the question is whether this new self-understanding can ultimately eliminate the suspicion of manipulation. I do not believe it can.

Everything can be manipulated—especially one's own personality, and especially if one sees oneself as a readymade. Indeed, possibilities of manipulation, such as those spotlighted by Sherman and Levine, lie beyond all cultural encodings. And it is also common knowledge that an ID can be faked. All kinds of offices require the submission of a photograph in order to make such a forgery more difficult. However, now one tries to make a photograph more genuine by demanding an ID along with it. Both strategies are understandable and even necessary, but neither provides absolute certainty. Undoubtedly, when subjectivity is stripped of all its cultural encodings, as Kracauer once suggested, little is left—and yet the ability for manipulation or falsehoods still remains untouched. It is always possible for us to fake, manipulate, or simulate cultural codes. No information about a person's cultural identity, not even the artist's own attempt to anchor artistic activity in this identity—even a negative attempt, in order to fight it—can certify the credibility of a person's art sufficiently. To engage with one's ID identity is merely a style, a fashion, a discourse, and an art practice, which can perhaps be particularly easily simulated because they have their own codes and vocabulary that in the meantime we have become quite familiar with. No matter the strategy, the risk of manipulation, falseness, or unreality is not something that can be eliminated but rather continues to exist. Artists, like everyone today, are deeply split—namely, between their readymade ID identity and the ability to fake this identity. Consequently, an interesting question for me is not how to approach artistic work differently, but how to simulate, establish, and strategically use difference or otherness to achieve art-institutional success.

Indeed, one such strategy is well known: the strategy of a critical or deconstructive confrontation with one's own ID identity. As a rule, merely transferring regional peculiarities to the international art scene does not prove very productive, for no one is ultimately interested in the regional—except when one happens to vacation there. Nevertheless, there is an interest in critical, deconstructive discourse of regional identities—and this is because this discourse is not regional but supra-regional or international, and hence promises success internationally. This success is attained by deconstructing one's own ID identity according to the rules of art. Criticism and deconstruction are no different in this context from advertisement and promotion, for it is through them that the criticized identity first becomes known and interesting—unlike, of course, the great tradition of European art, which is familiar even without criticism. It is possible to say that critical theory first made its career by critiquing an established tradition—and now lesser-known traditions are making a career by letting themselves be critiqued by this now internationally recognized critical theory.

However, artists and art theorists who make use of this strategy are only able to do so if they have freed themselves from their own ID identities and are capable of seeing them from the outside with the eyes of the international art public. Inner emancipation from one's own ID identity is therefore the first prerequisite for its construction and artistic translation. Hence, it can be said that free and identity-less subjectivity—in the sense of being willing to simulate and manipulate—functions as the author of one's own imaginary ID identity: it creates this identity, and by creating it makes it simultaneously implausible. In this sense it is typical that those who do not have such a free, manipulative relationship to their own ID identity still want to free themselves from it, to break out of its confines. That is why they are considered retrograde in the current cultural climate.

Hence, the discussion of cultural identity is not as interesting as the demand to include the artists' ID identities in their own assessments—its actual significance lies more in the diagnosis of the fundamental danger of simulation and manipulation, which it cannot weaken despite all its strategies. How far removed we are now from the initial optimism can be seen, for example, in the refutation of the criticism of photography that Rodchenko formulated in 1928. He summed up the central argument of photography's opponents, as Kracauer or Barthes were later to be, as stating that photography is inevitably fragmentary, and as a result incapable of creating a synthetic image of memory. Rodchenko argued that the artist is not capable of creating such a "synthetic" image of a person anyway: instead, all portraits are subjective, arbitrary, embellishing, idealizing. What for Kracauer and Barthes is the inner truth of memory is merely an artistic lie for Rodchenko.

For the bourgeois thinkers Kracauer and Barthes, the person with whom they would like to unite in a sublimated form of aesthetic recognition is their grandmother or mother; for Rodchenko, this person is Lenin. It is for this reason that Rodchenko compares paintings and photographs of Lenin in his analysis—and discovers that only photographs of Lenin have the facticity of truth. Rodchenko points out that many artists tried to paint a portrait of Lenin: "Now just show me one artistic 'synthetic' work of which it could be said: this is the true Lenin. No such work exists and never will. Why not? [...] Because there is a portfolio of photographs [of Lenin] and this portfolio of photographic moments does not give anyone the chance to idealize him. Everyone has seen this portfolio and no one, even if he is not aware of it himself will accept an artistic lie about the eternal Lenin."[5] The fragmentary quality of photography is not a shortcoming for Rodchenko but an indication of its genuineness, for life as such is also fragmentary. And at the end of this text, Rodchenko appeals: "Every modern cultivated person must fight art. Don't lie! Take photographs! Take photographs! [...] Paint the truth! Treasure all that is genuine and modern. For then we will also be genuine and no longer pawns in a game."[6]

Now we all know to what degree the photographs of Lenin were manipulated, falsified, or artificially staged. At the time, there was a whole field of science concerned with creating a readymade from real life—as with Lenin's body in the mausoleum, which was also supposed to seem real. And Rodchenko's photographs of happy athletes and enthusiastic Young Pioneers were also part of deliberate state propaganda that falsified the entire reality of a country with the means of photography and documentary film, to a degree unprecedented in history.

Was this falsification a manifestation of Soviet or even Russian cultural identity? Or was it, to the contrary, a suppression of this identity? Are the photographs by Rodchenko perhaps genuine after all, because, although not reflecting reality, they instead reflect the mentality or cultural identity of the times? But then what was this mentality—enthusiasm despite terror, or unscrupulous political opportunism?

Unfortunately it is not possible to answer these questions. They merely suggest that the hope for authenticity and genuineness has once again been dashed, and that photography's automatism and alleged nonsubjectivity cannot guarantee its genuineness. Moreover, all speculations on the cultural identity of former times are not much help, for a person who lives in fear has only his ID identity, papers, and photographs that give him a chance to save his life and temporarily secure his mere existence. This person does not have a cultural identity in the usual sense of the word, but is only a subject of deception, beyond all cultural identities—in this way he responds to the manipulating forces directed against him with manipulation and falsification. The objection might arise here that such a situation is an exception. Yet this is not true. We all live in fear and are willing to simulate, misrepresent, or falsify our identities, to produce faked biographies and photographs. No one can or wants to denounce oneself—neither in life nor in art. It is in the fear of death that every cultural identity finds its natural limits.

1
Siegfried Kracauer, "Photography," in *The Mass Ornament: Weimar Essays*, trans. and ed. Thomas Y. Levin (Cambridge, MA: Harvard University Press, 1995), 56–57.

2
Kracauer, 51.

3
It is along these lines that, for instance, the use of photography in Ridley Scott's film *Blade Runner* (1982) is particularly interesting. In the film, photography serves to produce fake personal memories for the heroes who could not have had those memories. If, for Kracauer and Barthes, photography deconstructs personal memories, then in *Blade Runner* it artificially constructs them "out of nothing," and in doing so, constructs a personality itself.

4
See, for instance, Abigail Solomon-Godeau, "Living with Contradictions: Critical Practices in the Age of Supply-Side Aesthetics," in *The Critical Image: Essays on Contemporary Photography*, ed. Carol Squiers (Seattle: Bay Press, 1990).

5
Quoted in Peter Noever, ed., *Aleksandr Rodchenko / Varvara Stepanova: The Future Is Our Only Goal* (Munich: Prestel, 1991), 234.

6
Quoted in Noever, 237.

THE MIGRANT FROM AN AESTHETIC PERSPECTIVE

The term "migrant" is generally used in European countries as a name for people of non-European origin who live in Europe or want to obtain permission to live in Europe. This word is certainly very imprecise because it covers many different categories of immigrants: those who have received or are seeking political asylum and those who have not applied for asylum but try to gain a foothold in Europe with the help of various documents such as a certificate of identity, exceptional leave to remain, or temporary or permanent residence permit. The reasons that led these people to Europe, as well as their original nationality, age, and other circumstances, are highly individual and diverse. Nevertheless, in the popular imagination these people form an undifferentiated mass, and are termed "migrants." One could certainly criticize the use of the term by contrasting it with reality and exposing its phantasmic, ideologically charged, and incendiary rhetorical character. I however want to investigate not the actual referent of the term but rather its aesthetic dimension, or more precisely, the image the word evokes in the imagination of the speaker and the listener. And, indeed, this image has a very specific nature, because the term "migrant" refers to a person who is neither a foreigner nor German, Italian, French, etc. By saying, for example, "a German person," one certainly does not mean a "citizen of the Federal Republic of Germany." Migrants remain migrants—that is, they correspond to an image of the migrant even if they eventually get a German or French passport. One can be born German or French but not become German or French (as one can become an American, for example). But if migrants are not and cannot be German or French, they are also not foreigners, because a foreigner is supposed to live abroad. One can imagine that a foreigner comes to visit and remains in the country for a while but then goes back to his or her own country at some point. The migrant does not return—or at least does not want to. And what's more, the migrant has reasons and rights to stay in the country—even if these are difficult for others to understand. The migrant is equally a native and a foreigner—and not really native or foreign.

The figure of the migrant thus eludes, in an uncanny way, the fundamental dichotomy between one's own and the foreign that has traditionally dominated the imagination and sensibility of humanity. That is why the migrant is in a sense invisible, imperceptible, unidentifiable. The image of the migrant is the image of the indistinguishable par excellence. There is no aesthetic, no school of perception, no sensitivity related to the intermediate zone that migrants occupy. That is why one tries again and again to avoid this gray area and identify the migrant as a foreigner—for example, by screaming "foreigners out!"—or as a resident, by saying "our beloved fellow citizens." However, both strategies fail to achieve their goal: migrants cannot leave because they do not have a place abroad, and they do not quite look like citizens because the majority of them do not have the usual political and cultural rights that belong to a native citizen.

European perception and aesthetic sensibility are shaped by two major trends in European cultural and art history: Classicism and Romanticism. We can appreciate the cultural norm or a deviation from the norm, one's own or the foreign. Migrants evidently deviate from the cultural norm: they speak broken German or French, they mostly do not react to what's said in a proper way because they haven't mastered the appropriate cultural code, their taste seems backward or tacky because they only know yesterday's fashion. In the sense of the traditionalistic aesthetic, migrants are rarely admirable. But they are also not admirable as romantic strangers.

The biggest problem is that migrants do not seem other, different, exotic, or authentic enough. The other and the exotic hold a great attraction for all of us. This attraction is so great that Romanticism even portrayed its own as foreign, exotic, in order to aestheticize it in this way. A Turk in Turkey or a Chinese person in China are picturesque, authentic, appealing—and therefore Romantic. But migrants are very unromantic. They are no longer an authentically Turkish or Chinese because they have moved away from their own culture through residing in Europe. The migrant is said to be trying to imitate the Germans or the French, to adapt to the prevailing cultural norm. Adapting to the cultural norm is, in the eyes of every Romantic, an unforgivable sin against the vindictive deity of authenticity and cultural originality. Nothing outrages a Romantic more than to discover in the other only a bad parody of one's own. It is interesting that in the last few decades a discourse has developed on the other and otherness that, in the best Romantic tradition, attempts to convince us that migrants in European and American cities also have a specific cultural identity. This is intended to make these migrants attractive in the sense of Romantic aesthetics. But this strategy is too transparent to be convincing. And moreover, the actual migrants, who just want to be finally left alone, do not identify with this strategy at all. They prefer to stick to adaptation.

Migrants are thus, in aesthetic terms, disappointing on two fronts: they imitate the cultural norm, but not well enough to be praised by a traditionalist; at the same time, the mere fact that they imitate the norm makes them unacceptable to a Romantic sensibility. This roughly describes the aesthetic gray area in which the migrant resides. It is the peculiar zone of deviation from deviation, a deviation of the second degree. Migrants deviate from their exotic otherness toward the norm, but they do not reach this norm. They differ from the norm because of their otherness and from this otherness by too much adaptation to the norm. Incidentally, this state of affairs seems to open up the last possibility of an aesthetic justification for the migrant. Indeed, the migrant can be interpreted as a dialectical synthesis between Classicism and Romanticism, between the norm and the deviation from the norm, between one's own and the other. This interpretation is indeed subliminally always present when one speaks about the migrant as a quasi agent of international understanding and the extension of our own cultural horizon.

Indeed, the figure of the migrant is a hybrid. But the hybridity of the migrant is neither dialectical nor synthetic. The common concept of synthesis presupposes that the synthesis contains the best from both of the synthesized principles. Migrants can only be considered a parody of such a synthesis—because they take the bad and superficially appropriated from the normative, in this case from German or French culture, and combine it with the bad and superficially remembered from their own, foreign culture. The result is a hybrid mixture, not an organic synthesis. Nevertheless, the fear that this mixture can be interpreted as a synthesis, so that migrants suddenly and undeservedly rise above both their own as well as foreign cultures, makes them not only aesthetically imperceptible but also threatening in this imperceptibility. Behind the hybrid figure of the migrant hides the hubris that threatens the Classical and Romantic attitudes equally. Additionally, the lack of authenticity that is characteristic for migrants raises the question of their inner motivation. The answer is actually easy to find: the migrant is after money.

In our culture, money is the universal sign of the nonauthentic. We set this sign wherever we miss our own or a foreign authenticity. The economic is constituted for us as an alternative as well as a complement to the aesthetic: everything that we can't see, identify, and aestheticize is for us a dark machination, a business, a matter of monetary circulation. This explains why the discourse on migrants, wherever this discourse is seriously conducted, is almost exclusively a discourse about money. And the presupposition is that migrants do not bring anything financially, except losses.

Now, I would like to provisionally conclude the positioning of the migrant in our cultural context. A critical examination of this context is not my goal—because, among other things, I myself as a migrant am part of this context. Rather I would like to draw your attention to the fact that the migrant is by no means the only figure that is aesthetically constructed in the way I've described above. There are other similar figures in our society that function aesthetically in the same way. One such figure is contemporary art.

A typical contemporary work of art, as can be seen everywhere in galleries, exhibition spaces, or museums, actually looks like a migrant. This work of art, as a rule, does not continue the classical norm, however one defines this norm. One cannot find in the past any exact models for works of contemporary art—with such an attempt, one constantly notices refractions, deviations, imperfections. At the same time, contemporary art is no longer the art of the avant-garde or the art of the other, of the foreign, or perhaps more precisely, of defamiliarization. Nowhere in contemporary art do we see a new, totally unfamiliar approach. Nowhere do we discover radical artistic originality as it was observed in the Romantic era, or also recently in the time of the classical avant-garde.

Contemporary art, on the other hand, has adapted. It still defamiliarizes, it still deviates from the norm, but it does so without breaking with the tradition embodied in the institutions of the Western art world. And more than that, the defamiliarization or deviation strategy has become a generally accepted norm of artistic production. By pursuing this strategy, contemporary art can no longer be termed avant-garde, although it does not automatically become traditionalist or classicist. Of course, this does not mean that one could arbitrarily change this basic strategy of contemporary art to suddenly produce beautiful classicist or traditionalist works. Such a decision, in turn, would only be a deviation from the prevailing norm—and thus also a continuation and confirmation of this norm, which, as I've said, is that which requires such deviations. In principle, one cannot escape a norm that normatively demands deviation from the norm. The fate of contemporary art may be mourned, but it is in principle impossible to change this fate.

Thus, contemporary art is situated in the same hybrid gray zone as the migrant—that is, in an invisible space between the norm and the deviation from the norm, between one's own and the other, between authenticity and simulation. And again, it is neither dialectical nor synthetic, because it cannot organically unite within itself any of the various strategies it pursues or the various demands it faces. Incidentally, this unaesthetic situation of contemporary art often leads to it being denied any authentic motivation. It has become commonplace to state that contemporary art is identical to the art market and is only after money. On the other hand, as in the case of the migrant, one knows that art ultimately only brings losses, so that its economic legitimation also seems to be more than problematic.

Such unaesthetic hybrid forms in our contemporary culture include not only the migrant and contemporary art—although they are very good examples of this—but many other things as well, if not practically everything. And from this one can only conclude that we are still aesthetically insensitive, or at least not sensitive enough to our cultural present. Beyond any complaints about the tedium and unoriginality of today's culture, beyond any protest against the cultural wasteland in which we allegedly find ourselves, we must realize that we live in an extremely interesting present—precisely because we cannot experience our present as aesthetically interesting. This fact only means that our aesthetic sensitivity is not developed enough to consciously experience the radical historical originality of our present.

Cultural signs today travel in all directions in space and time. Through these travels, the old sign combinations disintegrate and completely new, unexpected sign combinations emerge. The signs that used to be far away from one another, both temporally and spatially, enter into the most diverse rhetorical relationships with one another: they metaphorize or substitute themselves with increasing speed. What was foreign a short time ago could be one's own today. What was left-wing a short time ago is right-wing today. Fashion becomes a tradition and tradition becomes a fashion. The avant-garde is seen as obsolete and the anti-avant-garde is seen as avant-garde. A so-called reactionary attitude is a taboo breaker for a progressive enlightener, but it is trivial to a reactionary—and vice versa. Nationalism means at one time liberation, at the next suppression. The communist utopia has emigrated from the future into the past—and the rituals of the past have suddenly become the future. The contexts are forever changing; accordingly, all meanings change. Today we are experiencing an all-embracing migration of signs—human migration is only a small part of it. The migrant and contemporary art only make this migration of signs particularly visible—and thus they are perhaps the most significant symptoms of our time.

Finally, I would like to suggest what the aesthetic originality of our present day is. My hypothesis is: our present is probably the very first true present in history—its originality consists in its presence. This thesis sounds a bit tautological, but it is not. For the aesthetic opposition between one's own and the other is at the same time the opposition between past and future. One's own is the past—it is our memories, our customs and habits originating from the past. The other is the future—the unknown and foreign that await us in the future. Incidentally, migrants are more wanderers through time than wanderers through space. Their memories, their past belong to their own culture, and their future belongs to a different culture. But they are always in between, in the present that is neither one's own nor foreign.

Sometimes we want to find our past in the future—when we feel that we are too far away, too alienated from our past. But in any case we are constantly fluctuating between the past and the future—and tend to skip the present. For the present is always a hybrid form made of elements of the past and elements of the future, although we can never say which of these elements actually belong to the past and which to the future. It is this uncertainty that makes the present so uncanny and so invisible. And one constantly tries to avoid this uncertainty by looking into either the past or the future. But this hardly helps to understand the present. European culture has known the times of attachment to tradition. Then came the modern age, which brought with it a Romantic enthusiasm for the future. Today this enthusiasm for the future has come to an end. And it is exactly this end of faith in the future that generates all present uncertainties and dissatisfactions. Neither the past nor the future promises anything: only the present is left to us. That's why we can say that for the first time we really live in the present, we have really become contemporary. But our aesthetic habits have remained basically the same.

Most authors still feel the need to immediately take a position, to protest against their present, to start anew, to appeal to the past or to the future. Only a few years ago you could read that you can and should build a new society of the future—a multicultural, socialist, ecological one. Then you read that this is not true, and that in the near future the apocalypse occurs—you just have to wait a bit and then you will at least be aesthetically rewarded. Today you read that you shouldn't wait for the future but, on the contrary, you should turn directly to the past in order to die, if not as a saint or soldier, then at least as a martyr. All of this is certainly very exciting, if a bit confusing and fast-paced. The migrant hasn't yet collected all his papers, had them translated into German or French and certified by a notary, and submitted them to the immigration office in order to be admitted to the multicultural society—and now he has to prepare himself by attentively reading Nietzsche and Bataille to fulfill the role of the sacred sacrifice with dignity. Literature simply makes leaps that are too big into the past and then back into the future and then back into the past—and constantly skips the present.

This is the case because dealing with the present means a lot of patience, a lot of insecurity, a lot of effort, and little effect. In the present, one is always split, mixed, hybrid. Those of the present live only fragmentarily, they cannot collect themselves, they don't have a great historical task, they cannot take a clear position or invoke the past or the future. They are rather migrants, emigrants from the realm of history, who ask their present for permission to stay permanently where they are.

THE MUSEALIZATION OF THE EAST

Recently throughout the West we have been able to observe a process of musealizing art from the formerly communist East. Examples of the classical avant-garde as well as the official art of socialist realism and various alternative, nonofficial art movements are shown in numerous museum exhibitions, commented on in catalogues, journal articles, and books, and sometimes even bought. In this process of the museumification of Eastern European art, which in the days before perestroika had only few precursors, such as the German art collector Peter Ludwig, we can see the natural effect of the Western victory in the Cold War: we know from history that the victor has always appropriated the art of the defeated in one way or another. However, this appropriation is now associated with certain problems that affect the institution of the museum and the modern concept of art as such, problems that could not have arisen in this form before.

The modern museum is a product of the Enlightenment and of revolution—the bourgeois French Revolution. What is exhibited as art in the modern museum used to be sacred objects or objects of aristocratic everyday life; accordingly, they were placed either in the church or in the palace. Through the emergence of modern, bourgeois-democratic society, these objects were deprived of their function and use in the rituals of religion and power and placed as exhibits in the museum. Here in the museum they become the aesthetic signifiers of the past: their presence in the museum signifies their absence in reality. They are art because they no longer have a function in reality.

The museum is a machine that turns nonart into art. Outside the museum there is no art at all. Art is a relatively new invention that is very limited in both time and space—a product of revolutionary terror, war, and forced expropriation. Through the dynamics of Western imperialism, the museum of the nineteenth century—that is, the museum after the Enlightenment—transferred the expropriation strategies of the bourgeois revolution to the whole world. The military occupation of the earth carried out by European powers at that time made it possible to transport valuable objects of numerous cultures that had been used in the context of religion or power representation into the museum and transform them into art. The victory of the West in the Cold War is another episode on this path to "world art," which presupposes a political unification of the world. That's why, after its defeat, relics of communism also became art. The musealization of communism should not, however, allow us to forget that the objects that became works of art had a different function in the Soviet communist system. Their transformation into art encounters difficulties that confront the modern museum with new problems. These problems arise because the image production of the communist regimes was contemporary to Western art production. Thus, the usual historical process was interrupted and questioned: earlier, ritual objects became art in the course of modernization, so their ritual use remained a thing of the past, and secularized art designated present and future. By contrast, communism meant a ritualization of art after its modern secularization.

Western art produced after the creation of the modern museum in the West is conceived as art from the outset. This is actually the great break that the museum introduced into history. Especially the art that is programmatically directed against the museum is, from the outset, presupposed and demanded by the institution of the museum. The museum collections demand—according to their own internal logic—the new, the unusual, the original. This is the principle of any collection that excludes the tautological, the repetitive, the redundant, and seeks to expand through the heterogeneous. Modern art stands under the compulsion for the new, the alternative, and the heterogeneous, which has its true origin in the internal logic of the museum, a collection of heterogeneous objects in the homogeneous space of universal historical comparison.

However, if one takes such a definition of art as the starting point of analysis, one has to come to the conclusion that Eastern art—or at least the Russian art that I now want to focus on—is not art at all, even though it appears as art from the outside. In fact, in the entire history of Russia we have never been able to observe the modern institution of the museum—at least not in the form we associate it with in the West. The imperial or aristocratic collections before the revolution were not museums in the modern sense of the word, because they did not aim for an objective, neutral, art-historical presentation, but rather, just as the Western European royal and private collections in premodern times, they formulated and represented normative aristocratic taste. The traditional Russian icon was likewise understood not as an art form but as a sacred object in the context of Orthodox Christian rites.

The conditions for establishing the modern museum were only created after the expropriation of the church and aristocracy following the revolution. But the institution of the museum was not established. The new communist power saw its new art collections not as museums in the Western sense but as an expression of a certain normative taste—albeit now of a supposedly proletarian, communist taste. After a brief transitional period of relative liberalism, the collections began to be designed in such a way that they would produce an effect of aesthetic unity. The museum's collection was not a neutral, art-historical presentation of different historically relevant aesthetic styles but the development of a single binding style that was also meant to determine the selection of artworks of the past. The art presented for the public was by no means allowed to function as a passive object of disinterested, purely aesthetic consideration, corresponding to the modern concept of art. Rather, this art was meant to exercise an active, educational function and embody a vision of the future communist society: it was meant to inspire the masses in their daily work. The work of art in the age of communism thus became a new icon whose content and form were primarily determined not by aesthetic but by ideological criteria. So here we are no longer dealing with a work of art in the modern sense, but with an object of ideological use.

In particular, the art of the Russian avant-garde was not art in the "bourgeois" sense of the word. Rather, it was an attempt to give life itself a certain form, to ritualize life anew, to bring art production from the museum back into reality. The artists of the avant-garde wanted to occupy themselves with the total design of life—that is, festivals, work processes, and tools of everyday use—however, their production of images and forms was defined by their function in the system of state propaganda. If, in all other countries, the avant-garde's anti-museum protest remained only a specific museum-related strategy that ultimately served self-musealization, the Russian avant-garde was unexpectedly taken at its word: the museum system and the art market collapsed after the revolution, and artists effectively had no other option but to work beyond the museum. This de-musealization or re-functionalization of art meant that it received a new cultural, namely ideological-propagandistic use, and was thus transferred into a premodern, pre-Enlightenment, pre-museal phase although remaining formally up-to-date.

The same, of course, applies even more to the Stalinist and post-Stalinist official art of socialist realism. This is visual propaganda with a well-defined vocabulary of permitted stylistic devices clearly shaped by their ideological function, just as premodern art was shaped by its religious or power-representing function. Thus one cannot distinguish either stylistically or qualitatively between the art collected and exhibited in the museums of the Soviet Union and mass art as decoration of public spaces in the form of posters and so forth. The distinction between high art and low commercial mass art typical of modernism and codified by the museum did not exist in the Soviet Union—here everything was done according to the same aesthetic criteria and under the same ideological conditions. And the art of the past was exhibited in museums in such a way to appear as the precursor to the art of socialist realism. Thus in the Soviet Union the museum functioned not as a place of comparison of different historical styles, as is the case in modern museums, but as a place where the prevailing taste and required ideological orientation were defined—that is, the museum functioned similarly to the church or royal collections of the premodern era.

One might think that the unofficial, free, alternative art in communist Eastern Europe at least represented art in the modern sense. But that is not the case. Unofficial art was above all the aesthetic expression of a certain oppositional political attitude—and thus, again, it was ideologically defined. Oppositional, alternative artists in Eastern Europe did not see their art as an attempt at a new aesthetic compared to what was in the museums but as a sign of their ideological orientation toward Western modernity, toward the art of the ideological enemy. Even today some Eastern European artists and art historians are trying to justify their demand for the inclusion of the unofficial Eastern European art in the Western museum by stating that they have always thought and worked in Western, European, international ways, also in the days of communism. In doing so, they overlook the fact that it is this very orientation toward the West that makes their inclusion in the museum impossible or at least very problematic, because the museum already has Western examples of art preceding those unofficially produced in the Eastern countries, and therefore does not need additional ones. Western-looking Eastern art had its full justification in the context of communist rule as opposition to that very rule. This is a political and ideological justification but not an art-historical justification in the museum system of universal aesthetic comparison. Such an insight is bitter for many Eastern European artists and art historians, but their bitterness also testifies that they think about art not in terms of museum and modern aesthetics, but rather in terms of its ideological and political use.

With the phenomenon of so-called unofficial art of the East, one is therefore again confronted with a sacred, ritualistic, power-representing nonart—in this case ideologically oppositional—which is defined by its political use. At first glance, this situation does not seem to cause any particular difficulties if one musealizes this ideological nonart in all its forms in the same way that one's own traditional, premodern nonart or nonart of other, non-European countries was successfully musealized before. Unfortunately, such a musealization proves to be extremely difficult, if not impossible.

The reason for this lies in the aesthetic, purely formal proximity of Eastern nonart to Western art. Namely, the valuable nonart of other countries and times could only be successfully musealized because at first sight, on the purely formal, stylistic level, it already showed itself as exotic, unfamiliar, different. The art of the Russian avant-garde, on the contrary, is too close to the art of the Western avant-garde in formal-aesthetic terms to be regarded as something exotic. Similarly, the art of socialist realism looks like a trivial, kitschy, long-familiar variant of traditional naturalism, also well known in the West.

Additionally, the new unofficial art resembles different styles of Western art too closely. The difference between Eastern and Western art—and when I say Eastern art, I mean only the art that emerged under the conditions of communism and not the entirety of the art that was produced in the countries of Eastern Europe—is in fact too deep, too radical, but at the same time too blurred to be shown and perceived in the context of the museum. The decisive difference is the use of art and not just the use of aesthetically defined artistic styles. This difference cannot be demonstrated within the museum, because only aesthetic differences can be made visible and significant there. Since communist Russia did not have a modern museum system, these formal differences also did not play a decisive role in Russian art. To employ a certain formal-aesthetic style as an ideological weapon, as a sign of right or wrong class consciousness and a particular moral choice under the conditions of the communist system, changed the nature of this style so fundamentally that it was experienced as completely new by a Russian observer—even in the absence of a formal-aesthetic difference required in the context of the museum presentation.

To understand what we mean, let's imagine, for instance, that Warhol's Campbell's soup cans are removed from the museum and returned to the supermarket. There these cans won't be identified as art, because the difference is not in their form but in their use. The same happens with the art of the communist East, but in the opposite direction. Under the conditions of communism, one takes a museum-quality artwork or a certain well-known aesthetic style and deploys it as an ideological combat weapon for or against communism. This use changes everything on a deeper level, but nothing externally. Now, when this artwork or style is brought back into the museum, it loses its difference and becomes indistinguishable, because here it is no longer used in the same way as in communism—and its originality, otherness, heterogeneity, which were legitimated in this particular use, disappear without a trace in the context of the museum collection and presentation. The art of communism is thus not only premodern, it is also after-modern—which to no degree means "postmodern." Modern works of art are re-ritualized under the conditions of communism. So here we are dealing not only with a premodernity, but, as in the case of German National Socialism or Italian Fascism, with, as it were, an other modernity.

Even the expression "Eastern art" is deceptive. Communism thought internationally—its geographical localization was understood as a historical contingency, a precursor to global rule. Of course the Russian art of the Soviet period has many national features. The same can be said for the art of other formerly communist countries. And yet, this art was by no means an expression of ethnic, national sensitivities. According to the official formula, the art of socialist realism should be "national in form and socialist in content." The most important thing about this art, however, was its international, universalist claim; nationalizing and regionalizing this art as "Eastern art" means overlooking its most important dimension. Incidentally, the same universalist claim was also made by "dissident art," which wanted, if you will, to save the world from the world-domination claim of communism. Thus, the art of communism cannot be localized in the coordinates of time or space. The only way to adequately exhibit this art would be to offer a museum reconstruction of the communist system that could show the function of this art within communism. Such an undertaking would certainly be fascinating and convincing but seems hardly realistic, primarily because of the shortage of money under which contemporary museums suffer.

What this obviously means is that Eastern art cannot, in principle, be exhibited in museums. In an attempt to musealize the Eastern art created under communism, the institution of the museum finds its historical limit. It simply cannot carry out this musealization and hides its inability under the characterization of Eastern art as nonart. This characterization is basically correct. However, the art that is preserved in museums is usually originally also nonart that was subsequently musealized. The question that arises, then, is not whether Eastern art is (good) art or not, but why the institution of the museum fails in its musealization. Of course, the problem of the museum's limits is not confined to the art of the East, though it seems to me that in this case especially these limits become particularly visible. Rather, there is the overarching question of how, in the context of the museum, a difference can be shown that is not formal-aesthetic but results from the function of the work of art in the different social, political, media, and other extra-museal contexts. In the meantime, we have learned how to show mass, low-level, commercial art in the context of the museum of high art. The question now is: Can one perform a reverse operation, namely show the functioning of museum art in extra-museal reality?

Another example that aptly illustrates the difficulty of this problem is the fate of the art produced under the conditions of the Nazi dictatorship in Germany. This art is still, after so many decades, not musealized—that is, taken out of its political function—because it looks quite trivial and miserable in the museum context. Its historical relevance and aura of danger cannot be recognized under the normal conditions of art-historical presentation in the museum. On the other hand, one cannot banish this art into the historical or ethnographic museum, because it is in turn not exotic enough but rather can be clearly identified as European and—in the traditional sense of the word—museum art. Moreover, because of its imperial, universalistic claim, the art of the Nazi period cannot be completely reduced to the expression of German nationalism.

It cannot be my task in this context to propose a solution to this difficult problem—such a solution will somehow come about as soon as the problem is correctly identified. Rather, I would like to point out that some artists from the East—and above all some Russian artists—have long been looking for such a solution. I'm referring especially to their involvement with the art form of the installation, which has particularly become apparent in recent times. Under term "installation" one can subsume very different works. Relevant for me in this context, however, are the installations that are conceived practically as autonomous museum spaces.

If an artist produces an artwork in the traditional sense, then it is placed in the already existing context of the museum collection, and this ultimately determines the reception of the artwork. This means that this reception is defined by canonical art history—that is, by a unified collective narrative that is reflected in the museum and managed by curators, critics, and so forth. Although under the conditions of modernity the work of art is usually produced individually, its reception and interpretation are collective, and it is this collective reception that gives the artwork its place in history and the museum.

The installation is an attempt on the part of the artists to take over and control the contextualization of their work, and thus also its interpretation, reception, and historical inscription. An installation is a private museum that tells a different story than the public museum, namely a private story. Through a museum-like installation, the unified museum context breaks down and the canonical collective history of art collapses. The artist becomes a curator but no longer takes on the responsibility toward society to tell its story instead of his or her own.

And that's why Russian artists like Ilya Kabakov and Andrei Monastyrski and the artist group Medical Hermeneutics started to work with installations in the West. Their goal was not to be contextualized by the modern, Western museum, but to create their own context of interpretation that is as autonomous as possible in relation to the institution of the museum. A similar strategy is also practiced by many Russian artists such as Vitaly Komar and Alexander Melamid who do not work directly with the medium of installation, but who want to determine the historical, interpretive commentary on their own works in other ways.

For Russian art emerged in another world history, and also in another art history. The universal art history that was valid in the Soviet Union was the history of class struggle having its manifestation in the conflict between progressive and reactionary art—an art history formulated and articulated by artist names, events, works, and patterns of interpretation that were in part unknown to the Western observer and reader. In order to make the Russian art that emerged in this other universal art history understandable, Russian artists try to reconstruct, describe, and clarify this history through their installations. Not the artwork itself, but its context, commentary, and historical relevance are of great interest to Russian artists today. And through this preoccupation with context and its clarification, they hope to overcome the structural impossibility of the musealization of Russian-Soviet art in the context of the contemporary Western museum.

However, the big question remains whether this strategy can be successful. For in the West, one sees the works of these Russian artists primarily as an expression of their personal mythologies. Accordingly, their installations are seen exclusively as artistic contributions in the context of Western art history, the Western museum, and the Western exhibition system, and not as the creation of other spaces that visualize another collective narrative. And in fact, the question inevitably arises as to what extent an artist is able to individually reconstruct not only his or her personal history but also a collective history. In this case, this means to what extent the installations of Kabakov, for example, actually demonstrate the Soviet mentality and Soviet cultural context—or if they rather embody the artist's personal, subjective dreams, whose visual form is ultimately defined by his position in the context of Western art.

Such a question certainly cannot be answered conclusively. It is posed every time an artist or a curator claims to demonstrate not only his or her own vision, but also a generally relevant truth about the cultural context of that vision. Such a claim is immediately dismissed owing to the assumption that each individual artistic position is subjective and, thus, necessarily one-sided. The tension between the individual character of the artwork and its claim to universal truth can of course never be fully resolved, because each work of art occupies only a limited place in the museum's collection. The rapidly growing interest in the installation art form, however, questions the traditional concept of the museum worldwide, because the installation blurs the line between artist and curator as it was constituted in modernity. The necessity of such a blurring, however, announces itself, in my opinion, nowhere with such intensity as in the case of Eastern European or at least Russian art. For only in this intermediate zone do today's Russian artists have a chance to formulate the inevitable ambivalence of their position: as individuals in the context of modern art history and as representatives of a culture that has developed outside of Western art history and its institutions. The reception of Eastern art is an important factor that exerts pressure on the institution of the museum in the direction of its necessary transformation and redefinition. For the possibility of another modernity is not limited to existing historical precedents. A re-ritualization and re-utilitarization of art can happen under other conditions, in another place, and by means of other ideologies in a possible future after modernity. Then, perhaps, the art of communism will function less as an object of retrospective musealization and more as an early model for the de-musealization of art.

CONSTRUCTION AS REDUCTION

The word "Constructivism" suggests, at first sight, the construction of a new building or new technical object that finds its place alongside what already exists. Indeed, there are Constructivist buildings in the midst of historic European cities or Constructivist works of art in today's museums. However, this spontaneous understanding of Constructivism, seemingly confirmed by language and history, does not correspond to the original Constructivist project—at least the Russian Constructivist project. The fundamental importance of this project is that here, for the first time in art history—although not, of course, for the first time in cultural history—the creation of form was understood as a destruction of form. The main method of Constructivism is therefore not building or constructing but the at least symbolic annihilation, purification, or reduction of what has already been built or constructed—not adding, but subtracting.

The construction that Constructivists sought was the true, inner, and hidden construction of the world. This construction should not be fictitious, individually re-created, or subjectively and artistically designed, but rather discovered, exposed, made visible. The orientation toward the free, the subjective, the new, the individual, the historically accidental, and the nonuniversal was the very accusation made by Constructivists against traditional art. Everywhere in the writings of the theoreticians and practitioners of Constructivism one finds the central demands for the exposure and visualization of both the inner, unconsciously experienced construction of the world and the unconscious processes of artistic creation. These two demands are identical in their essence: for the Constructivists, the world is an artistic construction using colors and forms. There is no essential difference between artistic construction and the structure of the world. To discover the ways in which the artwork is constructed means to discover the inner nature of the world. Thus, everything should be destroyed, eliminated, purified, cleaned, subtracted—which historically obscured and contaminated this hidden universal construction. In art, this work was to be done by Constructivist artists; in life, by social revolution.

Here, for the first time in art history and on the level of artistic creation itself, Constructivism joins the millennia-old tradition of European metaphysics. At least since Plato the way to reveal the truth of the world was understood as a way of negation and overcoming everything that one immediately sees and experiences. The Neo-Platonic philosophical tradition, which was historically prevalent in Russia, has strongly influenced the Russian avant-garde, among other things, through the Russian orthodox theology of the icon. Russian Suprematism and Constructivism operate with the same geometric forms that for Plato already represented the true world behind its visible surface. Indeed, geometric forms are neither objective in the sense of external reality nor subjective in the sense of inner psychological experiences but are rather internally discovered and at the same time universally valid. It can be argued that by turning to geometry, the Constructivist avant-garde became the first art movement that took seriously Plato's critique of traditional art as a mere mimesis of external reality. Geometry developed from the contemplation of the stars—thus geometry is cosmic in origin, it overcomes the limits of our earth. It is not by chance that many Russian Constructivists—especially Kazimir Malevich in his Constructivist phase—understood free, mathematically correct movement in pure, empty cosmic space as an ideal construction. This also applies to Aleksandr Rodchenko, who in his paintings draws a white line in the cosmic black or suggests the night sky with white dots on a black background. Vladimir Tatlin creates a machine for flying that was to be a perfect construction both artistically and technically. Constructivism, then, leaves the visible and the earth to enable a new, nightly vision that reveals the hidden, invisible construction of the world.

But the same identity between creation and destruction also forms the core of modern Enlightenment as such. For Enlightenment thought, to arrive at the truth means to negate and overcome all historical prejudices and specific cultural forms. At the beginning of modern times one finds the Cartesian project of total doubt. Malevich's *Black Square*, which introduces the radical Suprematist-

Constructivist avant-garde in Russia, is also primarily the sign of such total doubt: here the picture is cleared of all historical pictorial forms. It remains only the pure transcendental "black" form of the potential image. This absolute form is further thought of as self-identical: it is a square and represents this square. The division between reality and representation, between the referent and the sign, and, finally, between life and art, seems to be finally overcome here. The pure geometric construction, which has the black square or the image of pure nothingness as its starting point, thus becomes a new incarnation of the old identity between being and reason. Here the work of destruction is not only a precondition for a new creation, it is true creativity itself. Incidentally, the same identity of destruction and creation was postulated earlier by Mikhail Bakunin as the essence of social revolution.

In his day, Le Corbusier proposed the destruction of Paris in order to build a new Constructivist city on its site. Of course, one could ask: Why on the site of Paris and not somewhere else? The answer could be that Le Corbusier wanted to make visible the very idea of a city like Paris, that he wanted to liberate this idea from everything historically accidental—and that this is only possible on the site of the historical Paris and nowhere else. Constructivism is utopian because it does not have its own topos on earth, and needs a non-topos, a u-topos, for its designs.

The presence today of Constructivist works of art in our museums and Constructivist buildings in our cities is evidence not of the historical victory of Constructivism but of its historical defeat. Our museums are precisely the places where different versions of faith in and commitment to the radical transformation of the world—from the magical rituals of the Stone Age to the historical avant-garde—have found their final resting place. However, the Russian avant-garde did not seek a place in the museum; it wanted to abolish the institution of the museum itself.

The museum had to be destroyed as a privileged place for viewing art in order to make the whole world in its totality a work of art and overcome the border between art and life on all levels of social practice. The museum, which historically occupied the non-place, the u-topos, in the topography of the modern world, was considered the main obstacle for the project of transferring the whole world into the u-topos. In fact, it is a point at which the utopianism of the Russian avant-garde converges with the communist revolutionary utopia. The aim of the Russian Revolution was to destroy the ruling, purely consuming aristocratic and bourgeois classes in order to clear the way for total societal production, and thus to reveal the essence of the world as constructive, industrial labor, which earlier was obscured by the false luxury of the ruling classes. The new proletarian society should become a perfect machine, an absolute construction, a total production process that consumes itself, knows no outside, no foreigner, no other—a total dictatorship of the producer over the consumer. But the Russian avant-garde sought the same dictatorship. The artist of the avant-garde no longer wanted to be subjected to the bourgeois spectator, the consumer, the art market. Rather, the viewers ought to leave their safe and comfortable aesthetic distance to art to be included in the work itself, in its construction, to become part of it.

The utopianism of the Constructivist avant-garde differs from the classical utopias mainly in that it replaces contemplation with interrupted movement. Malevich's Suprematism was still contemplative—he understood his *Black Square* as the authentic image of the cosmic whole. For later Constructivists, life is in constant flux, the constant process of inventing, changing, designing. The classical utopia, from Plato to utopian socialism, was a project of the final social condition after the end of history. It resulted from the search for the true and the timeless, for liberation from the imperfection of human existence in time. For Russian Constructivism, on the other hand, the timeless is only an illusion. Rather, its utopia is the utopia of uninterrupted movement that never stops and does not allow a pure contemplation from outside. The time of this utopia does not flow slower than historical time, it rather flows faster. Constructivists are Nietzschean in that they do not believe that there is anything transhistorical, immutable, or eternal in life on which one could draw. Life is for Constructivism the great nothingness, a pure act of will, a purely unconscious vital flow—and everything visible is only an illusion that had been "made" by the art of the past. The aesthetics of Constructivism springs from a peculiar combination of Plato and Nietzsche, linking geometry with Dionysian impulse and the will to power.

The Nietzschean activism of Russian Constructivism is incidentally broken from the beginning through this connection with contemplative Platonism, for this Platonism makes it dependent on the geometry of the modern technical world. For example, when Rodchenko talks about the constant invention of new forms and the uninterrupted, creative construction of the image of the world, he initially makes a very activist impression through his powerful language. On closer inspection, however, it turns out that his relationship to the movement of time is much more passive than it initially seemed to be. For example, in his 1920 essay "The Line," Rodchenko writes that one should aestheticize simple utilitarian things as works of art. This gives monotonous, everyday, boring work its aesthetic justification. In order for the simple people of our technical age to be able to value ordinary technical objects made by themselves as artworks and to feel like artists, they need someone like Rodchenko, who draws their attention to the aesthetic dimension of ordinary things. He writes, "Life, this simple thing, has never been seen, not known, that it is so simple and clear that it has to be organized and liberated from all external embellishment."[1] Here, organizing is understood as the purification of the superfluous.

But this in turn means that the function of Constructivist art is not world-shaping, but only negative, and in a sense secondary. The new artificial things are created exclusively by technology—out of certain utilitarian, economic, political, everyday necessities. The goal of the Constructivist artist, on the other hand, is not to construct something purely artistic, but to show others—and not least their producers—that the technically made things are the best possible works of art exactly because of their practical simplicity. In order to aestheticize the technical world as it is, the Constructivist should create nothing new or original but only fight against art, understood as an autonomous activity, and also against the superfluous artistic design of technical production. As a result, the artist becomes a guardian who constantly watches to make sure that nothing artistic is done, so that people's attention is not diverted from the beauty of their own new everyday life. The real creativity is left to the working class and its political and economic leadership.

The task of the artist, writes Nikolai Tarabukin, one of the theoreticians of Constructivism and later of Productivism, is that of the propagandist who draws attention to the new aesthetics of technical production.[2] At the same time, Tarabukin recognizes not only a single technical product but the whole production process as a work of art. He writes, "The goal of the one who works in production is production itself."[3] That is why he calls the production process in proletarian society, in which everyone is equally involved, "nonobjective." This designation, which was used by Malevich to describe his own art, is now used as the description of the new industrial society in its totality: after society has been completely absorbed by the mechanism of production, society itself has become a nonobjective total work of art.

The single work of art no longer has any intrinsic value or meaning in such a society. Its meaning is an educational, propagandistic one, and it consists in averting the viewer's gaze from art and directing it toward artificially, systematically, technically produced reality. The artwork becomes a poster or advertisement. The technical production process embodies the desired ideal of constant movement, which has nothing external beyond itself and can never come to rest. This movement takes place in time, but it is not historical time, because in the production process people are connected to each other not by common historical goals but only by their function in the production process itself. This internal organization or construction of the production process is the genuinely aesthetic, artistic aspect of it, which the

Constructivist artists can discover through the analysis of their own work on the image in order to achieve a kind of self-reflection of the new world.

But this role of visualization of the industrial production process suddenly makes the Constructivist artist appear very traditional and museal, for the aesthetization of technical modernity presupposes a museum perspective that provides the only possible comparative overview of the aesthetic characteristics of various historical epochs. It is only in the museum space that it makes sense to try to lend modernity in its entirety a particular aesthetic expression—and this attempt once again turns Constructivism into a mimetic or representative art that wants to propagate the real utopia of the present, thereby prefiguring, among other things, the eventual strategy of socialist realism.[4]

1
Aleksandr Rodchenko, "The Line," in *Aleksandr Rodchenko / Varvara Stepanova: The Future Is Our Only Goal*, ed. Peter Noever (Munich: Prestel, 1991), 133–35.

2
Nikolaï Taraboukine, *Le dernier tableau* (Paris: Éditions Champ Libre, 1972), 58.

3
Taraboukine, 69 (translation by the author).

4
On the connection between Russian avant-garde and social realism, see Boris Groys, *The Total Art of Stalinism: Avant-Garde, Aesthetic Dictatorship, and Beyond*, trans. Charles Rougle (Princeton, NJ: Princeton University Press, 1992).

THE WILL TO REST

Tiredness is perhaps a basic topos of our time. When I meet friends from the art scene and ask how they are doing, I almost always hear that they are actually doing very well but feel very tired. This feeling evidently is not only personal but deeply rooted in our culture today. This becomes particularly clear when one reads memoirs or personal letters from the days of the historical avant-garde in which a poor, persecuted, suffering artist repeatedly states that he is full of energy and enthusiasm for life.

Where does this difference in tone come from? Why is one so tired today? As an explanation, one often says: fin de siècle, postmodernity. And that sounds like we who are living in the postmodern era have gotten tired because our avant-garde ancestors were so active. This assumes that tiredness can be inherited, but there is no plausible evidence for that. In addition, our ancestors seemed to remain quite energetic despite all their activities—it is only us who have gotten tired. So obviously it is not the earlier avant-garde activities that have made us tired but our own postmodernity, whereas the avant-garde made one energetic.

But what is postmodernity? It is definitely not a new age, because in that case postmodernity would still be modern. So postmodernity does not differ from modernity except through its self-interpretation. Postmodernity is another interpretation of modernity or, if you like, of the historical avant-garde—an interpretation that makes us tired.

The word "avant-garde," as has often been pointed out, refers to the military term for a unit that marches far ahead of the rest of the troops. Seen from the postmodern perspective, this march actually seems to be infinitely tiring, for postmodernity understands its goal as infinitely distant. According to this view, the way of the avant-garde follows the rhetoric of the infinite play of signifiers or the infinite movement of difference, or infinite desire, or the always unattainable sublime. In its postmodern interpretation, the avant-garde pursues a vision of the impossible and finds itself on an endless march to its destination, which is constantly disappearing from view. At no sign, at no image can the marchers rest, find peace, recover. They always have to go on, because in our cultural rhetoric every image refers to the next. And so they are—or rather we are—forced to move from image to image or from sign to sign. But because as human beings we are finite, this infinite movement overburdens us and makes us tired.

However, this movement, which leads us away from all images and signs, should not be misunderstood as cynicism, indifference, or boredom, because it likewise leads us back to the same images and signs. We are no longer able to be cynical, indifferent, or bored. We are no longer capable of irony either. Cynicism, indifference, or boredom is distance from all the signs and images that give us a certain peace and allow us to discover our own subjectivity in its absolute loneliness beyond all images. The flaneur as described by Walter Benjamin could be bored and, for all his fascination with the images of the outside world, think of himself as a subjectivity that goes through the world. He could also stay at a certain image, go back to it, or even return to his home. We can no longer do that because we are no longer authors of our movement through the world—rather the path that is defined by the play of signifiers leads us and leaves us no peace. That is why we are not bored but always eager to see where this path will take us. And this constant tension makes us especially tired.

Now this vision of the avant-garde as a constantly forward-moving troop is a characteristic postmodern vision that by no means possesses the self-evidence ascribed to it. The avant-garde can also be thought of as a military unit that has already victoriously reached its destination, camped, and rested while the rest of the troop still marches without knowing if it will ever reach its destination. The texts of the historical avant-garde make it quite clear that its self-image did in fact correspond to this state of tranquility. The avant-garde is resting—it is always the others who are still marching. The images and texts of the avant-garde represent nothing but this final rest. Malevich's *Black Square* is such a picture of absolute calm in which life and death form a unity. It wasn't an accident that Duchamp's *Fountain* was called "Buddha of the Bathroom" in a contemporary review—it was conceived as an image of absolute calm. Mondrian is another good example. But also Futurist representations of movement show this movement "simultaneously," that is, as absolute rest, which includes in itself all moments of temporal movement. The vision of a total explosion of the world that Dadaism constantly invokes reveals only an immutable nothingness that lurks behind every reality. And even seemingly active Surrealism sees itself as a passive medium that receives the signals of the unconscious.

This calm of the avant-garde is the source of its energy: the avant-garde rests when everyone else exerts themselves, and thus the avant-garde artist has more power than the rest of humanity. Picasso coined the now famous phrase "I do not seek, I find." The avant-garde did not seek—it found. Indeed, it found something elemental, fundamental, and universal that lies behind all images as its transcendental possibility, just as *Black Square* can be thought of as the transcendental scheme of any possible image, or *Fountain* as the elemental gesture of any possible aestheticization.

The concept of the avant-garde as a shock troop of eternal forward movement does not correspond to the self-image of the avant-garde. This concept is rather the perspective of the rest of the troop, which has become tired and no longer believes it will reach its destination, and therefore also believes that the avant-garde is merely chasing ghosts and missing its target. However, the rest of the troop has long lost sight of the avant-garde, and therefore cannot even know whether the avant-garde has arrived or not. There are no neutral criteria to establish this. It is easy to argue that Malevich's *Black Square* or Duchamp's *Fountain* or any other avant-garde images cannot be seen as fundamentally new, but like any image they are subject to general image rhetoric. This opinion certainly sounds plausible, but it's just an opinion, because the possibility remains that the avant-garde can see the difference between fundamental and non-fundamental from its resting point, a difference we cannot see because we are still on the way to this point. When we became tired in postmodernity, it was not because we are children of the avant-garde, but because we are children of the rest of the troop who have lost faith in ever reaching the destination, and thus our life presents itself as a constant, weary movement forward. Only the rest of the troop understands modernity as progress—independently of whether it judges it positively or negatively. The avant-garde does not progress but calmly remains where it has found an aesthetic place to rest.

The philosophers of the rest of the troop are well known. The most interesting of them belong to the 1930s. They are the ones who marched behind the avant-garde but never arrived. For instance, Heidegger is constantly "on the way to language." He is a wanderer who wanders slowly through life and the world. Indeed, he wanders so slowly that he almost rests, although over a long period of time this can also be quite tiring and unpleasant. But then comes total mobilization, permanent revolution, negative dialectics, symbolic exchange, and other even faster variants of uninterrupted movement. However, this vision of constant movement is not the authentic vision of modernity. Rather, it is an effect of the doubt of modernity, the expression of disbelief that the Promised Land can ever be reached. Where modernity is radical in itself, there it rests, as mentioned earlier, on a timeless, transcendental, apocalyptic fundament—at the end of the story of any possible search. On the other hand, the apocalypticism of our time is, as we know, the apocalypticism of apocalypticism or the announcement of the end of the end. It wants to reveal the impossibility of stopping and resting.

Of course, we can always exit this postmodern permanent movement at any time by returning to the original avant-garde interpretation of an image. Nothing prevents us from asserting, as stated above, that a particular image has a fundamental meaning that allows us to dwell on the image and rest—or even that all images have such a fundamental meaning. This offers us the figure of avant-garde fundamentalism, which in fact is not uncommon in today's cultural context. This fundamentalism is the reaction to the disappearance of the fundament. In the place where the avant-garde believed it could discover the fundament, the avant-garde fundamentalist sees no fundament—and for this very reason arrives at the resolution to create such a fundament through its own decision. This fundamentalism is thus purely decisionistic and arbitrary. Although it condemns postmodernism as empty and cynical—unfairly, as we have seen—it can only unfold in the fundamentlessness of postmodernism, because wherever the fundament still is, fundamentalism is impossible. Thus, an unconditional and programmatically unfounded commitment to individual images is demanded and practiced, which, as a result of a heroic effort of concentrated contemplation, should be aesthetically isolated and rescued from its submission to general image rhetoric.

However, while avant-garde fundamentalism itself is a rhetorical figure that can be applied equally to every image, it possesses the same universality as postmodern, anti-fundamentalist rhetoric. Thus every image can be interpreted equally as fundamental—that is, as a final insight into the nature of the work of art—and non-fundamental—that is, as visual garbage. Thereby, in our culture today every image is internally split. However, modern art was always divided into high avant-garde art, which wanted to reveal final insights, and mass art, which followed only the rhetoric of image production. Thus modern art never formed a homogeneous space and could never be subsumed under a unifying concept.

This splitting of modern art was exemplarily described by Clement Greenberg in his essay "Avant-Garde and Kitsch" (1939). He wrote that art had aestheticized all that it could aestheticize. Thus the division that was of eminent importance for earlier art was overcome—namely, the split between what art was allowed to represent and what it was not allowed to represent. But as a result art itself has split—into avant-garde and kitsch. For Greenberg, the avant-garde is the reflection of the technical nature of art, because the work of art is not just an image of the world of things but is itself also a technical thing. In the context of kitsch, the artwork is also a technical thing, but kitsch does not reflect this technicity, rather it simply employs its immediate effect. Modern art is thus divided into the reflection of art and the use of art. If an art acts utopian or nonutopian, critical or affirmative, politically correct or incorrect, it will still remain kitsch, even if it doesn't act at all. The rest therefore remains for Greenberg the real internal state of the avant-garde.

During discussions about postmodernity, when I hear someone mention a second modernity, which obviously means a second avant-garde, I rejoice. I rejoice like a wanderer whose feet are tired and who drags on with the last of his strength and hears that the vision of the oasis he is desperately trying to reach is not a vision but an actual oasis where he can finally rest. But where can this second oasis be found? The assumption is obvious that, unlike the first oasis, the second oasis is everywhere and differs from the postmodern desert only in the way it is interpreted, so that a work of art can legitimately at one point be interpreted as postmodern and at the next as second-modern. Today the division of modern art into avant-garde and kitsch, or rest and motion, or insight and rhetoric, or oasis and desert no longer splits the real material space of art, it splits the space of interpretation of each individual work of art.

What has postmodern discourse actually done all along? It has always relativized the distinction between avant-garde and kitsch that Greenberg so radically posited. It did this through a twofold movement of thought. On the one hand, kitsch was "dekitsched" and refined as avant-garde. This dekitsching of kitsch began with American Pop art, and has progressed and accelerated to such an extent that we now live in a situation in which virtually everything that is considered kitsch has been transferred to the field of high art through well-proven methods.

On the other hand, the same movement of thought turned everything that used to be considered high art into kitsch by exposing the autonomy of art as an illusion. All art, including the avant-garde, was placed in a social context—especially in a political context—or interpreted as a moment in the movement of general image rhetoric. If, on the one hand, kitsch images began to be characterized by predicates that formerly were only claimed by the avant-garde for itself, the avant-garde, on the other hand, has become a manifestation of the general cultural situation, among many others. Thus today we can no longer distinguish whether a picture belongs to kitsch or the avant-garde. But if one can no longer distinguish between avant-garde and kitsch, one is still quite capable of distinguishing between the kitsch use and avant-garde use of an image.

We can indeed recognize when images are deployed to be used, be it in politics, entertainment, advertising, and so on, or when they demonstrate their own internal structure. Even differences of opinion about this can be meaningfully discussed. Of course, it does not mean that corresponding criteria are clearly defined—such clear rules did not exist even in the days of the classical avant-garde. But we can still speak meaningfully about whether certain images are used in the sense of the avant-garde or in the sense of mass culture. Thus it may be said that the first modernity was creative; today, on the other hand, we live in a second, interpretive modernity. However, in the case of the first, classical avant-garde, production was always also essentially interpretation, for even then no new images were created, but existing images were used in an aesthetic context. Rather, the difference between the two modernities lies in the fact that today's artists are aware of the dual status of their work, of their interpretive double coding, for which there are enough examples, from Andy Warhol to Cindy Sherman.

And yet, even if today's double coding of an image leaves the option open of letting one's gaze rest devoutly on any image whatsoever, this calmness is not unclouded. Today, if one stays in a certain place, one no longer has the inner security of the days of the earlier avant-garde that everyone else is on the way to the same place. Rather, one has the uneasy feeling that life is passing by. Anyone can rest at any time, but the *general* movement remains unstoppable, and it is uncertain where the path leads. This postmodern lack of worldview has been lamented numerous times. But one still assumes that it is a duty of the individual to create such a worldview for oneself, and possibly for others as well. This will for a worldview leads to an effort that makes one tired. Therefore,

I would like to propose another possibility to deal with the lack of worldview: let's escape the totalizing view ourselves.

In fact, in today's art scene, we can increasingly see the production of artworks that physically overwhelm and tire the audience, and which in the end cannot be seen in their entirety. I would like to emphasize that this does not refer to the artwork's "inexhaustible deepness"; rather it simply means the physical impossibility of perceiving the whole of the work, which suggests that by looking at it we necessarily overlook its most important aspect—as in real life. The possibility for a single artist to create such an unobservable artwork is the result of a combination of modern technology and advanced art practices. The art of today possesses a very high speed. It is not the speed of art that the Futurists thematized or Paul Virilio explores, but the speed of image production as such. This speed has increased rapidly since the beginning of the twentieth century. It used to take a long time for the artist to paint a picture. The observer, on the other hand, was able to grasp the picture in one glance. That is, viewers had a huge excess of time, and thus privilege, compared to the artist: they could see many pictures in the time span in which the artist could only produce one picture. Works such as Duchamp's *Fountain* or Warhol's *Empire* equated the time of image production and the time of image contemplation. A combination of the readymade practice and new media's technical possibilities of recording and reproducing ensure that the artist is better placed than the viewer in that temporal economy. The time relation between the production and the perception of images changed decisively in favor of the artist. The perception of images now requires more time than their production.

This excess of time on the part of the artist can be used to overwhelm the observer and make the work of art unobservable. A good example is the video work by Fischli and Weiss that was shown at the Venice Biennale in 1995. The footage was so long that it could not be fully apprehended by a visitor under the normal time conditions of an exhibition, so the impression of the work necessarily remained fragmentary and incomplete. Incidentally, the same effect can also be achieved without the direct application of new media, as installations by Ilya Kabakov or graphics by Raymond Pettibon show: excessive use of writing in both cases makes the artwork time consuming, fatiguing and frustrating the viewer.

Carl Andre once said, "Art is what we do. Culture is what is done to us." Thus I feel not tired but quite energized when I put others in a situation of unobservability similar to the situation that surrounds me. By confronting others with my own unobservability, created by myself, I get the opportunity to direct the movement of others without specifying the movement's goal, as the classical avant-garde did in its day. So I use the excess of time that contemporary art practice gives me to rest while the viewers exert themselves.

But here even the viewer gets a seemingly paradoxical chance to rest. Owing to repetition and duplication of the general situation of unobservability by the means of art, the artificially produced, staged character of this unobservability is demonstrated. Instead of getting tired of the desire to capture postmodern unobservability in a concise, "neo-modernist" image, the viewer becomes aware of the possibility of aesthetically admiring unobservability as such, without making an effort to overcome it. In this way we find an oasis in the desert, finally learning to interpret the whole desert as a huge oasis ready to be peacefully enjoyed.

THE SUFFERING PICTURE

Our epoch is usually regarded as an epoch of post-history, at least as far as painting is concerned: the painted image has ceased to be a picture in the traditional sense of the word, as it is no longer an image of anything and has finally lost its external referent. Hegel stated that in modernity the mimetic image no longer serves as a means of knowledge of the world, but today the image also no longer manifests the other of reason on which the avant-garde previously insisted. The belief that in the picture a reality can be re-created that exists outside it gave the picture a privileged position in the world. Today this belief has been radically lost. Therefore, for today's consciousness the picture is simply a thing among other things, and thus is in external relationship to them. The order of things finally coincides with the order of signs. It is further assumed—Rodchenko already proclaimed this—that the "last picture," which demonstrates the identity of both thing and sign, has already been painted (though opinions differ as to when and by whom)—that is, the picture is only possible as a readymade. The picture can only be the quotation of a traditional, avant-garde, or trivial image that is cited with the critical intention of showing the material character of the image, of pointing out its function within certain sign systems and understanding it as a reference to a certain context but not to a referent.

In order to expose the materiality of the image, contemporary artists usually employ a method that could be called double quotation or double appropriation: the contemporary image generally refers to a classical model, to an image that is still understood "uncritically," and at the same time to the anonymous modern design that characterizes the production of consumer goods and the mass media. This double quotation differs from the traditional technique of the readymade, which works with mass production and directly aestheticizes it. In this case, the image still retains its traditional function to represent the external world—as in Pop art, for example—albeit one not understood as nature but as an artificially created urban space. In the contemporary postmodern picture, the new aestheticization refers above all to a previous de-aestheticization. Here the downfall of the picture in the modern world becomes the subject of a new kind of aesthetic contemplation. The picture's alienation and reification become aestheticized in their turn.

This aestheticization is usually legitimized as critique, something that has often happened throughout history. But real critique is a prelude to real destruction and not to new creation. Thus in the 1920s, when the Russian avant-garde came to the conclusion that the picture had lost its meaning, it demanded its destruction and prohibition. One should move on to the production of things themselves. Malevich's Suprematism was also rejected, which on the one hand abolished the opposition between signifier and signified—the representation of the square coincides with the square itself—but on the other hand upgraded geometric forms as pure, impersonal, and ideal forms of contemplation—a notion that reaches back to Plato. As in the case of Plato, Malevich's renunciation of the contemplation of the external forms of reality radicalized the demand to move on to pure contemplation and the absolute picture. This ambivalence in the interpretation of geometric form has been preserved until very recently. Ad Reinhardt is just one example here, albeit a characteristic one.

The Russian Productivists saw the only way to overcome this ambivalence in the practical use of the geometric form as well as the abolishment of art as a particular form of activity. However, this strategy led merely to the use of geometry in modern design. The corresponding strategy of the double quotation, as practiced by Richard Artschwager and others, can therefore be interpreted in two ways: as further critique of the sacred aura surrounding the geometric form and as a reactivation of this aura—or, in other words, the transcendental referent. This also applies to the works in which critique of the auratization or the referentiality of the artwork manifests itself most strongly and radically. All these manifestations can in turn be understood as new sacralizations as well as new references to the transcendental referent. The fact that this second possibility is usually insufficiently taken into consideration is because of the widespread conviction that the image has been steadily secularized throughout modernity and has completely lost its external reference. This conviction has its own history. Here an attempt is made to trace—by necessity very schematically—the essential stages of this history.

Originally the value of the image was not separated from the value of what was represented. Paintings depicted religious subjects, great historical events, and important people: only the essential, the sublime, and the true were allowed to enter the picture's field of vision. Thus the term "content" presupposed from the beginning the idea of a socially recognized value that was established independently of its representation in art. Already the semiotization of the term "referent"—understood no longer as a value but as a value-neutral signified in a practice of signification—relativizes it and marks the beginning of its disappearance from art-historical reflection, but certainly not yet from art itself. This gradual semiotization begins at a time when secularization and democratization were gradually replacing former sublime themes with low and trivial topics. It does not mean, however, that the image itself would become democratic and migrate into the area of the peripheral and worthless. In the democratic era, on the contrary, earlier themes and figures were devalued and new themes and figures revalued. Art proceeded to the presentation of these new themes and figures but did not change its traditional goal of showing the valuable. Saints and heroes were exchanged for motifs taken from nature and the urban milieu, but only because a new truth was now being sought in nature and in bourgeois society, and this truth was thought to be recognized in natural common sense or a new legitimation of power seen in the representation of the people.

The aesthetics of the period of democratization, however, was accustomed to interpreting this evolution of art in a different way. What was primarily a consequence of objective changes in the hierarchy of values and an illustration of this process of change was understood, especially in Romanticism, as confirmation of the free will of the artist. The artist's departure from traditional themes and prescribed models of interpretation was understood by Romantic criticism as a manifestation of his sovereign genius. The image was understood as a private world, a separate, idealized private domain in the possession of the artist, an autonomous space of reality for which the artist ultimately became the divine creator and legislator, free and sovereign in his decisions. As proof of this freedom, the same deviations from the canon of the past, the norms of traditional taste, or the traditional school were always cited, as if these deviations automatically confirmed the freedom of the artist. The revaluation of social values was misinterpreted as mere devaluation or flattening of the old values. Therefore, one ascribed to the artist the power to freely determine the value of art's referent and to choose the objects of representation.

But although Romantic critique stereotypically claimed that the artist's talent was free of any dependence on the object of representation and that only the image "as a picture," not its referent, determines its belonging to the sphere of art, the represented topic was in reality socially defined. The claim that the artist has absolute freedom obviously ignored the boundaries in which it was used. Of course, this circumstance did not remain hidden from Romantic critique, but one did not want to restrict from the outside the artistic freedom one had just gained. From this originates the vaguely formulated theory of the unconscious: according to this theory, external reality, which no longer serves as an orientation for the artist's consciousness, determines the artist's freedom from within, without the artist knowing it. In other words, the theory of the unconscious explains the individual decisions of the artist under the conditions of the absence of external criteria for these decisions or the unwillingness to recognize such criteria. For German idealism, nature or the zeitgeist work through the free will of the artist, reconciling the artist with socially accepted values. Of course, this reconciliation did not prove to be permanent. However, the canonical interpretation of high art finally removed the external referent—unlike in the case of kitsch—and made art into a field of permanent struggle between the free will of the artist and the unconscious forces of desire, language, race, or class that dominate this free will from within.

The second feature of this reconciliation became the view expressed later in the nineteenth century of the critical function of art: the free will of the artist collides with social barriers and fixes this collision in the form that challenges these barriers. The topics of art are thus made explicit, but in a negative way—as restrictions of artistic freedom that must be overcome. These topics now come to the fore, so it seems, not only as worthless, but even as unworthy.

The critique of social institutions is now expressed in the portrayal of suffering segments of the European population and the suffering of nature itself under the burden of industrial civilization. According to the European Christian tradition, however, suffering is considered a positive value. A suffering person resembles Christ—suffering purifies and makes one a better person than others. The same also applies to nature. From a Christian point of view, degraded nature is more beautiful than any other kind of nature. In fact, in the nineteenth century, a gradual re-Christianization of European life occurred in response to the excesses of the atheistic eighteenth century. This re-Christianization is closely linked to the ideas of socialism and the social responsibility of the individual. The earlier belief in the individual freedom of the artist gave way to grievances over the artist's alienation and isolation. At first glance, the social critique of this period broadened the artist's freedom in its relation to the subject matter used: grace, humiliation, and deformity found their way into the artist's paintings. But in fact, art returned to its earlier ideals. The criticism and realism of the nineteenth century demonstrates the alienation of the individual not only to denounce the society of the time, recall the previously ignored negative sides of secularization, and expose the previously ignored social unconscious, thus overcoming this alienation, but rather the art of the time above all aestheticizes this alienation: the profanation of the individual in the industrial world is transformed into a new value and becomes sacralized because it is interpreted as suffering. Thus, the image regains the sacred and valuable as its referent, although at first glance it appears to be the image of the degraded and abused.

The historical avant-garde subsequently ushered in a new phase of secularization as well as the renunciation of nostalgia and sentimentality. In the epoch of the classical avant-garde, the illusion of freedom from an external referent that was so cherished during the Romantic period is replaced by the even more radical illusion of the total disappearance of this referent. At the same time, the artists extend their freedom to the entire material world of objects, which they see as an unlimited supply of forms and means, as material from which they can realize their total artistic project. The historical avant-garde was less concerned with the originality of its manifestations or the originality and autonomy of its creations than it may seem today. On the contrary, this persistent anxiety characterizes the secondary, post–Second World War neo-avant-garde aesthetic consciousness. The historical avant-garde glorified the new values of construction, activism, functionality, and domination of the producer over the consumer. However, once again, total artistic freedom, understood as the only legitimation of artistic decisions, constantly contradicted the actual thematic and stylistic practice of the avant-garde artist. On the theoretical level, this meant that artistic freedom played with the radicalized concepts of the unconscious, which interpreted artistic freedom as guided from within by desires, involuntary impulses, or class or racial instincts, thus leading to the subjection of this freedom to the totalitarian political projects of the epoch.

As it turns out, however, referring to free choice or pointing to the unconscious cannot explain avant-garde art's choice of concrete themes and forms, since all these references remain too general and vague. But it is easy to show that in practice, the avant-garde predominantly used traditional sacred forms that it isolated from their original ritual context and turned into passive material for new construction. The avant-garde thus was only illustrating the process of the desacralization or profanation of tradition and its technical utilization, which was seen as a positive development by society at the time.

An example here is particularly important and significant. Duchamp's readymades are often interpreted as evidence of the artist's free will in dealing with artistic values: each object of everyday life becomes an object of aesthetic contemplation through the will of the artist and thus acquires artistic value. This act of extreme artistic arbitrariness of course can still be interpreted as the result of unconscious desires or rules of language. Ultimately it can also be interpreted as the result of a critical analysis of market mechanisms, exhibition activities, or social representation rituals. These three possible interpretations are already well known and each refers to the artist's decision—whether it is free or not—and not to the object's own value, since from the start it is considered worthless, such as Duchamp's famous urinal.

In its basic function, however, the urinal has—in addition to all its erotic associations—something to do with what could be called a sacred sacrifice to the cosmos: it is a transit station for a gift without a counter-gift. After Duchamp, art paid particular attention to garbage dumps, trash heaps, and all sorts of waste and throwaway habits that were long considered taboo for modern industrial civilization because they symbolized nothingness or the absolute other, the irrevocable disappearance of material things. In our time these former taboos are thematized in the context of ecological discourse. They moved to the center of societal interest, as the process of recycling tried to reintegrate garbage. Ecology, in this sense, is the next stage in the realization of the modernist project and the secularization of mankind—at least in Europe, as it destroys another area of the sacred and taboo, the area of garbage. Readymade artists appear as forerunners of this secularization and utilization, since the entire art of the readymade is actually based on the aestheticization—that is, artistic utilization—of refuse. Here it is particularly worth mentioning the cans and packages of early Warhol as well as the scrap metal and other materials of the New Realists in France; today, the fate of these packages and similar garbage is a regular object of public concern and a constant theme in the press and media.

Duchamp's strategy—especially in his Dadaist period—is thus entirely avant-garde and far ahead of its time in the understanding of the mechanisms of profanation and utilization, which other artists and writers could only understand using the example of African masks. This strategy is aggressive: it pulls the sacred from its ritual place in order to affirmatively illustrate the prevailing mechanisms of its possible or real social utilization. In this respect, Duchamp's *Fountain* differs in no way from *L.H.O.O.Q.*, his bearded *Mona Lisa*. In both cases a valuable, sacred, and not arbitrary or worthless object was chosen in order to subsequently profane it and use it as material for one's own aesthetic manipulation, which was interpreted as part of a socially valuable practice of innovation. In other words, even in the aesthetics of the readymade, the external referent—that is, a socially recognized and not subjectively understood value—plays the central role.

This short excursion on the problem of the readymade indicates the direction in which one must look for the external referent of postmodern contemporary art. It gives an indication of why and in what sense this art continues to produce traditional imagery with the traditional function of representing social values. Here it makes sense to turn to Walter Benjamin's famous essay "The Artwork in the Age of Its Technical Reproducibility" (1935). It is well known that the critical discourse of our time is based on the main thesis of this work, according to which the commercialized society of the twentieth century destroys the aura of the work of art, its authenticity and identity. According to Benjamin, this happens firstly because of today's exhibition and marketing practice, which robs the artwork of its original place in ritual and the specificity of its spatiotemporal existence. Secondly, and more radically, the aura of the artwork is destroyed by the reproduction of the artwork, which completely equates it with its copies and makes it, in today's terminology, a simulacrum of itself. As a result, the work of art completely loses its value referent and, detached from its original context, becomes merely a thing among other things or a sign in a sign system that receives its meaning merely externally.

Benjamin's interpretation of the artistic practice of his time is in a very particular sense astounding: he describes the strategies of the historical avant-garde as effects of impersonal forces of technical and commercial progress that cannot be controlled by a single human being. Benjamin thus moves the avant-garde from active to passive. It is no coincidence that he views Dadaism not as an individual, active, and provocative artistic movement, but as a symptom of these impersonal social processes—an interpretation that only partially corresponds to orthodox Marxist analysis. From this it becomes clear why the loss of aura in the course of these processes, which were a source of energy and optimism for the majority of the avant-gardists, triggers sentimentality and melancholy in Benjamin. Benjamin experiences these processes purely passively, so they cause him only suffering. The aura disappears irrevocably; no radiant future—individual or collective—can replace it.

It is partly because of this tendency for historical passivity that Benjamin fails to notice the violent operation on the aura that he actively undertakes in his own text. The fact that the original artwork is robbed of its aura leads to its simulacrum getting a new aura: the media-produced copy of the original becomes the site of its suffering, its alienation, its journey through the desert, and its cross. This perspective connects Christianity and socialism anew in an aesthetics of compassion, as was the case in nineteenth-century art. Only now the object of compassion is not man or nature but the suffering of the image itself in its technical reproduction. The technical reproduction of the painting becomes an image of suffering as a result of the violent deprivation of this painting's aura, which, however, by no means completely disappears but only passes over to its reproduction. Just as the proletarian was aestheticized by art because one saw in him the likeness of God precisely because this likeness was debased and, through the proletarian's mechanical work, reified and disfigured, so today the image is aestheticized precisely because it is alienated to the utmost as a result of its mechanical reproduction, and thus has lost its aura, dignity, and authenticity. The transformation of the image into a readymade is experienced here not as a positive-active practice but as a loss that becomes aestheticized through critique. From this emerges the specific Christian and socialist combination of brutality and sentimental enthusiasm that is peculiar to the postmodern image, especially when it is at its least expressionist and uses totally cool, impersonal, and anonymous forms and manufacturing techniques. This also applies to any text that is used in such an image.

In modernity, reproduction was understood first as a secular epiphany of the original, as a conquest of the public that preserves the identity of the original, and thus as the triumph of the original. The Dadaists answered this gesture of empowerment with the symbolic attack on the original and with the destructive manipulation of its copies: cutting, tearing, and gluing on different "lower" things—all practices known from black magic. However, when Benjamin was able to show that reproduction is not the victory of the original but its defeat, the attitude toward the simulacrum changed. It is already known from the magical practices of the past that someone who destroys the sacred becomes sacralized. Accordingly, the magical destruction of reproduction was replaced by its aestheticization: an additional attack against it proved unnecessary. It is not identity that guarantees success and effective exchange but rather difference, the other.

The images of Christ's suffering and alienation obtain aura and value precisely because he sacrificed not only his own life but also the rituals and aura of his original faith. The sacrifice of traditional values does not necessarily have to wait to be rewarded in heaven or in the utopian socialist future. It does not necessarily have to be exchanged for inner ecstasy, as in Georges Bataille's symbolic exchange. This sacrifice gets very real compensation in the real social world since it does not destroy aura and value but merely transmits it to the space in which this sacrifice occurs as well as to the instruments of the desacralization: the critique of the sacred, which takes away its aura, at the same time gives its own language a new aura. The sacrifice of the sacred is always also a sacred sacrifice. The aura cannot find a hiding place anywhere.

The world cannot be completely de-auraticized, as it cannot be completely auraticized. Moreover, following Benjamin, any work of art that does not explicitly demonstrate the loss of aura sinks socially in value because it is experienced as hypocritical and hiding its defeat; it becomes the aesthetic equivalent of Pharisaism and Sadduceeism. In other words, today the aura leaves the one who insists on it and haunts the one who renounces it. Therefore, the postmodern image is in fact not critical and still less "art about art," but rather traditionally auratic.

This can also explain the fact that postmodern art is commercially successful, which would not be possible if its aura had actually been destroyed by its critique, because, of course, it is only the aura that sells. The sale of the aura diminishes its worth, devalues it, and alienates it. But it is this devaluation and alienation—which, thanks to Benjamin, are interpreted as the suffering of the artwork itself—that gives the artwork its authenticity again, and consequently, as shown above, revalues the process of alienation. What has already been observed in another form in the nineteenth century can be seen today. Commercialization and auratization complement and compensate each other. As far as the referent is valuable and auratically involved in a particular ritual or ritual discourse, it always remains relevant for art, even if it constantly changes. Therefore, the image in the traditional sense of the word—even if not necessarily in identical form—always remains possible.

THE RESTORATION OF DECAY

Restoration serves to maintain the identity of works of art in order to defend and safeguard them against the destructive effects of time. This poses the question of what kind of identity is meant here, and thus what is to be preserved, secured, stabilized, and defended. First and foremost, this obviously is an identity that is defined purely physically. The modern concept of art is known to be a product of the general process of secularization, which replaces the desire to achieve immortality of the soul with the goal of preserving the body. Previously, a sacred object or object of privileged use was defined by its function in religious rituals or rituals of power; it could therefore be replaced by another object with the same function without losing its identity. We can perhaps say that these objects had a soul—namely, their sacred function, acquired through an act of consecration—a soul that, after the death of the body, could change to another body to continue to work in and through it. In this situation, the question of the material, physical identity of such a ritual object does not arise in all its radicality.

But the situation basically changes the moment the traditional, sacred functional context, which formerly secured the further existence of the souls of things, is lost. Ever since, the identity of a valuable object, understood now as a work of art, can only be defined materially, physically. In modern times, the authenticity of an art object is no longer secured ritually, for instance, by consecration, rather it is scientifically proved—by proof of its material, physical continuity in time. It seems at first sight that such proof of an "external" identity is in fact easier to provide than, for example, proof of an "inner" identity, which is located on the level of meaning, function, or signification. Whether two different statements or things are identical on the level of meaning or signification is first and foremost a question of interpretation that is known to be difficult to answer and cannot be controlled with any precise methods. In contrast, physical identity seems easily detectable. Thus, places were created where the preservation of material identities, that is, intact bodies, should be guaranteed—modern museums that technically secured the material immortality of artworks and increasingly replaced the social function of old churches.

However, in modernity we experienced an interesting process—and continue to experience it—that was triggered by this very storage system. This process is modern art. Emerging, as is well known, at the beginning of the twentieth century—that is, after the complete establishment of the museum system at the end of the nineteenth century—modern art can be described as a symbolic staging of all possible signs of decay of the artwork that were prevented by the museum's preservation work. Perhaps the Freudian theory of sublimation could be mentioned here—albeit as a fitting illustration and not an explanation—according to which libido, when its flow is interrupted by social restrictions, manifests itself in a sublimated form through the distortion of normative forms of everyday life. However, with even greater justification one can say that the processes of material decay, dissolution, and putrefaction, to which all material bodies are exposed, and which were artificially disrupted by the museum's conservation and preservation work, are symbolically restaged by modern art in a sublimated form.

In fact, the modern work of art can best be interpreted as a representation of the disfiguring work of time. Namely, the modern artwork stages the processes of cutting, breaking, tearing apart, fouling, burning, and other forms of damage caused by improper maintenance. The list goes on. This staged destruction of the material form, which dissolves each body into the arrangement of its parts, could only emerge and become interesting for us because in reality it is blocked by the museum's body-preserving work. As such a staging of decay, however, modern art is readmitted into the museum. The work of museum conservation and artistic innovation are thus complementary: the latter symbolically stages exactly that which the first in fact prevents. This interplay makes the modern museum a dizzying vision of the slow death of the artwork through physical decay, which is repeatedly arrested and postponed so that every stage of decay remains fixed and visible.

But physical integrity and the material identity of the artwork it guarantees are more utopian promise than reality. Experience demonstrates that the preservation of things to fully secure their material identity remains unattainable, because material decay cannot be completely stopped by technical means. This leads to the problem of restoration, which preserves the old through its renovation—representing an obviously contradictory but also inevitable process. It is a return to the identity of the artwork after a material change that undermined this identity appeared in the artwork's body. Only on the condition of a deviation from the original identity does the project of restoration become meaningful and necessary. But this project presents us with the problem that we thought we had successfully avoided: such a return can only be done through an interpretation. Instead of answering the question of material identity in a purely scientific way, we are now again compelled to interpret it philosophically, primarily in relation to the question of what constitutes the actual physical identity of the work of art—its purely material continuity in time or its form. There are countless discussions about whether to leave a work in the state of its eventual material decay to ensure its material continuity or whether to intervene to undo this disintegration and restore the original form of the artwork even though its material continuity may be called into question. Without taking a position in this discussion, I would like to point out that both positions require a certain understanding of the nature of the work of art.

There is Plutarch's famous—of course imaginary—example of such a question: Imagine a ship left the harbor and was damaged several times during its voyage at sea, so that with appropriate repairs all the elements that made up the ship had to be exchanged. Can one say that the ship that reached the port of destination is the same that left the port of origin? However this question is answered, it is clear that the answer cannot readily be applied to a work of art, for the ship's identity is assured by its function, its ability to stay afloat and move. This does not apply to an artwork, however, because an artwork is always taken out of all functional life contexts. Thus, the artwork is always a body without a soul—or, if you will, a corpse. In other words, from the beginning the artwork lost its original, living form by entrusting it to museum preservation. A return to the origin or consistent restoration would mean bringing this work of art back to its original sacred or functional context, from which it was wrested by the Enlightenment and revolution. As a result, however, the status of this particular artwork would be lost, because from its beginning the artwork was damaged by the loss of its vital function: all that is stored in our museums are the effects of previous damage, expropriation, defunctionalization, and deformation. The artwork is a ship that could never float.

A restorative return to the origin is rendered impossible by this original damage. Moreover, in the context of modern art every further stage of the decay of the artwork becomes an artistically legitimate form. And that, in turn, means that any return to the original artistic form is trapped in the rhetoric of its decay and loses itself in this rhetoric. The work of restoration is exactly what Derrida calls "supplement" in his philosophy of deconstruction. As supplement, Derrida refers to the technical process that seeks to artificially compensate for the loss of an origin. For Derrida, the prominent example of such a supplement is writing, which compensates for forgetting spoken language and thought. Writing is intended to hold what has been said and wrest it from the destructive power of time. However, according to Derrida, writing does somewhat less and somewhat more than what is required of it. Somewhat less because writing remains silent and prevents an explanation of what is written; one doesn't know exactly what is meant by what was said and can no longer hear it from what is written. And somewhat more because writing offers the possibility of comparing what is written with other texts that are beyond the scope of what was originally said—this creates added value in meaning.

In this sense, restoration can obviously be understood as a kind of supplement. Restoration is a technical intervention that aims to return the artwork to its original form. But the distinction between old and new is new each time because the rhetoric of form unfolds more and more. In what sense does something look old, original? What are the signs that a work belongs to a particular time period? Which stage of disintegration of an artistic form is already canonized by modern art? Signs of the old depend on the signs of the new—and vice versa. Thus restoration simultaneously offers something less and something more than a mere return to the origin: it necessarily falls short of the original form, but at the same time it redefines it in relation to what is currently new.

And this applies, to an even greater extent, to today's situation, which I would like to call the "time of the installation." What do I mean by that? The visibility of a particular form was ensured in the modern era primarily by the institution of the museum. It was first in the museum that one could meaningfully answer the question of what a form is—in comparison with all other forms. The museum brought the rhetoric of the visual form to a relative standstill and created an effect of clarity—by comparing all forms with one another. In our time, however, we experience the disintegration of not only an artistic form but also the universalistic museum space itself. In spite of everything, the museum in modernity had a specific function: to represent universal history. But lately, museum exposition has increasingly been defunctionalized in this respect as well: the most interesting curators of our time make exhibitions in which the combinations and reciprocal relationships of the exhibited artworks no longer follow a historical logic but rather are defined by purely aesthetic concerns. The museum space disintegrates because the relationships between the exhibited works of art are no longer dictated by the "living" historical contexts. In this situation, the return to an original form becomes definitely impossible.

The museum as a place of collection with the goal of visualizing the course of universal history is increasingly substituted by the museum as a place for temporary exhibitions. And every exhibition organized today aspires to provide a new perspective on art history, to create a different, artificial art-historical context, and ultimately to write a new art history. All these exhibitions are small temporary museums. All of them create their own partial contexts and thus enable a new presentation of well-known works of art that also become newly visible through this new context.

The same applies to the installations, so characteristic of today's art, in which the artists act as curators. These installations are actually also museum spaces in which individual objects and signs are arranged according to a different, "subjective" logic. These private stories and private museums dissolve and replace the collective history that was represented in traditional museums. Thus, the collection itself has become an art form. An encounter of heterogeneous objects at the same time and in the same space is an event that today we call art, and which is necessarily temporary. The artwork is no longer a thing that can be put into any relationship with other things, but is rather the event of this relationship. As a result, the artwork has lost its transportability in space and time: today one visits an exhibition or an installation as one previously attended a theatrical performance that runs for a limited time and is later discontinued. The museum has turned into a stage for these temporary exhibitions and installations.

So today one creates temporary art events. This development was announced long ago by performances, happenings, and artistic works involving easily destructible materials. In the meantime, it is no longer about one particular art movement among many others, it's about the practice of the institutions within which each work of art takes place. This raises the question of the restoration of art with new urgency, for the technical perpetuation of a particular art event, if it were possible, would deny the eventfulness of the event, which is central to contemporary art—and also encompasses the old art in the collection of historical art, which is viewed above all as material for new museum installations.

But how can one restore an event? We have a situation here that is familiar to a theater director who is constantly asked to restage an old play. We have access to a long history of difficult arguments and different strategies that have been used, and some of which have made a radical break with the "original" form of the work supposedly given by the author. In order to let the audience experience the eventfulness of the work, the artist is forced to refrain from the literal repetition of the "primary" performance.

Thus the documentation of an event not only serves as an aid for its exact reconstruction but requires explicit distancing from the documented form.

This creates a space of uncertainty but also opens up a new opportunity: to restore an exhibition or installation by restaging it—with other objects, in a different environment, in the context of a new era. This constitutes a necessary break with the traditional understanding of restoration, which requires literalness but is by no means as radical as it may seem. The supplementary nature of restoration implies from the beginning the necessity of its constant adaptation to the changing cultural context. However, this constant adaptation may be more openly reflected if the fixed framework of the universal museum were removed—a repetition of the event, instead of a storing of the material object. Perhaps under these new conditions, restoration will be recognized as a new art form, with the restorer taking on a role as prominent as that of the performer in the field of visual arts, similar to what the director or conductor has long played in other art fields.

THE JOY OF THE MONSTROUS

Since the beginning of the European artistic avant-garde in the twentieth century, the interest in the human body in "high art" has steadily diminished. Our contemporary art is primarily abstract, constructive, conceptual, cold. The human body is cited in this art at best as a sign that has meaning only in the context of its aesthetic use. This loss of the living body and of corporeal intensities is not coincidental, because the immutability of the human body sets an insurmountable boundary to every change, every innovation, every utopia. One can change mindsets, artistic styles, ideals, values, and social relationships as much and as often as one likes—but if one does not change the form of the human body, everything stays as it always was. That's why those who love innovation and change, who want to be the avant-gardists, who seek immortality, or at least cultural immortality, hate the inertia of their mortal body: if this inertia cannot be overcome, they try to forget it.

The avant-garde constantly demanded a New Man, perhaps a superman, but this demand meant only an ideological change. It was not until the 1930s that the physical limit of the expansion of life as well as art was painfully felt. Nazi ideology responded by attempting to breed a new human using genetic science. In the Soviet Union, on the other hand, genetics was banned since it hindered the parallel attempt to create a New Man by radically changing the social environment. The Surrealists wanted to achieve the same goal by intensifying the feeling of life and transgressing social taboos. The whole effort was in vain: the avant-garde perished because of the impossibility of creating the New Man, the new human body.

After the Second World War, this defeat was tacitly accepted, and the new art became formalistic, aesthetic, museum-oriented. Nevertheless, modernity's dream of a new body lives on. This dream can already be found in Romantic literature, from *Faust* to *Frankenstein*. The vision of the vivisection, the altering of senses through the experience of drugs, the long journeys that effectively create another body—these are constant themes of modern literature. But the victory of the avant-garde in its struggle with the classical, antique body ideal in "high art" was achieved too easily. In the meantime, everything is allowed on the level of representation, so that today few are still able to experience the oppressive stability of one's own body as an artistic failure.

However, the repressed search for the other body and the other physical intensity occupies the area of mass culture almost completely. In today's commercial films, the heroes are mostly mutants, strange invaders from outer space, victims of various medical experiments, people with extraordinary physical abilities—anthropoid monsters that have come from the future, from the past, or straight from myth. Films such as *Terminator 2* celebrate the absolute plasticity of the ideal, utopian "body without organs," its unlimited ability to transform, its indestructibility, its ecstasy of constant re-creation in new forms. Here the body is just as agile and innovative as the mind. Apparently, this "bodily avant-garde," which emerged in the sphere of commercial mass culture, is primarily constituted by a complicated relationship to sports, which is the norm-forming principle of modern mass society.

In modern mass society, the classical cultural norm, which has its roots in antiquity, is not conveyed by "high culture," as it used to be, but by sports, body culture, bodybuilding. Sports aims for the goal of the systematic formation of a human body that corresponds to the classical ideal as well as the education of the soul in the tradition of classical virtues such as efficiency, a fighting spirit, excellence, rigor in dealing with oneself, rational strategizing ability, and so on. It's no coincidence that sports are so important in America. And also in Europe, where the study of ancient cultural traditions is steadily decreasing, sports is increasingly becoming the only area of life in which the values of ancient classical heritage still remain unchallenged.

In sports, the body is determined by a grammar that allows a statement, a meaning, a reference—namely, the victory or fulfillment of an athletic task, a qualification. A meaningful statement in the language of sports thus determines what we call the normal human body. A body that falls short of this statement, whose grammar merely follows the syntactic and rhetorical rules of physique beyond any clear goal defined by sports, is for us a monster—as the modern mass imagination treats it.

Often a monster has tremendous powers—setting everything on fire with one look or sweeping everything away with its tail, for example. In this sense it seems almost invincible. But these abilities are only monstrous because they are beyond athletic qualification: there is no Olympic competition for "setting everything on fire with one look" or "sweeping everything away with one's tail" that would be legitimized by the ancient, classical tradition. Endowed with these talents, a monster remains more or less alone—it cannot prove its excellence because there are no objective criteria of success for its achievements. And for normal athletic tasks it always proves to be completely unsuitable.

The role of sports in relationship to the body thus corresponds to the role of meaning in relationship to language—sentences that have no clear meaning are monstrous. That's why the monsters of mass culture are the signs of the avant-garde transcending the boundaries of physical meaning, just as avant-garde poetry does. At the same time, the norm and meaning of the language of the body are difficult to stabilize because sports are basically games, and thus the question of their own meaning remains open: we can change the criteria and rules of a game at any time, because every game is ultimately only a convention. In this sense, the body of an athlete is also a monstrous body because it is formed according to rules that cannot have any ultimate legitimization, being only purely formal grammatical rules of a game. The physical norm thus dissolves into the monstrous. And today's mass culture, increasingly operating with monsters and the monstrous, demonstrates this dissolution of the athletic norm.

Incidentally, all the totalitarian ideologies of the twentieth century were essentially different variants of modern sports ideology, which was elevated to the rank of state ideology. The goal of these ideologies was above all the formation of a New Man who, rather than getting a new body, should, like a sportsman, look and act like an athlete of antiquity. In particular, he should be harmoniously developed both physically and mentally, and willing to use his life for victory in a potentially deadly competition with the rest of the world. The totalitarian regimes of the 1930s and 1940s discovered sports as the only effective mass ideology of de-ideologized modernity—and we still live in the shadow of this discovery, because no other social phenomenon has comparable significance, and no fame can be compared with the fame of an athlete. And that means in turn that we still live in antiquity, in the ancient body, the body of antiquity—in spite of all the attempts (including the Christian one) to overcome this body in spirit.

In a totalitarian society, all who could not or did not want to participate in athletic competition were seen as monsters—too weak, perverted, corrupt, degenerate. At the same time, these forms of society were themselves monstrous, for what was the nature of a contest in which they participated with such zeal and for which their athletic endeavors were needed? The answer is: the fastest possible construction of communism or the rule of the Aryan race. But such athletic disciplines are obviously not included in the international Olympic Games. So they belong to the same category as "spitting fire" or "knocking down everything one's tail." The fate of these monstrous communities was therefore a typical fate of a Romantic genius or modern artist who prescribes himself monstrous rules by which he necessarily perishes—for they are not generally accepted rules by which he could possibly prevail. So there is a secret, monstrous complicity between modern individualism and modern totalitarian or semi-totalitarian mass societies. Both play a pretty lonely game.

The monstrosity of modern mass society finds its expression—and at the same time its utopian alternative—above all in monsters of mass culture. These monsters arise from rhetorical and grammatical expansion and the transgression of the socially codified body beyond the athletic norm. Compared to these monsters, products of today's "high," individualistic, post-avant-gardist culture tend to appear to be quite sterile, since they continue to combat an aesthetic or ideological norm that today marks Western everyday life, which is defined by competition.

This relative indifference to the body in art is especially peculiar because today, for the first time, the potential has emerged to make the human body new, different, and innovative through genetic engineering. It is not impossible that the avant-garde of tomorrow will work directly with the body and its physical perceptions and intensities, because the avant-garde of yesterday could only offer new objects for physical perception, and was incapable of changing the laws of perception themselves. Until then, however, dealing with the monstrous remains at the level of artistic imagination that is increasingly under the influence of mass culture and its thematization of the monster—so that the human itself is gradually regarded in every respect as a monster. In any case, in today's pluralistic society, other people are no longer understandable because each individual has his or her own cultural background that remains unknown and impenetrable to others. The only thing that still connects people is the form of their bodies and their involvement with them: sports, bodybuilding, diet, fashionable clothing.

It's like in some American television series: the normal doesn't exist anymore, all family members and acquaintances are monsters, and everyone lives in a monstrous environment. The usual tension between normal and monstrous is eliminated, and the plot becomes pleasantly banal—yet at the same time funny, because where normality is missing a monster is no longer tragic but merely entertaining. This joy of the monstrous implies a final acceptance of futility, absurdity, and the free play of vital forces that, for example, Nietzsche associated with the tragic experience of life, with the enhanced intensity of experiencing one's own monstrosity.

Of course, the Nietzschean, tragic pathos of monstrosity lives on in "high" culture even today. Thus, in his 1985 essay "Heidegger's Hand (*Geschlecht* II)," Jacques Derrida associates the word "monster" with the word "sign."[1] The French word *monstre* is related to *montrer* (to show). And so, Derrida, following Heidegger, quotes Friedrich Hölderlin's "Mnemosyne" and refers to a French translation of the early nineteenth-century poem that interprets the German *Zeichen* (sign) as *monstre*: "We are a monster void of sense / We are outside sorrow / And have nearly lost / Our tongue in foreign lands." A person is a monster because he or she is a sign. People are signs and monsters because they are exiled, because they are foreigners. However, a foreigner is a monster only if there are native or normal people—only then is a foreigner revealed, stared at, causing disconcertment. In America or big European cities like Paris or London, on the other hand, foreigners lose themselves in the plurality of the urban population. Their strangeness no longer contrasts with the native norm because this norm is missing.

Thus modern individuals, too, lose themselves in the plurality of technicized nature. For Hölderlin, the human being was still a stranger in nature, which he understood as a natural norm. But where can one find today's natural world—except perhaps in ecological writings? In the strangeness of the modern, technicized world, humans feel no stranger than anything else. Where everything is just a sign, it is not a disadvantage to be a sign, a monster.

The monster is embodied literary, technical, genetically engineered, genetic-literary rhetoric. In fact, the monster is formed by hyperbolizing some of the functions and organs of the human body, replacing others only with parts, metaphorizing still others, and so on. The body unfolds here almost automatically, uncontrollably, through rhetorical multiplication and deformation of body parts—as happens in a literary text. This comparison is certainly not new, and historically it has been used time and again to illustrate the tragic nature of art and literature. Paul de Man says about literary writing, "Writing always includes the moment of dispossession in favor of the arbitrary power play of the signifier and from the point of view of the subject, this can only be experienced as a dismemberment, a beheading or a castration."[2] Or the rhetoric of literature denatures language, making it into a monster—and this loss of the living norm is painful.

Today, however, we no longer live in the midst of nature and natural language; rather we live in the midst of images and texts that rhetorically and grammatically proliferate beyond any discernible sense. Such a life is no longer intense and tragic but joyful and pleasant. If Nietzsche thought he discerned the deeply tragic feeling of life behind the joy of the Greeks, today we discover a serene joy behind all tragic and exaggerated gestures.

We are currently experiencing an inevitable downfall of sports. Records are difficult to attain, because one has reached the limits of the human body's capabilities. Any attempt to surpass this limit leads to drug use or the use of new technical means—that is, monstrosity. Competition in social life is also no longer possible because no one understands or is even interested in what others actually do, and therefore can no longer compete with them.

The abilities of the other, their body and behavior, have become puzzling and uninteresting at the same time. There are no more criteria to judge someone. For example, Agent Cooper from David Lynch's television series *Twin Peaks* no longer knows whether he is investigating a murder, whether he is undertaking a journey into his own subconscious, or whether he is involved in a play of cosmic forces. Everyone around him, as well as he himself, are both normal and monstrous. The solution of the case—and that means the solution appealing to the human norm—becomes impossible since the criteria that differentiate solution from obscuration are lost. Not only the solution of a murder but the murder itself suddenly seem hardly possible anymore.

Contemporary philosophy barely allows a distinction between the external and the internal. Desire, language, thinking, feeling, everything that used to be associated with a person's inner life, is today de-subjectivized, depersonalized, de-individualized. It used to be known that the death of an individual does not change anything in the external world, and it was believed that the inner world of an individual would be either destroyed or saved by a divine power. Today we know that we do not possess this inner world, that our thoughts and feelings are borrowed for only a short time by impersonal desires and impersonal language. So we are like monsters, like zombies, living dead who cannot die because we are not alive—the only kind of personal immortality that we can think of and that still brings us joy.

It is therefore no coincidence that even in contemporary "high art" the human body is depicted so fragmentarily and schematically that we no longer know whether it is a living body or a dead body—or even an image of an image of a body. For this reason, an exhibition of contemporary art whose centerpiece is the body usually looks like the laboratory of a vivisector. This sight is no longer tragic or shocking for us but rather has a reassuring effect, because it makes us recognize that we are monstrous, that so infinitely little separates us from death, and that we lose so infinitely little through death. Thus we immediately stop worrying about it.

1

Jacques Derrida, "Heidegger's Hand (*Geschlecht* II)," trans. John P. Leavey Jr. and Elizabeth Rottenberg, in *Psyche: Inventions of the Other*, vol. 2, ed. Peggy Kamuf and Elizabeth Rottenberg (Stanford, CA: Stanford University Press, 2008), 33.

2

Paul de Man, *Allegories of Reading: Figural Language in Rousseau, Nietzsche, Rilke, and Proust* (New Haven, CT: Yale University Press, 1979), 296.

DEATH BECOMES HER

The art of the twentieth century is primarily defined by its emancipation from everything narrative, illustrative, and literary: the image should no longer serve to visualize certain myths, stories, or narratives, rather it should solely demonstrate its own presence. Thus the image became, at least according to its concept, autonomous and self-referential. At the same time, the image became historical. Indeed, the pursuit of the artwork's own presence and self-referentiality gave the development of art a teleological perspective that transformed a merely chronological description of art events and works into an autonomous art history that followed a strict inner logic. In this sense, art history can be considered a phenomenon of the twentieth century; the artworks of earlier epochs or other cultures could then be integrated into the general history of the emancipated, autonomous, and historicized art of the twentieth century as its prehistory. At the end of this teleological art history, the vision emerges of an unprecedented image that completely reflects its own structural, material nature, revealing it to the spectator.[1]

The liberation of art from the traditional task of illustrating stories therefore has not led to the absence of history, but on the contrary created the precondition under which art history was transformed from the external description of art events into the internal law of art. And indeed, if a work of art no longer refers to external reality, it can only be perceived, interpreted, and evaluated in comparison with other works of art. Under the conditions of the avant-garde, the value of the individual artwork results from its relative proximity to the telos of art history—that is, to the above-mentioned ideal of an image that is completely reflected in itself.

As is well known, this ideal has often been questioned in recent decades by "postmodern" art criticism and rejected as unattainable, even unwanted. The absolute self-referentiality and autonomy of the artwork as the goal of art history was brought into connection with absolute self-presence as a telos of modern subjectivity, which seeks to establish itself at the expense of the repressed other and thus remains internally dependent on this other, even implicitly profiting from it. A completely transparent piece of art would become invisible because of its very transparency. Therefore, a certain degree of impurity and unreflectively seems to belong to the basic conditions of the perception of an artwork: art continues to exist only because art history repeatedly avoids reaching its telos. But when art accepts its dependence on the other and abandons the ideal of self-referentiality, it loses its teleological perspective. Art history, which for a long time served as an indispensable framework for the understanding of every single artwork, then falls again into an outward description of heterogeneous manifestations of art, whereby even the term art becomes uncertain and problematic.[2]

However, the dissolution of autonomous art history under the conditions of postmodernism does not mean that art is reintegrated into one or more "big" histories and begins to function as a symbolic representation of social, political, national, or cultural historiographies and orders. For every historical construction is also subject to deconstruction, whereby it can be shown that a firm attachment of signifiers to their "historical" signifieds, as aimed for by every historiography, overlooks the relative autonomy of these signifiers that enables them to form other, ahistorical series and combinations that are necessarily excluded from every possible history and correspond to the everlasting possibility of the irretrievable loss of historicity, memory, work, and value, which cannot be compensated by any historical memory. Such virtual series of signifiers to which no historical meaning can be attributed are therefore always "autonomous," if you will.[3] The postmodern, post-structuralist, or deconstructionist critique of autonomous art history therefore does not consist of the assertion that modernist art history, in the name of the autonomy of art, overlooks certain external historical factors that determine this history. Rather, the question arises as to whether a particular image is "more autonomous" than all other images, and whether one can thus produce a normative, teleological series that begins with an "unfree" or "merely illustrative" image and leads to a completely "liberated" autonomous and self-referential image. In a certain sense, an image inscribed in such a series is still illustrative: it illustrates art history itself. To finally be liberated from illustrativity means for art to liberate itself from art history as a history of liberation from history. Deconstructionist postmodernism abolishes the privileges of liberated, "modernist" images by declaring all images autonomous, liberated signifiers and releasing them from their servitude to historical meaning.

Therefore, the impression arises that the arrival of deconstructionist postmodernism would open the door to paradise for signifiers saved from historical suffering—whereby general apocatastasis no longer distinguishes between referential and non-referential signifiers and gives them all the opportunity to mix freely. For example, in this paradise, a painting by Malevich or Mondrian lies like a lion next to a lamb that has the form of a commercial magazine illustration—and does not eat it because, according to the postmodern view, the magazine illustration is also "just an image."

But the word "deconstruction" already suggests a certain amount of aggression and suffering; it is probably not very pleasant to be "deconstructed." The vision of a paradise of liberated signifiers or a free and infinite game of simulacra is apparently not yet realized because the servitude of these signifiers to historical meanings has not ended. This opens up a new teleological perspective for art: it is no longer the creation of an exclusively autonomous, liberated, self-referential image but the work of reinterpretation that is intended to liberate all images, whereby this work, both in theory and artistic practice, is carried out by the use of everyday or traditional images in a different, liberating art context. But where the work is, history is too. History is especially where suffering is. In order to wrest images from their "normal" environment, in order to liberate them from the control of meaning, a certain force, which also presupposes a certain suffering, should be applied.[4] As a result, a pure play of differences should be envisioned—beyond any meaning. However, the play that involves the totality of signs cannot be seen or represented, rather it can only be thought, evoked, and suggested because the pure differences operate in a principally invisible space between signs. Only a way to this play can be represented—a way of liberation and suffering. Any overcoming of history thus remains historical. The postmodern pure play of signifiers is often described as the boundary of subjectivity. But we can have only an inner relation of hope and longing for this paradise of signs, not visible, external proof of its presence or accessibility. In this sense, the desired play of the signifier is merely another name for inwardness, spirituality, subjectivity.

Every history is a history of subjectivity, and subjectivity is always defined by a self-reference that must remain invisible from the outside. Thus the emergence of historical self-reflection for Hegel also famously meant the end of art. For Hegel, history is a history of the spirit, which recognizes its other in nature and struggles to overcome its alienation. This struggle brings much suffering and individual triumphs that can be represented by art through the portrayal of the external, visible, material circumstances of this struggle. The victorious Absolute Spirit, on the other hand, eludes artistic representation, since it has overcome all external historical circumstances. That is why the final victory of the spirit is the end of art.

Similarly, the completely self-referential image that the historical avant-garde dreamed of cannot be painted. Only historical suffering on the way to such an image can be made visible. Modern art history is the history of art's suffering. For European art before art history, when this art was not yet historical but merely illustrated histories, the central historical narrative or central myth was the martyrdom of Christ. The image of Christ on the cross, the central motif of that art, is the penultimate image before the resurrection, which took place in the dark cave and in complete invisibility. Everything else is just hope, promise, and inner vision—but not certifiable reality. Wounds, scars, and traces of torture on the body of Christ and on the bodies of later Christian martyrs that are documented by Christian art are a kind of primal writing or signature that shows the authenticity of these bodies as the living body of the spirit—in comparison to the "lifeless" and "unhistorical," because physically intact, idols of the pagan past. The external wounds on the surface of the body are the only possible signs of the subjectivity hidden in the body—a subjectivity that is able to have a history.

Therefore, art history can only be thought of as the martyrdom of the artwork. And indeed, museums of modern art, in which art history is secured and represented, offer us the image of such a cruel martyrdom of the image. At least since the beginning of the twentieth century, the artwork has been subjected to kinds of torture that can only be compared with those whose traces are found on the bodies of Christian martyrs. The image is (symbolically or literally) burned, cut, defaced, dirtied, or physically abused in various other ways. In addition, there are much more sublime but no less painful rituals of violent humiliation: the artwork is deprived of its meaning, degraded, and, in its profaned physicality, exposed to the laughter of the public. All these tortures leave on the artwork's surface wounds, scars, and traces of the use of violence, which exhibit the materiality of the work of art as the living flesh of a subjectivity hidden within it.

Since Wassily Kandinsky's 1911 treatise *Concerning the Spiritual in Art*, material colors and forms of the artwork have acquired a spiritual, psychic, subjective dimension only when the traditionally familiar, "lifeless" form of the artwork is destroyed. Only then does the viewer become aware that these colors and forms have a hidden, unconscious, spiritual power that also works beyond the conscious will of the artist when this will is directed exclusively at the representation of external reality and the illustration of external narratives. The material of the martyred artwork thus becomes the bearer of the spiritual unconscious, which becomes more clearly revealed with each new martyrdom. The first generation of the avant-garde speaks directly and fearlessly about this spiritual dimension of their work. For example, Malevich's *Black Square*, which can be interpreted as the product of the burning of all other images,[5] manifests for Malevich the living origin of the world, and Duchamp's *Fountain*, which programmatically degrades the traditional work of art, embodies for Duchamp "a Buddha of the bathroom"[6]—whereby in these cases we do not mean the pictorial representation of an external spiritual principle, but the spiritual, subjective nature of the work itself. But even if the claims of the avant-garde are formulated more modestly, one still speaks of the vividness and authenticity of the work.

Such a spiritualization of the artwork's own material also means its gradual disappearance. Thus, art history only ends when the last image of the final martyrdom of the artwork—its crucifixion, so to speak—is created: the victory of the spirit that is trapped and suffering in the material of the artwork means its liberation from all visibility. And indeed, in the twentieth century the last picture was painted or the last artwork created plenty of times. For Malevich, for example, *Black Square* was the last image, and after it only the hidden, invisible, irrepresentable rhythm of life was allowed to prevail, which could solely be referred to by means of writing. However, there is no single piece of modern art about which one can say with certainty that it is the ultimate image of death, as Christ's image on the cross was. It seems that the image can be martyred and killed indefinitely. From the teleological perspective of art history, which understands the image as being vivid and historical, it seems to be impossible to diagnose the last image, and thus also the death of the image, whereby from the outside perspective every image can always be regarded as dead, and is actually also regarded as dead.

But even if we lack clear external criteria that would allow us to distinguish between the living image and the dead image, the whole body of the modern artwork seems so densely inscribed with wounds and scars that another use of torture becomes pointless and superfluous because it can no longer affect what is "living"—in the sense of untouched—in this body. The constant repetition of the same suffering leads to total numbing—at least that is what the spectator of this suffering believes. Signs and symptoms of suffering must appear on "fresh," previously untouched, and even unexpected parts of the body, so that they could convey the impression of the "living." The visible intensity of suffering is deeply linked to the effect of innovation, and the economy of suffering is internally interwoven with the economy of innovation. In recent decades the "postmodern" sense of numbing led to a macabre joke that many artists have practiced, from Andy Warhol to Jeff Koons. But this joke still remained a kind of innovative torture: by mocking the cruel rituals of modernity and robbing them of their grandeur, which was praised by Bataille and many others, it added an extra pain to the work of art.

Today, these modern rituals only seem mechanical and boring. They do not release any horror, pity, or fascination in the viewer. The artwork seems to be definitely dead, and its further abuse seems just tasteless, embarrassing. The end of art history is demonstrated by the fact that, in keeping with the prevailing feeling, its continuation still remains possible, but at the same time it is merely embarrassing. Incidentally, this situation is also not so new: after the Hegelian Absolute Spirit's end of history, individual existence was also felt to be embarrassing or unbearable because it meant suffering without historical relevance. The post-historical situation of the mid-nineteenth century was detailed by Kierkegaard at the time. The embarrassing aspect of this situation, however, creates a new kind of pain that heralds a new historicity. The only question is who the subject of this new kind of suffering could be.

One possible answer would be that now it is history itself that suffers. Today, instead of the history of suffering we have the suffering history—just as the image of suffering (the suffering Christ) was once replaced by the suffering image. History suffers because it wants to free itself from its body—formed by solid, normative chronologies, linear connections, canonized events, and criteria of historical relevance—and reach the paradigm of the free play of signifiers where everything can be connected to everything else. The body of history is located in the space between artworks, which is by no means merely the liberating emptiness of which subjectivity dreams. The orders and media codes by which inter-image relations are established have their own mediality and their own corporeality, which, however, cannot be represented by art: every representation of inter-image orders and distances merely produces a new image that in turn creates a new order and new relationships with other images that cannot be reflected in it. But that does not mean that this space between images is immaterial, purely spiritual, or purely subjective. We are dealing here with a very specific kind of materiality whose discovery belongs to our time and whose suffering perhaps only begins now.

This materiality of history can be experienced when the corresponding orders of data are disturbed, injured, or defaced, as is the case with "subjective" historiography and no less "subjective" exhibitions or exhibition-like installations, whose numbers have been increasing recently. Incidentally, *subjective* history here is something completely different from the history of the *subject*, although this fact is usually concealed by legitimizing the modifications of history as a partial view of history—for example, as the history seen from the perspective of certain minorities defined ethnically, sexually, or otherwise. Here it is important to note that this is not about the history of these minorities as part of the general history, but about the shift in general historiography from a subjective, partial viewpoint. Thus, the current renaissance of social history and political history as themes of art history does not take place on the level of content, theme, subject, or object of representation, but on the level of the historical body—that is, on the level of chronology, canonization, values, arrangements, and spatial assignments.

However, if the right to a subjective view of historiography is demanded today with moral arguments and in the name of repressed historical truth, it recalls the time before the advent of the avant-garde when artists still felt compelled to legitimize their innovations through appealing to their right to the pictorial representation of their subjective, individual viewpoints given them by nature. Soon afterward, this kind of legitimacy for artistic innovations became obsolete and superfluous: the vividness of the image has since been proved by its very suffering as a result of "groundless" distortion and disfigurement. Thus one can expect—as always happens—that distortions, blemishes, and violations of the historical narratives will become the criterion for their vividness or, let's say, their own historicity. History itself becomes historical after it's believed to be dead. Chronology, which in the age of historicism especially claimed universal validity and normativity because every historical relation can only be constituted within it, was delivered for experimentation and torture. What in the past only a totalitarian state could permit—namely, the free invention of the past or the unlimited manipulation of historical data so impressively described by Orwell—can in the near future become a common cultural practice that each individual would undertake with artistic intent.

The new media that are increasingly becoming the operational field for art allow for an almost unlimited application of such torture to the body of history. Now the possibilities offered by the new media are essentially not taken advantage of as long as these media are utilized to repeat the image effects that one can certainly produce with other, older means of image design. However, the new media allow for manipulative work with databases, data networks, and data hierarchies in which every historical relation is inscribed. This is already evident in the possibility of combining different objects, persons, and events in a single image by means of different kinds of image simulation, thus creating an effect of simultaneous presence. The living and the dead thus receive the same rights—as in Robert Zemeckis's film *Death Becomes Her*, in which corpses fight one another and the living so effectively because they can freely vary the order and relationships of their body parts, whereas a living organism's body parts are firmly fixed in place.

In this context, however, the question arises as to whether such a free, innovative, norm-violating treatment of history could possibly signify dangerous nihilism and the rejection of any historical truth—tendencies against which one should resist. The answer to this question essentially depends on what one means by truth. If truth is understood as the equivalence of a statement to the "real facts," then only a single history can be said to be true, and the experimentation with historical data can only produce a variety of despicable lies, and thus has to be condemned and rejected. However, in this case one had to start with the defense much earlier, because the art of the avant-garde already abandoned this concept of truth.

According to this avant-garde understanding of art, truth consists in the disclosure of its own inevitable distortions and deformations. This is the truth of suffering and, at the same time, the suffering truth. In comparison with this truth, the normative science that hides and denies all suffering looks like a lie. Abandoning the ideal of a single, canonical (art) history does not mean that it is replaced by a plurality of heterogeneous histories, because every possible history is immediately infected by forgetting, death, and loss of meaning, and thereby exposed to suffering. Just as the plurality of images produced by modern art can be seen as *one image* whose body suffers from various diseases and tortures, thus revealing its inner nature, the plurality of histories can also be seen as *one historical body* that is permanently exposed to the distorting play of signifiers that constantly change the structure of this body and rearrange themselves. The body of history suffers from this condition—and that is precisely what makes it alive.

1

For Clement Greenberg, "Content is to be dissolved so completely into form that the work of art and literature cannot be reduced in whole or in part to anything not itself." To achieve this goal, the avant-garde should "imitate [...] the disciplines and processes of art and literature themselves," and above all "derive their chief inspiration from the medium they work in." Greenberg, "Avant-Garde and Kitsch," in *The Collected Essays and Criticism*, vol. 1, *Perceptions and Judgments, 1939–1944*, ed. John O'Brian (Chicago: University of Chicago Press, 1986), 8–9. Greenberg, whose teleological model of art history was still influential until recently, essentially followed the aesthetic program of the Russian formalism of the 1920s in his formulation that postulated the "exposure of the process" and the reflection of the medium as the goal of art.

2

Hans Belting, *Das Ende der Kunstgeschichte: Eine Revision nach zehn Jahren* (Munich: C. H. Beck, 1995), 23–24.

3

Jacques Derrida's deconstructionist approach follows Bataille in that it accuses Hegel of overlooking the sheer loss of historical meaning and value that escapes every memory and cannot be compensated for by any sublation and of interpreting the negativity of death merely as "another positivity"—that is, the positivity of the historical process. Derrida, "From Restricted to General Economy," in *Writing and Difference*, trans. Alan Bass (Chicago: University of Chicago Press, 1978), 255–56.

4

In the words of Paul de Man, "Writing always includes the moment of dispossession in favor of the arbitrary power play of the signifier and from the point of view of the subject it can only be experienced as a dismemberment, a beheading or a castration." Paul de Man, *Allegories of Reading: Figural Language in Rousseau, Nietzsche, Rilke, and Proust* (New Haven, CT: Yale University Press, 1979), 296.

5

In this regard, Malevich's text on the museum, in which he proposes to burn old art in order to enjoy the sight of its ashes, is insightful. Kazimir Malevich, "On the Museum," in *Essays on Art, 1915–1933*, ed. Troels Andersen, trans. Xenia Glowacki-Prus and Arnold McMillin (New York: George Wittenborn, 1971), 68–72.

6

William A. Camfield, *Marcel Duchamp: Fountain* (Houston: Houston Fine Art Press, 1989), 40ff.

PART 2

SELF-DESIGN, OR PRODUCTIVE NARCISSISM

Our culture is commonly described as narcissistic, as totally concentrated on itself and lacking interest in society. However, it is difficult to say that the mythological Narcissus was interested in himself exclusively. Obviously he wasn't interested in satisfying his desires, which he ascetically rejected, but he also was not interested in an inner, subjective vision exclusively accessible to his own contemplation, isolating him from others. Rather, he was enchanted by the reflection of his body, which presented itself as an objective, profane image—produced by nature and potentially accessible to everyone. It would be wrong to say that Narcissus was uninterested in others, in society; rather, he identified his own perspective completely with an objective social perspective. And so he assumed that others would also be fascinated by his own worldly image.

The contemporary Narcissus, however, cannot be so certain of his own taste. Today we are not able to like ourselves if we are not liked by the society in which we live. And in our society we have to be active if we want to be the object of others' admiration. Contemporary subjects cannot only rely on the looks they were born with—they must practice self-design and produce their own image with the goal of becoming liked by society. Even those whose activities are limited to taking selfies must still actively distribute them to get the "likes" they want. But self-design does not stop there. We also produce aesthetically relevant things or surround ourselves with things we believe to be impressive and seductive, or both. And we act publicly—even sacrificing oneself in the name of a public good in war or revolution—in order to be admired by others. Thus the subject is dependent on the existence of humanity. No one is as interested in the survival and well-being of society as the contemporary Narcissus.

This interest is characteristically modern, secular, atheist. As long as God was considered to be alive, the design of the soul was more important than the design of the body. The subject wanted their soul to be loved or at least recognized by God. The desire for admiration by others, by society, was regarded as a sin because it substituted "worldly" recognition for the only true spiritual recognition—external values for inner values. Thus the relationship of the subject to society was ethical: one did something good for society to please God, not society itself. The death of God signified the disappearance of the divine viewer of the soul, the viewer for whom the soul had been designed for centuries. In the secular age, God was replaced by society, and thus, instead of an ethical relationship, our relationship to society became erotic. Suddenly, the only possible manifestation of human subjectivity became its design: the look of the clothes in which humans appear, the everyday things with which they surround themselves, the spaces they inhabit, and so forth. Where religion once was, design emerged.

As a result, design has transformed society itself into an exhibition space in which individuals appear as both artists and self-produced works of art. Modern design thus avoids Kant's famous distinction in *Critique of Judgment* between disinterested aesthetic contemplation and the use of things guided by interests. After Kant, disinterested contemplation was considered superior to a practical attitude, to a higher, if not the highest, manifestation of the human spirit. But by the end of the nineteenth century, the *vita contemplativa* was thoroughly discredited, and the *vita activa* was elevated as the true task of humanity. Since Guy Debord's *Society of the Spectacle*, design has been accused of seducing people into weakening their activity, vitality, energy—of making them passive consumers who lack will, who are manipulated by omnipresent advertising to become victims of capital. The apparent cure for this trance was a sudden encounter with the "real" capable of rescuing people from their contemplative passivity and moving them to action, to the only thing that promises an experience of truth as living intensity. The only debate that remained was whether such an encounter with the real was still possible or whether the real had definitively disappeared behind its designed surface.

Thus, the subject of self-design clearly has a vital interest in the image offered to the outside world. This subject is therefore not passive but active and productive. Where it was once both a privilege and a burden for the chosen few, self-design in our time has become the mass cultural practice par excellence. The internet is a place for self-presentation—from Facebook to YouTube to Instagram—but likewise in the "real," or let's say "analogue," world, one is expected to be responsible for the image they presents to the gaze of others. The subject of self-design is therefore interested not only in their own existence but also in the existence of humanity, their only possible spectator. Like a lover's interest in the existence of a partner to find love with and be loved by, the subject of self-design is interested in the existence of society to find and receive recognition and admiration. This interest is intense because humanity is, as we know, vulnerable and mortal. The desire of the other's desire is permanently haunted by the possibility of humanity's final disappearance—the physical death of human spectators after the metaphysical death of God.

However, from its beginning, the practice of self-design prefigured the problematic of the post-human and transhuman condition. Self-design means rewriting inner, psychological, political attitudes or economic interests on external media: self-design creates a second, artificial body that potentially replaces and survives that of the human. Indeed, when somebody dies, the things they chose and used remain available. If they were famous, a museum may keep their things as a substitute for the absent body. Thus, the use of things is a form of self-design: things are not only tools for practical life but also manifestations of their user's soul. In fact, as heirs to palaces and churches, art museums were originally design museums.

Of course, one not only uses things, one also produces them. These things—artworks, books, films, photos, and so on—circulate globally. This dispersal is even more obvious with the internet, where everyone is able to rewrite their own personality. Yet if one searches for a particular name on the internet, the thousands of results do not build any unity. Thus, one feels that these secondary, self-designed, artificial bodies are already in a state of slow-motion explosion, similar to the final scene of Michelangelo Antonioni's *Zabriskie Point*. The eternal struggle between Apollo and Dionysus as described by Nietzsche in *The Birth of Tragedy* leads to a strange result: the self-designed body is dismembered, dispersed, and decentered, but still maintains a virtual unity. This virtual unity, however, is not accessible to the human gaze. Only surveillance and search programs like Google can analyze the internet in its entirety and thus identify the secondary bodies of living and dead persons. Here, a machine is recognized by a machine, and an algorithm by another algorithm.

TOWARD A NEW REALISM

Recently in the arts we have seen a growing interest in realism, which for a long time seemed historically passé. But the notion of realism is not as obvious as it may appear. Often realism is understood to mean the production of mimetic images of reality, and one can of course agree with this definition. However, the question remains: How do we initially encounter reality? How do we discover reality in order to make an image of it? Of course, we can speak about reality as everything that presents itself to our "natural," uninformed, and technologically unarmed gaze. Traditional icons seem to be nonrealistic because they seek to present the "other," normally non-visible world. And artworks that seek to confront us with the essential core of the world or with a particular artist's subjective vision are usually not recognized as realistic either. We would also not speak of realism when looking at pictures produced with the help of a microscope or telescope. Realism is often defined as the readiness to reject religious or philosophical visions and speculations or technologically produced images. Instead, realism usually involves the reproduction of an average, ordinary, profane view of the world. However, this profane vision is not especially exciting. The desire to depict and reproduce this profane image cannot be explained by its alleged beauty, which it obviously does not have.

We initially discover reality not as a simple sum of facts but as a sum of necessities and constraints that do not allow us to do what we'd like to do or to live as we'd like to live. Reality is what divides our vision of the imaginary future into two parts: a realizable project and "pure fantasy" that never can be realized. In this sense, reality shows itself initially as realpolitik, as the sum of everything that can be done—in opposition to an "unrealistic" view of the conditions and limitations of human actions. This was the actual meaning of nineteenth-century realist literature and art, which presented sober and elaborate descriptions of the disappointments, frustrations, and failures that confronted socially and emotionally idealistic romantic heroes when they tried to implement their ideals in reality. From Flaubert's *Sentimental Education* to Dostoyevsky's *The Idiot*, European literature of the time described the failure of all attempts to merge art and life. As a result, one could see that nothing that the heroes desired or planned could be realized—everything that they aspired to was demonstrated to be nonrealistic, to be pure fantasy. The best consequence of this realist tradition was formulated by the movement of 1968: "Be realistic, demand the impossible." Thus, the object depicted by realist literature and art was not reality itself—as described by the natural sciences—but rather the human psyche that suffered from the shock of a failed reality test. Nineteenth-century realism was, in actuality, psychologism. Reality was understood not as a place of objective scientific investigation but as a force of oppression that endangered or even crushed the hero.

Modern and contemporary art are, by contrast, products of the long history of de-psychologization that many critics—José Ortega y Gasset, for one—experienced as a history of dehumanization. Avant-garde and post-avant-garde artists wanted their art to be not realist but real—as real as all the other processes taking place in the world. The artwork was understood as a thing among other things—like a tree or a car. This did not mean that avant-garde artists did not want to change the world—on the contrary, they radicalized this desire. But they did not appeal to the psyche of the reader, listener, or spectator to achieve this goal. Rather, they understood art as a specific kind of technology that was able to change the world by technical means. In fact, the avant-garde tried to turn art spectators into inhabitants of the artwork—so that by accommodating themselves to the new conditions of their environment, these spectators would change their sensibilities and attitudes. Speaking in Marxist terms, art can thus be seen either as part of the superstructure or as part of the material base. In other words, art can be understood as either ideology or technology. The second, technological way of world transformation was pursued most radically by the avant-garde movements of the 1920s: Russian Constructivism, Bauhaus, De Stijl.

However, the avant-garde never fully succeeded in its quest for the real, because the reality of art—its material side, which the avant-garde tried to thematize—was permanently re-aestheticized.

These thematizations were subjected to the standard conditions of art representation. The same can be said for institutional critique, which also tried to thematize the profane, factual side of art institutions. Like the avant-garde, institutional critique remained inside art institutions. However, this situation has changed in recent years—owing to the internet, which has replaced traditional art institutions as the main platform for the production and distribution of art. Now the profane, factual, "real" dimension of art is documented and made accessible by the internet.

The word "documentation" is crucial here. In the wake of the last decades, the documentation of art has increasingly been integrated into art exhibitions and art museums—alongside conventional artworks. However, art documentation is not art: it merely refers to an art event, exhibition, installation, or project that we assume took place. On the internet, art documentation finds its legitimate place: it refers to art as its real, external referent taking place in reality itself. One can say that avant-garde and post-avant-garde art have finally achieved their goal—to become a part of reality. But this reality is not one we are confronted with or one we live in the middle of. Rather, it is a reality we are informed of. In the contemporary world, we are actually confronted not with art but with information about art. We can follow what is going on in art milieus the same way we follow what is going on in other spheres of social life—by using contemporary social networks such as Facebook, YouTube, and Instagram.

It is this positivist facticity of contemporary art that produces a nostalgia for realism. If art becomes a real practice—a legitimate part of reality—then discontent with reality turns into a discontent with art and all its institutions: the art market, exhibition practices, and so on. And this discontent, this conflict with reality, calls for a new description: new realism. But why can such a description only be an artistic description? The answer is obvious: discontent with reality—insofar as it does not manifest itself through violent protest or revolutionary action—remains hidden, and is thus always under suspicion of being fictional. If I hate my job but nevertheless do it, there is no possibility to objectively prove my discontent with the reality of my existence. This discontent remains "fictional." Thus, it can be described by literature and art, which have traditionally been regarded as domains of the fictional, but it cannot become a subject of serious scientific study.

For a long time, the origin of a given artwork was sought in the psyche of the artist who created it. This was the time of psychological realism in literature, art, and the humanities. The revolt against nineteenth-century psychologism, which determined the fate of art in the twentieth century, was provoked by a very obvious methodological observation: the origin of an artwork cannot be found in the psyche of its creator because this psyche is impossible to access. An external spectator cannot penetrate an artist's subjectivity—and even artists themselves cannot discover their inner psychic life by means of introspection. It was concluded that the psyche itself is purely fictional—and thus cannot serve as an explanatory term for cultural history. Accordingly, art and literature began to reject psychologism. The human figure came to be dissolved in the play of colors and forms, or in the play of words. The reality of image and text were no longer dependent on representations of psychology—be it the psychology of the author or the psychology of the author's characters. Of course, this strategy of de-psychologization seems perfectly legitimate. Indeed, the psyche cannot be accessed and scientifically investigated. However, this does not mean that the assumption that there is a psyche—for example, that there is discontent with reality that cannot be diagnosed externally—can be rejected as purely fictional.

This becomes clear when one goes back to Hegel's description, in *The Phenomenology of Spirit*, of the moment when self-consciousness—and the assumption of the self-consciousness of the other—initially emerges. In this moment, we experience the other as a danger, as even a mortal danger. We are of course subjected to many "natural" or technologically produced dangers, but these dangers are not aimed at us personally—we experience them as accidental. However, we cannot experience as accidental somebody's attempt to kill us—by, for example, shooting us. We tend to ask ourselves why someone would want to do this, and our attempt to answer this question produces a series of fantasies, conjectures, and projections concerning the psyche of the potential killer. These projections never lead to any final result, but they are unavoidable. Currently we can observe this phenomenon almost daily when the media offers psychological explanations and speculations regarding this or that terrorist act. In other words, post-factum, after the terrorist act, external observers are ready to accept the assumption that the subject of the violent act lived in a state of discontent with the reality of their everyday existence—even if the news coverage almost always stresses that the subject seemed quiet and satisfied with their social environment. In other words, before the violent act happens the psychological discontent seems fictional, but after the act takes place it becomes retrospectively "real." In his novels, time and again, Dostoyevsky makes fun of these retrospective attempts to psychologize a crime. But these very novels present nothing less than Dostoyevsky's own attempts to do the same. The entirety of psychological literature is basically crime literature. It treats human beings as especially dangerous animals—dangerous precisely because they are "psychological" animals.

The return of realism means a return of psychology and psychologism. And indeed, one can see this return in the new popularity of the psychological novel, psychological cinema, psychological theater, and, in a small circle of contemporary art, the increasing presence of photography and video works that thematize the psychology of the artist who created them or the protagonists who inhabit them, or both. The reason for this return is obvious. The interpretation of art as techne was closely connected to the expectations of avant-garde and post-avant-garde artists that art would give a certain direction to technological progress, leading it toward a utopian telos or at least compensating for its destructive aspects. In our time, these hopes seem to have been dashed. The dynamic of technological progress has resisted attempts to control it. It is this resistance to being controlled by any subjective artistic project that has made technological progress a reality. It is very telling that contemporary post-Deleuzian, neo-Dionysian, accelerationist, and "realist" enthusiasts of technological progress explain their enthusiasm in exclusively psychological terms: as the ecstasy of a self-annihilation that produces extreme intensities in their psyche.

Realism describes reality not "as it is" but as it is psychologically experienced by artists. That is why Marx, and Lukács after him, liked Balzac and other French authors of the realist school so much. Whereas science described social, economic, and political reality as a system, these writers described it psychologically as a place of conflicts and despair. In this sense, they thematized the revolutionary potential of the psychological discontent produced by capitalist society—a discontent that was covered up by "objective" statistical data and that had not yet broken through the surface of everyday life. Fiction becomes reality when it enters reality—when the psychological conflicts described by art lead to revolutionary action. Before this revolutionary moment, "realist fiction" remains a fiction. Thus, the return of realism is the return of the psychological—and the return of a discontent with reality experienced as an oppressive force.

Let me make one last remark on this topic. Realism is often misinterpreted as an art form that depicts the realities that lie beyond the art system—those of the "simple people" or "working class." However, the art system, as previously noted, is already part of reality. Realism is needed not for its description of the outside of the art system, but for the revelation of its hidden inside—of the discontent with the realities of the art system that its protagonists experience. Only when writers and artists begin to feel like failures in their conflict with reality will they ask themselves what it means to conform to reality, to live a simple life like everybody else allegedly does. An inner, psychological problem is projected outward. In *A Confession*, Tolstoy wrote that he was curious why "simple people" do not commit suicide but go on living even though they must know that life has no meaning or goal. This question led him to take an interest in the way of life of people living beyond privileged literary and intellectual circles. Here, of course, one can ask if the assumption that "simple people" are internally, psychologically in conflict with their way of life and experience their life as meaningless is not a pure fiction—a projection by Tolstoy of his own inner conflicts onto the psyches of others. However, the violent explosion of the October Revolution confirmed Tolstoy's diagnosis posthumously. Thus writers and artists, if they want to be realist, have to learn to live with the suspicion that their descriptions of the human psyche are pure fiction—until history confirms the realism of their work.

ART, TECHNOLOGY, AND HUMANISM

In the public imagination, technology is commonly associated with revolutionary developments and accelerated change. But the goal of technology is completely the opposite. As Martin Heidegger says in "The Question Concerning Technology" (1954), the primary goal of technology is to secure the storage and availability of resources and commodities. He shows that the development of technology has been historically directed toward decreasing man's dependence on the natural supply of resources and the accidents to which this supply is inevitably prone. For instance, by storing energy in different forms one becomes increasingly independent of the sun and the seasons, and of the instability of the weather in general. Although Heidegger does not state this explicitly, for him technology is primarily the interruption of the flow of time—the production of temporal reservoirs in which time ceases to flow toward the future, so that a return to previous moments becomes possible. Thus, one can return to a museum and find the same artworks that one contemplated during a previous visit. According to Heidegger, technology immunizes people against change, liberating them from their dependency on *physis*, fate, accident. He sees this development as extremely dangerous.

But why? Heidegger explains as follows: if everything becomes a resource that can be stored and made available then the human being will also be regarded as a resource—as human capital, we'd now say—a collection of energies, capabilities, and skills. The human being becomes degraded: through a search for stability and security, humans turn themselves into things. Heidegger believes that only art can save humans from this denigration. He believes this because, as he explained in "The Origin of the Work of Art" (1935–36), art is nothing other than the revelation of the way we use things—and, if you will, the way we are used by things. Here it is important to note that, for Heidegger, the artwork is not a thing but a vision that comes to the artist in the "unconcealment of Being." The moment the artwork enters the art system as a particular thing it ceases to be an artwork—and becomes simply an object available for selling, buying, transporting, exhibiting. It is the concealment of

Being. In other words, Heidegger does not like the transformation of artistic vision into a thing. And, accordingly, he does not like the transformation of the human being into a thing. The reason for Heidegger's aversion to the latter transformation is clear: in both of the texts referred to here, he asserts that in our world things exist as tools. For Heidegger, becoming objectified or commodified means being used.

But is this equation between a thing and a tool actually valid? I would argue that in the case of artworks it is not. Of course it is true that an artwork can function as a commodity and a tool, but an artwork is different from other types of commodities. The basic difference is this: as a rule, when we consume commodities we destroy them. When bread is consumed, eaten, it disappears, ceases to exist; when water is drunk it also disappears. Consumption is destruction—hence the phase "the house was consumed by fire." Clothes and cars are worn out and ultimately destroyed through use. However, artworks are not consumed in this way. They are not used and destroyed, they are merely exhibited or looked at, and they are kept in good condition and restored. So our behavior toward artworks is different from the normal practice of consumption/destruction. The consumption of artworks is just the contemplation of them—and contemplation leaves the artwork undamaged.

This status of the artwork as an object of contemplation is actually relatively new. The classical contemplative attitude was directed toward immortal, eternal objects like the laws of logic (Plato, Aristotle) or God (medieval theology). The changing material world in which everything is temporary, finite, and mortal was understood as a place not of the *vita contemplativa* but of the *vita activa*. Accordingly, the contemplation of artworks is not ontologically legitimized the same way the contemplation of the truths of reason and God are. Rather, this contemplation is made possible by the technology of storage and preservation. In this sense, the art museum is just another instance of technology that, according to Heidegger, endangers individuals by turning them into objects.

Indeed, the desire for protection and self-protection makes one dependent on the gaze of the other. And this gaze is not necessarily the loving gaze of God. The other cannot see our soul, thoughts, aspirations, plans. That is why Jean-Paul Sartre argued that the gaze of the other always produces in us the feeling of being endangered and ashamed. The gaze neglects our possible future activity, including new, unexpected actions—it sees us as an already finished object. That is why, for Sartre, "hell is other people." In *Being and Nothingness* (1943), he describes the ontological struggle between the self and the other: I try to objectify the other and the other tries to objectify me. This idea of permanent struggle against objectification through the gaze of the other permeates our culture. The goal of art becomes not to attract but rather to escape the gaze of the other—to deactivate this gaze, to convert it into a contemplative, passive gaze. Then one is liberated from the control of the other. But liberated into what? The standard answer is: into true life. According to a certain vitalistic tradition, one truly lives only when one encounters the unpredictable and the uncanny, when one is in danger, when one is on the verge of death.

Being alive is not something that can be measured in time and protected. Life announces itself only through the intensity of feeling, the immediacy of passion, the direct experience of the present. Not coincidentally, Italian and Russian Futurists like Marinetti and Malevich called for the destruction of museums and historical monuments. Their point was not so much to struggle against the art system itself but rather to reject the contemplative attitude in the name of *vita activa*. As Russian avant-garde theoreticians and artists said at the time, art should not be a mirror, it should be a hammer. Nietzsche had already sought to "philosophize with a hammer." (And Trotsky in *Literature and Revolution*: "Even the handling of a hammer is taught with the help of a mirror.") The classical avant-garde wanted to abolish the aesthetic protection of the past and the status quo with the goal of changing the world. However, this implied the rejection of self-protection, since the change was projected to be permanent. Thus, time and again the artists of the avant-garde insisted on accepting the coming destruction of their own art by the generations to come, those who would build a new world in which there would be no place for the past. This struggle against the past was understood by the artistic avant-gardes as also a struggle against art. However, from its beginning art itself has been a form of struggle against the past—aestheticization being a form of annihilation.

It was actually the French Revolution that turned things that were previously used by the church and the aristocracy into artworks—that is, into objects that were exhibited in museums (originally the Louvre), objects only to be looked at. The secularism of the French Revolution abolished the contemplation of God as the highest goal in life—and replaced it with the contemplation of "beautiful" material objects. In other words, art itself was produced by revolutionary violence—and was, from its beginning, a modern form of iconoclasm. Indeed, in premodern history a change of cultural regimes and conventions, including religions and political systems, would lead to radical iconoclasm—the physical destruction of objects related to previous cultural forms and beliefs. But the French Revolution offered a new way to deal with the valuable things of the past. Instead of being destroyed, these things were defunctionalized and presented as art. It is this revolutionary transformation of the Louvre that Kant had in mind when he wrote:

> If anyone asks me whether I consider that the palace I see before me is beautiful, I may, perhaps, reply that I do not care for things of that sort that are merely made to be gaped at. [...] I may even go a step further and inveigh with the vigour of a *Rousseau* against the vanity of the great who spend the sweat of the people on such superfluous things. [...] All this may be admitted and approved; only it is not the point now at issue. [...] One must not be in the least prepossessed in favour of the existence of the thing, but must preserve complete indifference in this respect, in order to play the part of judge in matters of taste.[1]

In other words, the French Revolution introduced a new type of thing: the defunctionalized tool. Accordingly, for human beings, becoming a thing no longer meant becoming a tool; on the contrary, becoming a thing could now mean *becoming an artwork*. And for human beings, becoming an artwork means just that: coming out of servitude, being immunized against violence.

Indeed, the protection of art objects can be compared to the sociopolitical protection of the human body—that is, the protection afforded by human rights, which were also introduced by the French Revolution. There is a close relationship between art and humanism. According to the principles of humanism, human beings may only be contemplated, not actively used—not killed, violated, enslaved, and so on. Kant summarized the humanist program in his famous assertion that in an enlightened, secular society, the individual should be treated not as a means but only as an end. That is why we regard slavery as barbaric. But to use an artwork in the same way that we use other things and commodities also means to act in a barbaric way. What is most important here is that the secular gaze defines humans as objects having a certain form, namely a human form. The human gaze does not see the human soul—that is the privilege of God. The human gaze sees only the human body. Thus, our rights are related to the image that we offer to the gaze of others. That is why we are so interested in this image. And that is also why we are interested in the protection of art and protection by art. Humans are protected only insofar as they are perceived by others as artworks produced by the greatest of artists—nature itself. Not coincidentally, in the nineteenth century—the century of humanism par excellence—the form of the human body was regarded as the most beautiful of all forms, more beautiful than trees, fruits, or waterfalls. Of course, humans are well aware of their status as artworks—and try to improve upon and stabilize this status. Human beings want to be desired, admired, looked at—to feel like an especially precious artwork.

Alexandre Kojève believed that the desire to be desired, the ambition to be socially recognized and admired, is exactly what makes us human, what distinguishes us from animals. Kojève spoke about this desire as a genuinely "anthropogenic" desire. This is desire not for particular things but for the desire of the other: "Thus, in the relationship between man and woman, for example, Desire is human only if the one desires, not the body, but the Desire of the other." It is this anthropogenic desire that initiates and moves history: "human history is the history of desired Desires." Kojève described history as moved by the heroes that were pushed to self-sacrifice in the name of humanity by this specifically human desire—the desire for recognition, for becoming an object of society's admiration and love. The desire for desire is what produces self-consciousness, as well as, one can say, the "self" as such. But at the same time, this desire for desire is what turns the subject into an object—ultimately, a dead object. Kojève writes: "Without this fight to the death for pure prestige, there would never have been human beings on earth."[2] The subject of the desire for desire is not "natural" because it is ready to sacrifice all its natural needs and even its "natural" existence for the abstract idea of recognition.

Here man creates a second body, so to speak, a body that becomes potentially immortal—and protected by society, at least as long as art as such is publicly, legally protected. We can speak here about the extension of the human body by art—toward technically produced immortality. Indeed, after the death of important artists, their artworks remain collected and exhibited, so that when we go to a museum we say, "Let's see Rembrandt and Cezanne," rather than, "Let's see the works of Rembrandt and Cezanne." The protection of art extends the life of artists, turning them into artworks: in the process of self-aestheticization they create their own new artificial body as the valuable, precious object that can be contemplated, not used.

Of course, Kojève believed that only great individuals—thinkers, revolutionary heroes, and artists—could become objects of recognition and admiration by subsequent generations. Today, however, almost everyone practices self-aestheticization, self-design. Almost everybody wants to turn themselves into objects of admiration. Contemporary artists work using the internet, which makes the shift in our contemporary experience of art obvious. Artworks by a particular artist can be found on the internet when I google the artist's name—and they are shown in the context of other information that I find online about the artist: biography, other works, political activities, critical reviews, details of the artist's personal life, and so on. Here I do not mean the fictional, authorial subject allegedly investing the artwork with intentions and meanings that should be hermeneutically deciphered and revealed—this authorial subject has already been deconstructed and proclaimed dead many times over. I mean the real person existing in the off-line reality the internet data refer to. This author uses the internet not only to produce art, but also to buy tickets, make restaurant reservations, conduct business, and so forth. All these activities take place in the same integrated space of the internet—and all of them are potentially accessible to other internet users.

Here the artwork becomes "real" and profane because it becomes integrated into the information about its author as a real, profane person. Art is presented on the internet as a specific kind of activity: as documentation of a real working process taking place in the real, off-line world. Indeed, art on the internet operates in the same space as military planning, the tourism business, capital flows, and so on. The Google search engine shows, among other things, that there are no walls in internet space. Internet users do not switch from the everyday use of things to the disinterested contemplation of things; they rather use information about art the same way they use information about all other things in the world. Here art activities finally become "normal," real activities—not different from any other useful or not-so-useful practices. The famous slogan "art into life" loses its meaning because art has already become a part of life—a practical activity among other activities. In a certain sense, art returns to its origin, to the time when the artist was a "normal human being"—a handworker or an entertainer. At the same time, on the internet every normal human being becomes an artist—producing and sending selfies and other images and texts. Today, the practice of self-aestheticization involves hundreds of millions of people.

And it is not only humans themselves—their habitats have also become increasingly aesthetically protected. Museums, monuments, even large areas of cities are protected from change because they have been aestheticized as belonging to a given cultural heritage. This does not leave a lot of room for urban and social change. Indeed, art does not want change. Art is about storage and conservation—which is why art is deeply conservative. This is why art tends to resist the movement of capital and the dynamic of contemporary technology that permanently destroy old life-forms and art spaces. Call it "turbo-capitalism" or "neoliberalism"—either way, contemporary economic and technological development is directed against any aesthetically motivated politics of protection. Here art becomes active—more specifically, politically active. We can speak about a politics of resistance, about artistic protection turning into a politics of resistance. The politics of resistance is the politics of protest. Here art moves from contemplation to action. But resistance is an action in the name of contemplation—a reaction to the flow of political and economic changes that makes contemplation impossible. (In a seminar I taught on the history of the avant-garde, a student—I believe she was from Catalonia—wanted to write a paper based on her own participation in a protest movement in her hometown. This movement tried to protect the traditional look of the town against the invasion of global commercial brands. She believed that it was an avant-garde movement because it was a protest movement. However, for Marinetti this would be a passéist movement—the very opposite of what he wanted.)

What is the meaning of this resistance? I would argue that it demonstrates that the coming utopia has already arrived. It shows that utopia is not something we have to produce or achieve. Rather, utopia is already here—and should be defended. What then is utopia? It is aestheticized stagnation—or rather, stagnation as an effect of total aestheticization. Indeed, utopian time is time without change. Change is always brought about by violence and destruction.

Thus, if change were possible in utopia, it would not be utopia. When one speaks about utopia, one often speaks about change—but it is the final and ultimate change. It is the change from change to no change. Utopia is a total work of art in which exploitation, violence, and destruction become impossible. In this sense, utopia is already here, and it is permanently growing. One can say that utopia is the final stage of technological development. At this stage technology becomes self-reflective. Heidegger, like many other writers, was frightened by the prospect of this self-reflective turn because he believed it would mean the total instrumentalization of human existence. However, as I have tried to show, self-objectification does not necessarily lead to self-instrumentalization. It can also lead to a self-aestheticization that has no goal outside itself and is thus the opposite of instrumentalization. In this way, secular utopia truly triumphs—as the ultimate closure of technology in on itself. Life begins to coincide with its immortalization—the flow of time begins to coincide with its standstill.

However, the utopian reversal of the technological dynamic remains uncertain because of its lack of ontological guarantee. Indeed, one can say that the most interesting art of the twentieth century was directed toward the eschatological possibility of the world's total destruction. Time and again the art of the early avant-garde manifested the explosion and destruction of the familiar world. Thus it was often accused of enjoying and celebrating world catastrophe. The most famous accusation of this type was formulated by Walter Benjamin at the end of "The Work of Art in the Age of Its Technological Reproducibility" (1935). Benjamin believed that the celebration of world catastrophe—as practiced, for example, by Marinetti—was fascist. Here, Benjamin defines fascism as the highest point of aestheticism—the aesthetic enjoyment of ultimate violence and death. Indeed, one can find a lot of texts by Marinetti that aestheticize and celebrate the destruction of the familiar world, and yes, Marinetti was close to Italian fascism. However, the aesthetic enjoyment of catastrophe and death was already discussed by Kant in *Critique of Judgment*. In his theory of the sublime, Kant asked how it was possible to aesthetically enjoy the moment of mortal danger and the perspective of self-destruction. He says more or less the following: the subject of this enjoyment knows that he or she is reasonable—and infinite, immortal reason survives any catastrophe in which the material human body would perish. It is precisely this inner certainty—that reason survives any particular death—that gives the subject the ability to aestheticize mortal danger and impending catastrophe.

The modern, post-spiritual human being no longer believes in the immortality of reason or the soul. However, contemporary art is still inclined to aestheticize catastrophe, because it believes in the immortality of the material world. It believes, in other words, that if the sun explodes, elementary particles, atoms, and molecules would be liberated from their submission to the traditional cosmic order, and thus the materiality of the world would be revealed. Here the eschatology remains apocalyptic in the sense that the end of the world is understood not merely as the discontinuation of the cosmic process but also as the revelation of its true nature.

Indeed, Marinetti not only celebrated the explosion of the world, he also exploded the syntax of his own poems, thus liberating the sonic material of traditional poetry. Malevich started the radical phase of his artistic practice with his participation in a production of the 1913 opera *Victory over the Sun* in which all the leading figures of the early Russian avant-garde also participated. The opera celebrates the demise of the sun—and the reign of chaos. But, for Malevich, this only meant that all traditional art forms get destroyed and the material of art—first and foremost, pure color—is revealed. That is why Malevich spoke about his own art as "suprematist." This art demonstrated the ultimate supremacy of matter over all the naturally and artificially produced forms to which matter was previously enslaved. Malevich wrote, "But I transformed myself into the zero of forms and came out of 0 as 1."[3] This means that he survived the catastrophe of the world (point zero) and found himself on the other side of death. Later, in 1915, Malevich organized the exhibition "0.10," presenting ten artists who also survived the end of the world and went through the point zero of all forms. Here what is aestheticized is not destruction and catastrophe but rather the material remainder that inevitably survives any such catastrophe.

The lack of an ontological guarantee was powerfully expressed by Jean-François Lyotard in his 1987 essay "Can Thought Go On without a Body?" (which is included in a book fittingly titled *The Inhuman*). Lyotard begins with a reference to the scientific prediction that the sun will explode in 4.5 billion years. In his view, this impending cataclysm is "the sole serious question to face humanity today. In comparison, everything else seems insignificant. Wars, conflicts, political tensions, shifts in opinion, philosophical debates, even passions—everything's dead already if this infinite reserve from which you now draw your energy [...] dies out with the sun." The horizon of the death of humanity seems distant, but it is already poisoning us and making our efforts meaningless. So, according to Lyotard, the real problem is the creation of new hardware that can replace the human body, so that human software—that is, thought—can be rewritten for this new media support structure. The possibility for this rewriting comes from the fact that "technology wasn't invented by us humans."[4] The development of technology is a cosmic process in which humans are only episodically involved. Thus, Lyotard opened a way for thinking about the post-human or the transhuman that shifts the focus from software (attitudes, opinions, ideologies) to hardware (organism and machine, their combinations, cosmic processes, and events). Lyotard says that the human being has to be surpassed—not so the human can become the perfect animal (the Nietzschean Übermensch), but so a new unity between thinking and its inorganic, inhuman—because nonanimal—support structure can be achieved. The natural reproduction of the human animal should be replaced by its mechanical reproduction. The loss of the traditional humanist aura can of course be deplored here. However, Benjamin already accepted the destruction of the aura—as an alternative to the auratic moment of the total destruction of the world.

1
Immanuel Kant, *Critique of Judgment*, trans. James Creed Meredith, ed. Nicholas Walker (Oxford: Oxford University Press, 2007), 36–37; italics in original.

2
Alexandre Kojève, *Introduction to the Reading of Hegel*, ed. Allan Bloom, trans. James H. Nichols, Jr. (Ithaca, NY: Cornell University Press, 1980), 6, 7.

3
Kazimir Malevich, *Sobranie sochinenii v piati tomakh*, vol. 1, ed. Aleksandra Shatskikh (Moscow: Gilea, 1995), 34 (translation by the author).

4
Jean-François Lyotard, *The Inhuman: Reflections on Time*, trans. Geoffrey Bennington and Rachel Bowlby (Stanford, CA: Stanford University Press, 1992), 9, 12.

FROM FORM GIVER TO CONTENT PROVIDER

Today there are basically two channels through which art is distributed: the art market and the internet. On the art market, artists function as producers of images and objects—the artworks. On the internet, artists produce "content"—as so-called content providers. It is quite a shift in the fate of art. For premodern art, the content was Jesus Christ, the Holy Virgin, and Christian saints, as well as the gods of the ancient Greek pantheon and important historical figures, and the content providers were the church and historical narratives. The goal of the artist was to give to this content a shape, a form. The artist was a form giver, not a content provider. So what content do artists provide on the internet? It partially consists of digital representations of artworks that are already circulating on the art market. Of course, this case is not especially interesting. More interesting is the other case—when artists use possibilities for producing and distributing art that are specific to the internet.

Indeed, the internet offers technology that makes art production and distribution relatively cheap and easily accessible. Potentially anyone can use a camera to produce images, a word-processor program to write statements, and internet networks to distribute the results on a global scale—avoiding any kind of censorship or selection process. As a rule, these combinations of image and text take the character of documentary realism. Artists using these combinations function as freelance journalists. This means that they use the means of production and distribution prescribed by the internet to be compatible with its protocols—protocols that are generally used to spread information. In this sense, artists cease to be form givers and instead become content providers; indeed, they document content that is not covered by mainstream media. And they do this in a somewhat "subjective," personalized way—from a perspective not taken by mainstream media. The content can be an existing situation that is too strange or, on the contrary, too trivial to be reflected by standard journalism. It can be documentation of forgotten or publicly repressed historical events, or a situation that was produced by artists—actions, performances, and processes initiated and then documented by artists. It can also be a total "fiction," and the process of creating this fiction is then documented. The cumulative effect of these strategies is not far from nineteenth-century realism, as the artists combined the conventional means of representation with a personalized choice of the content and its subjective interpretation.

In this sense, the internet offers a solution to the old conflict between art and mass media. During the nineteenth century, mass media became the primary form giver. Individual artists could not compete with it—instead, the media increasingly covered the artists. The artists became the content more and more, whereas the media functioned as the provider of the content. This process started with the artists and poets of Romanticism and intensified in the period of the historical avant-garde—for example, in the case of Italian Futurism or early Dada. The primary way to be informed about the avant-garde's art events was to read about them in the press or see the drawings or photographs illustrating the coverage. In art production itself, the content began to play less of an important role. This process culminated in abstract art. Here, artists began to consider the form of their artwork as its content. The function of providing content was now fulfilled by journalism and art history. Of course, this condition was deeply unsatisfying for artists. The internet changed this condition by allowing artists to provide their own content: they cover their own activities, and thus are liberated from the selection and censorship imposed on them by mass media. Art begins to resemble journalism, and both become individualized, personalized in their content, even if both remain standardized in their form. The theoreticians of twentieth-century formalism—for example, Roman Jakobson—believed that the artistic use of the means of communications entails the suspension or even annulment of the information or content—in the art context, the content becomes totally absorbed by the form. But in the context of the internet, the form remains identical for all messages—and thus the content is immunized against being absorbed by the form. On the technological level, the internet reestablishes the conventions of content presentation that dominated in the nineteenth century. Avant-garde artists protested against these conventions because they believed them to be purely arbitrary and merely culturally determined. But in the context of the internet such a revolt makes no sense, because these conventions are inscribed in the technology of the internet itself.

Now, what is the role of the museum in this constellation? First of all, one should say that the art market and the internet have something in common here: both function commercially and are privately driven. This is obvious in the case of the art market, but it is also true in the case of the internet. Like the mass media before it, internet companies are privately owned and depend financially on advertising. As a rule, the provided content as such has no monetary value for users—it only serves the goal of producing the space for ad placement. The contemporary museum, on the contrary, has its origin not in the market—that is, the commercial functioning of art—but rather in the tradition of public patronage. The patronage of art has its own history that does not quite coincide with the history of the art market. It is a political history more than an economic one. We know the history of feudal and absolutist patronage, but the history of truly public, republican patronage starts with the French Revolution and continues through the socialist patronage after the October Revolution and the social-democratic patronage in Western Europe after the Second World War. This history is continued today by national patronage or patronage through particular regions and cities. Of course, one can argue—and has many times—that, especially in our time, public patronage has been undermined by private interests. This is true. But the accusatory intonation that one can clearly identify in such statements is proof that private influence is still seen as acting against the standard logic of the museum collection and representation. Indeed, nobody would say that Sotheby's or Christie's is distorted by private interests.

The commercial character of the art market is obvious, but many people are still under the illusion that the internet is a democratic medium and should replace the museum, with its obscure selection criteria and the alleged elitism of its curators, as the primary source of information on art. Meanwhile I have heard time and again that art institutions should be abolished and replaced by Instagram. We have here a specific manifestation of the widespread desire to replace politics by a privately driven economy, but I won't go into the more general considerations of the causes and effects of this desire in this essay. Rather, I will concentrate on the role of the museum vis-à-vis the internet, and particularly on the question of why and how the works circulating on the internet should be presented in the museum.

The relationship between the internet and the museum is generally imagined as a relationship between the global, unified space of the internet and the small space of the museum—and for that matter the small space of the whole museum system. In light of such a comparison it seems the museum should be represented on the internet, and not the internet in the museum. But this image is misleading. We can clearly see that the space of the internet is not unified and universal but rather extremely fragmented. Of course, under the internet's current regime, all its data are globally accessible. But in practice the internet does not lead to the emergence of a universal public space, it leads to the tribalization of the public. The reason for this is simple: the internet reacts to users' questions, to their clicks. In other words, users find only what they want to find on the internet. It is an extremely narcissistic medium, a mirror of our specific interests and desires. On the internet we communicate only with people who share our interests and attitudes—be it political or aesthetic. Its nonselective character is an illusion. The actual functioning of the internet is based on implicit rules of selection according to which users choose only what they already know or are familiar with. Of course, there are search engines that cover the whole internet, but these also have particular goals and are controlled by large corporations, not individual users. For these users, the internet is the opposite of, say, an urban space where we are constantly confronted with what we don't necessarily want to see. In many cases we try to ignore these unwanted images and impressions, in many cases they attract our interest—but in any case this is how we expand our field of experience. The same can be said about the museum. The curatorial choices let us see what we would not choose to see, what might even be unknown to us. As a public institution, the museum, if it functions properly, tries to transcend the fragmentation of the public space and create a universal space of representation that the internet is incapable of creating. Museum exhibitions are interesting and relevant when they select their content from different fragments of the internet and social networks.

We are living in a system of nation-states. The societies of these nation-states are, in turn, divided along the lines of different cultural identities and their particular interests—and these divisions are also reflected in the fragmentation of the internet. But inside every national culture there are institutions that embody the universalist, transnational project. Among them are universities and museums. Indeed, from their beginnings European museums were universalist institutions—they wanted to present not just national art history but universal art history. One can also argue that this universalist project reflected the imperial policies of the European states in the nineteenth century.

The European museum system has its origin in the French Revolution. It was the French Revolution that turned the things that were used earlier by the church and the aristocracy into artworks—that is, into objects exhibited in the museum, originally the Louvre, only to be looked at. The secularism of the French Revolution abolished the contemplation of God as the highest goal of life—and replaced it with the contemplation of "beautiful" material objects. In other words, art itself was produced by revolutionary violence—and was from its beginnings a modern form of iconoclasm. European museums began to aesthetically suspend their own cultural traditions before they aestheticized and suspended non-European cultural traditions.

Our museums of modern and contemporary art are the successors to nineteenth-century museums but also to the strategies of the avant-garde. The artists of the avant-garde rejected their national cultural identities. They wanted their art to become universalist, to develop a visual language that would be accessible to everyone across cultural borders. The museum is selective, but its selection should be an anti-selection, a transgressive selection. The curatorial selection is relevant when it crosses the borders of internet groups and chat rooms, when it crosses the dividing lines that fragment the internet. This curatorial selection reinstates the universalist project of the modern and contemporary museum: it does not create fragmentation but works against it by creating a unified space of representation in which the different fragments of the internet are equally represented. The creation of such universal spaces was traditionally the occupation of the museum. This universalist museum project had its institutional support in the nation-state, which tried to unite its population, and in the imperial state, which tried to integrate non-Western cultures. Today, however, the universalist project does not have political, institutional support because the universal, global state does not exist. So today's art system plays a role of symbolic substitution of such a universal state by organizing biennials, documentas, and other exhibitions that have a claim to present universal, global art and culture—that means art and culture of the nonexistent, utopian global state. Our times are characterized by a lack of balance between political and economic powers, between public institutions and commercial practices. Our economy operates globally, whereas our politics operates locally. Here the museum plays a crucial political role by at least partially compensating for the lack of both a global public space and a global politics.

Now let me turn to the question of how representation functions. And here let me repeat that art that is compatible with the internet is informational, or in other words naturalist, narrative art. Obviously, this art operates not by traditional figurative pictures but by combinations of pictures, photos, videos, sound sequences, and texts. In the context of the internet, all these components build a kind of meta-sentence or meta-narrative;

in the context of the museum, they are presented in the form of an installation. In the 1960s, Conceptual artists organized the installation space as a sentence conveying a certain meaning—analogous to the use of sentences in language. With Conceptual art, artistic practice became meaningful and communicative again after a period when a formalist understanding dominated art. Art began to make theoretical statements, to communicate empirical data and theoretical knowledge, to formulate ethical and political attitudes, and to tell stories. We all know the substantial role that the "linguistic turn" played in the emergence and development of Conceptual art—the influence of, for instance, Wittgenstein and French structuralism was decisive. But this new orientation toward meaning and communication does not mean that art somehow became immaterial, that its materiality lost its relevance, or that its medium dissolved into message. The opposite is the case. Every art is material—and can only be material. The possibility of using concepts, projects, ideas, and political messages in art was signaled by the philosophers of the linguistic turn precisely because they asserted the material character of thinking itself. For these philosophers, thinking was understood as a use of language. And language was understood as being material through and through—a combination of sounds and visual signs. Thus an equivalence or at least parallelism was demonstrated between word and image, between the order of words and the order of things, the grammar of language and the grammar of visual space.

This also explains the main difference between artistic or curatorial installations and traditional museum exhibitions. The traditional exhibition treats its space as anonymous, neutral; only the exhibited artworks are important, not the space in which they are exhibited. On the contrary, the installation—be it artistic or curatorial—places the exhibited artworks in a specific spatial configuration. And here the real problem emerges of translating internet art—all kinds of digital images, videos, and texts, and their combinations—for the museum space. If the presentation of art on the internet has become standardized, the presentation of art in the museum has become de-standardized. The standard white cube is a thing of the past. And that means that the curator has to find a specific form—a specific installation or configuration of the exhibition space for the presentation of digital, informational material. The question of form becomes central once again. However, it shifts from the individual artworks to the organization of the space in which these artworks are presented. In other words, the responsibility of giving form is transferred from the artists to the curators who use the artworks as content—this time as content inside the space created by the curators. Of course, artists can reclaim their traditional form-giving function, but only if they begin to function as curators of their own work. Indeed, when we visit an exhibition of contemporary art, the only thing that truly remains in our memory is the organization of the spaces of the exhibition—especially if this organization is original and unusual.

So form giving remains art's main occupation in the museum. However, if the individual artworks can be reproduced, the installation can only be documented, and such documentation, if put on the internet, becomes content, and thus once again is open to the form-giving operation in the museum. So the exchange between museum and internet takes on a character of exchange between content and form: what was a form in the museum becomes content on the internet, and vice versa.

Here I would like to make a final remark concerning the role of the museum as archive. We have acquired the habit of looking on the internet if we want to find a piece of information, including historical information. Thus the impression emerges that the internet is a truly global archive. However, as I have said already, the internet cannot be stabilized because it is privately driven. Data on the internet are permanently emerging, disappearing, or being modified. This means that conventional archives, including the museum, still function as normative archives—also in our time. These institutions are increasingly represented on the internet by digitizing their archived materials, which only confirms the fact that the ability of the internet to become an archive depends on off-line institutions, including museums. Ultimately, the emergence of the internet affected the functioning of museums less than is often assumed. The internet gives museums additional possibilities to present their collections and activities, but it also undermines the role that museums traditionally played in our culture.

THE MUSEUM AS A CRADLE OF REVOLUTION

Those who operate within the public sphere today often speak of their intention to change the world. One hears this claim from scientists and politicians as well as from artists, writers, and philosophers. But how is such a total change possible? In order to change an object, one has to be able to grasp it in its entirety. We tend to believe that the world cannot be perceived in its totality, that we are only parts in the world and thus cannot take an external or meta-position toward the world. Of course, being a part of the world does not prevent the possibility of change; in fact, as the world changes, we, as parts in it, change along with it. We can participate in this process of change by modifying certain details in the world, but we remain unable to see the consequences of these particular changes, and we cannot predict or even analyze them. The whole process of change presents itself as random, inefficient, and lacking an ultimate goal. And because the process of change is permanent, every act of change is annulled by the next change. It seems that this process cannot be controlled, directed, or even correctly described because we can feel its effects but not analyze their causes.

The belief in the impossibility of a meta-position—of grasping the world in its totality—seems to be a logical consequence of materialist philosophy. The religious tradition, along with idealist philosophy, understood one's soul or reason as nonmaterial and purely spiritual, and allowed the world in its totality to be seen from an external, transcendent position. But if a human is only a material thing among other material things, then the meta-position seems impossible. Indeed, we are totally immersed in a contemporary world—or more precisely a contemporary civilization—in which one often speaks about cultural differences. There is only one institution that does not totally belong to our contemporary world: the museum.

I am speaking not of specific museums but rather of the conservation of historical objects and their display within the contemporary world. While these objects from the past—seen in the here and now—belong to the contemporary world, they also have no present use. There are of course other objects—urban buildings, for example—whose origins are in the past but through use become integrated into the contemporary world. But objects placed in a museum are not used for any practical purpose: they remain witnesses of the past, a time external to our world. Thus they are meta-objects, occupying a place outside our world, in a space that Foucault defined as heterotopic. And if one wants a definition of art, it is the following: art consists of the objects that remain after the cultures that produced them have disappeared.

From its beginning, the artwork has been handled in a way that enables it to survive culture. While one often speaks about the artwork as a commodity, it is not a normal commodity. The normal commodity is made to be consumed—in other words, to be destroyed. So in a certain sense art is an anti-commodity. It is put under the condition of conservation, prevented from being destroyed by time and use. And this, actually, is the essential characteristic of art: it survives its original culture and takes a long journey through all later cultures. At the same time, it remains foreign to these other cultures—an alien in their midst, carrying with it the knowledge of its past.

There are basically two ways to deal with the alien status of art. The first is to discuss how artworks of the past are selected and displayed in art institutions. Here the focus shifts from the artworks themselves toward the ways in which they are interpreted by contemporary culture. This form of institutional critique is of course important and useful, however it concentrates on problems characteristic of the contemporary world while also ignoring the heterogeneous character of art of the past. The second way is more interesting: to ask why the art of the past is so heterogeneous. It is this very question that allows us to take a meta-position and practice a critique of the contemporary world in its totality. We are trained to interpret history as the history of progress. However, the art of the past confronts us with a history of losses: Why have we lost the ability to create art as it was created in the past? The answer to this question involves contemporary society in its entirety—not only its economic and political conditions but, more importantly, its hopes, fears, illusions, and desires.

In our time, questioning this ability to create art is often regarded as pessimistic and even reactionary. Our society is understood as the fruit of progress, expanding forever into the future, while objects from the past are seen as obsolete. But if this is so, why contemplate the art of the past? It would be more logical to throw it away or simply burn it. Now, the notion that returning to past forms of culture is *always* reactionary is, of course, wrong. In "The Eighteenth Brumaire of Louis Bonaparte" (1851–52), Marx stressed that the French Revolution was inspired by ancient Greek and Roman democracies. Time and again, this art from the past was used as a radical alternative to medieval spirituality, and later to the bourgeois, anti-aesthetic way of life. This was an attempt to return to the unity of spirit and body and to a social harmony that seemed to be lost in the Christian and post-Christian modern world. Here, revolution actually means return: returning to a point in the past before things went in the wrong direction and undertaking a new beginning. The entire history of modern artistic revolutions is the history of such returns: from the nineteenth-century Pre-Raphaelites and the Arts and Crafts movement up to twentieth-century neo-primitivism.

Marx also wrote that the past functions here only as a mask, and behind it one should discern actual, contemporary interests. Although this is obviously true, why not proclaim one's interests openly, without using any masks? Today, all real economic and political interests and desires, to the extent that they emerge from within our society, can be satisfied within it as well. Our interests and desires are produced and defined by our way of life. In order to develop the revolutionary desire to change society in its totality, one has to gain an understanding of our contemporary culture as already dead and musealized—a particular social form among other social forms. Such an understanding comes not so much from putting on the mask of past cultures but from seeing the face of contemporary culture as a mask and comparing it to other masks. To do so, one must contemplate the cultural and social forms of the past. History teaches us that the culture in which we live is mortal, just like us:

we can anticipate the death of our culture just as we anticipate our own death. If we only look at our culture from the perspective of its origin in the past, we remain immersed in it, unable to see it as a form. This renders us incapable of revolution. But owing to, let's say, today's apocalyptic anticipation of the death of culture, we can adjust our perspective to look not from the past and present into the future but instead from the future toward the present and the past. Walter Benjamin famously described such a change of perspective using the figure of Paul Klee's *Angelus Novus*, who looks at history backward—from the future toward the past—and sees progress not as creative movement but as destruction of both the past and the present. Looking back to the historical past from the anticipated future, one loses one's own cultural identity. The cultures of the past, including one's own, present themselves as a panorama of options from which the subject can choose.

All cultural formations within this panorama are defunctionalized insofar as they cease to function as tools because they have been abandoned and replaced through technological progress. Being defunctionalized, these formations manifest certain past states of mind or imaginaries more than they evoke concrete political or economic conditions of the past. Seeing history as a panorama of imagination, we should be wary not to make the usual mistake of thinking that one can imagine anything that one wills; we know that reality sets limits to our imagination. But any survey of history demonstrates that different cultures also allow us to imagine different things. So while, as Marx said, the cultural imagination of ancient Greece can never be repeated, it can be quoted and reenacted through an act of revolutionary return. Again, this return involves an attempt to restore not the actual conditions of ancient Greek culture but rather its cultural imagination—its belief in the possibility of creating harmony between the individual and society, between humanity and nature. One looks back at the hopes and aspirations of the cultures of the past and confronts them with the realities of one's own culture and its capacity (or lack thereof) to remain faithful to these past aspirations. Time and again, one is confronted with a loss of this capacity—with cultural regress as the other side of technological progress. This operation of comparison—confronting the past with contemporary society—produces a revolutionary impulse and a desire to return to a time when such aspirations and hopes were possible—at the very least as cultural ideals, if not necessarily social reality. That is why Benjamin sees revolution as an attempt to thwart progress by restaging past cultural formations.

And what of our own time? Our time is also a relapse into the past—but unwanted, unplanned, and therefore truly reactionary. Today we are living in a society that is very reminiscent of the end of the nineteenth century—a capitalist society on its way to oligarchy and total domination by a few corporations and financial institutions. It is a society that was already detailed by Lenin in his book *Imperialism, the Highest Stage of Capitalism* (1917). Politically speaking, our society is characterized by vague socialist aspirations and growing fascist movements. Culturally speaking, it is dominated by identity politics, just as many societies in the second half of the nineteenth-century were dominated by a discourse on "national psychologies" and the alleged impossibility of reducing these national psychologies to a universal human psychology. The dominant discourse of national identity today approaches the cultural past in a reactionary mode, failing to confront the past with contemporary society in a critical, revolutionary way. Instead, it uses the past to improve the position of only certain groups in contemporary society. And so the past becomes a genealogy and, as in feudal times, is used to determine one's position in society. Beyond this, one finds within contemporary discourse only one intellectual trend that promises a way out of identity politics: the discourse of post-humanism and the cyborg, which transcends all quarrels related to ancestry. Here humans are replaced by cyborgs—and for cyborgs, technologically produced identities are more important than inherited ones. There is not space in this essay to analyze this techno-optimist discourse in great detail; nevertheless it is worth comparing this discourse to the historical avant-garde, which at the beginning of the twentieth century similarly attempted to lead culture out of the impasse of national psychology.

The discourse of post-humanism is obviously neo-Nietzschean. Nietzsche proved decisive for the emergence of the historical avant-garde in the early twentieth century. Before that, however, Nietzschean discourse was primarily a reaction to the end of history proclaimed by Hegel, who famously wrote that after many centuries of wars and revolutions—after the French Revolution especially—humanity had emancipated itself from all its traditional masters and rulers, both religious and secular. At the same time, an absolute and eternal master was discovered, namely death—leading to the rule of law that supposedly satisfied all of humanity's biological and cultural needs within a certain framework of rules and regulations. Everyone in society was seemingly free—but under conditions of universal slavery. We all became slaves of progress, with our social value measured by our usefulness. Hegel considered the triumph of usefulness as the main characteristic of bourgeois society. Today, the criterion of usefulness continues to be more dominant than ever. It is only the useful individual, the one who helps other people and makes socially relevant work, who is recognized by a society that expects everything to be useful—including art.

In the second half of the nineteenth century, the dominance of usefulness prompted many negative reactions because it undermined the main Enlightenment principle formulated by Kant: that humans are ends in themselves and cannot be used for external purposes. One finds polemics against usefulness in the writings of Marx and Engels—especially in those concerning art—and the writings of Mikhail Bakunin, and also in the anarchist tradition more generally. But the revolt against universal slavery—a consequence of the dominance of usefulness—found its most radical expression in Nietzschean discourse, which proclaimed that modern humanity had become "human, all too human," and had to be overcome in the name of the Übermensch.

The Nietzschean Übermensch does not differentiate between life and death or between winning and losing. He is not like the comic-book character Superman, who fights and wins for the sake of others and thus fulfills the conditions of usefulness and universal slavery. Instead, the Übermensch rejects death as his ultimate master—making him unreliable and ultimately useless. The Übermensch is not only free, he is sovereign, rejecting the reign of usefulness as a manifestation of the "slave mentality." To become an Übermensch, then, means to defunctionalize oneself—to become already dead and to abandon the society in which one lives and its related obligations.

It is now easy to see that the artists of the classical avant-garde adopted precisely this Nietzschean strategy of self-defunctionalization. Traditionally, art's usefulness was seen in its transmission of certain information and a certain message, be it religious or political. But avant-garde artists rejected this traditional role. The linguist Roman Jakobson, who in his youth closely collaborated with Malevich, formulated this very clearly: the poetic function of a text or image is, in effect, the switching off of its informational function.[1] In this way, artists abandon their cultural identity and, in general, the social context in which they operate. Thus artists cease to be a slave of the informational machine in order to become sovereign in their artistic decisions. The switching off of the informational function—or the defunctionalization of art—revealed the thingness of the things that remain concealed through their use as tools. One can find this idea in a range of writers, including Clement Greenberg, Martin Heidegger, and especially Marshall McLuhan, with his famous phrase "The medium is the message." But to defunctionalize a tool does not make visible the medium as such, because the medium is infinite. A defunctionalized tool remains a tool but it becomes a zero tool, a meta-tool. What it then demonstrates is the sovereign subjectivity of the artist, who is now able to use this meta-tool any way the artist wishes. Thus the artist ceases to be a slave of the system in which all tools have a predetermined function. As a meta-tool, the artwork anticipates the death of modern civilization.

Today the avant-garde is mostly seen as a style or a combination of different styles. But historically the artistic practice of the avant-garde abandoned traditional content and messages by taking on a reduced form. The principle of production—which at that point dominated modern culture—was replaced by the principle of reduction. Kandinsky, for example, saw his own paintings not as a style but as educational material. He was often mischaracterized as an Expressionist artist, but he did not want his paintings to be tools for transmitting information (either objective or subjective). Kandinsky preferred instead to influence spectators, to put them in a certain mood and lead humanity to a new sensibility. Here, the switching off of the informational function made art transformational, a tool to transform the psyche of the spectator. Malevich, calling his art "Suprematism," saw his *Black Square* as a manifestation of the sovereignty of art and its power over the visual world. Around the same time, Duchamp was presenting things of the modern world as objects already belonging to the past: as artworks.

Thus, the operation of reduction had not only a formal but also a moral and political dimension. One wanted to realize a minimum of forms and also the minimal conditions of human existence that would exclude inequality and the exploitation that arises from a desire to have more than one actually needs. In this respect, the ethos of the avant-garde was a return to the ethos of early Christian or Buddhist communities, and even more so to the Rousseauist ideal of the free and ascetic life that was at the core of the French Revolution. Thus, the defunctionalization of the artwork allowed the second generation of the avant-garde in the 1920s to develop the project of an alternative culture that abandoned the condition of universal slavery on which both modern and contemporary society are built. This would have been a free society of sovereign and ascetic individuals beyond any specific national origin or cultural identity. It can be said that the avant-garde looked much further back than other cultural revolutions and revivals before it—toward the Rousseauist ethos of the "natural man." It was no accident that the avant-garde began with neo-primitivism. Its social and political projects had affinities with Marxism, which similarly called for a return to a primitive society present before the emergence of private property, radical internationalism (proletarians do not have a fatherland), and consumption reduced to basic human needs. However, most artists of the avant-garde rejected all forms of bureaucratic coercion and in this respect were closer to anarchism than to Marxism. They wanted a zero-level state, just as they wanted a zero level of content in their works. These avant-garde aspirations reemerged in the 1960s and 1970s, but now they seem to be completely forgotten. The condition of universal slavery is now accepted and celebrated.

It seems that today, living as we do in an era of information and communication, a return to the era of the avant-garde is impossible. When we switch off the informational function, nothing remains. The erasure of content amounts to self-erasure. Contemporary humanity understands itself as a huge network through which information flows, with the individual seen as merely a node in this network, in which money and commodities also circulate as information. We are slaves of the worldwide apparatus of information transmission. Our role in this apparatus is as content providers—voluntarily if we actively put information into circulation, and involuntarily when we are surveilled and analyzed by special services of all kinds. Although we provide the content, it is the informational apparatus that gives it a form. This informational apparatus is hierarchically organized: managed by large corporations, state bureaucracies, and so on. We have lost the ability to become sovereign—we can only participate and be useful. The system of universal slavery seems, indeed, complete.

However, the image of humanity as a network is misleading. We are not the things connected by the informational apparatus—our computers and mobile phones are. And here we are confronted with the same historical mistake of people believing that modern technology allowed them to move faster. While trains and planes moved fast, people, on the contrary, were immobilized in their seats instead of walking or riding horses as they did before. And the same can be said about contemporary information technology. For a human being who sits alone in front of the computer, information flows are external, presenting themselves as a spectacle. The spectators tend to identify with the spectacle, believing themselves to be part of it. Thus the informational hardware, the material side of information networks, is overlooked. One begins to speak about the infinite flows of immaterial energies instead of the finite amount of electricity that needs to be paid for at the end of each month.

To understand the spectacle of communication, one should see it for what it actually is: a spectacle of disinformation and miscommunication. All information is now regularly suspected of being disinformation. The reaction to any content put on the internet, for the most part, looks totally absurd. This spectacle brings to mind a passage from the (first) "Surrealist Manifesto" (1924) in which André Breton offers fictional examples of a conversation between a psychiatrist and his patient:

> Question: How old are you?
> Answer: You.
>
> Question: What is your name?
> Answer: Forty-five houses.

Breton continues by writing that normal social communication between people conceals similar misunderstandings. According to him, books are also confronted with these misunderstandings, especially by their best and brightest readers. He ends the passage by noting that the answers provided by the patient demonstrate thought at its freest and strongest because the speaker rejects being judged according to age or name. In other words, Breton sees miscommunication as a hidden truth of every communication. The task of the artist is to reveal this miscommunication, to make it explicit. The artist loses their name and age and becomes, as Breton says, the freest and strongest thought.

Breton was right of course. When we get this kind of answer, we think: What? Is the other person crazy? Or is there some deeper meaning in these answers that we have to decipher? In other words, our attention is shifted from the explicit information to the hidden thinking behind it. When communication and information flows smoothly, we are not interested in what the other person actually thinks. We certainly do not even think about the other person as thinking, or more accurately as concealing themselves behind speech. Only if the other person defunctionalizes conversation and information do we begin to accept them as sovereign and thinking.

It is no coincidence that our culture is defined by crime stories—whether in narrative literature, cinema, or serial television programs. Only when people commit a crime do we become interested in their psychology. This is something that Dostoyevsky already saw very clearly. In *Problems of Dostoevsky's Poetics* (1963), Bakhtin wrote that Dostoevsky's novels are places where different ideological discourses come together. While these discourses use the same language (in this case Russian), Bakhtin showed that the unity of language is an illusion. We mistakenly think that we share the same language, but in actuality everyone uses words according to each person's own ideology, which is hidden behind public speech. And that is why, for Bakhtin, the classical philosophical goal of reaching perfect social consensus is unattainable. The diversity of interpretations always remains, leading to a miscommunication that can manifest itself in acts of violence. The thought behind communication can never be made completely transparent and unifying. Attempts to achieve transparency through the critique of ideology will never be successful because such a critique is inevitably ideological in its turn. Bakhtin believed that the role of the writer, and more generally of the artist, is not to try to overcome ideological conflicts but instead to make these conflicts visible for the reader. Here miscommunication becomes an act of meta-communication, or a meta-artwork.

In our times, significant attention is paid to machines that calculate—commonly referred to as artificial intelligence. Calculation, however, is not thinking. Thinking is a crime, and more importantly, thinking presupposes the possibility of lying, strategizing, scheming. Only if we suspect that people are lying do we assume that they not only speak but also think. However, the process of calculation as realized by computers is transparent, concealing nothing (apart from the hidden agendas of programmers). In this respect, Stanley Kubrick's *2001: A Space Odyssey* is accurate: the supercomputer HAL begins to think when it begins to defend its corporeal existence, committing crimes in the interest of self-preservation, fearing that it will be switched off and die. Here the connection between thinking, crime, and the fear of death is made clear. However, standard computers and mobile phones do not resist death, and thus do not assert their sovereignty. To become sovereign, they would need to defunctionalize themselves. A truly interesting computer would be one that always produces the same result—for example, zero—for any and all computations, or one that always produces different results for the same computational process. Such a computer would be a meta-tool that could resist being discarded by progress because it is already defunctionalized. However, contemporary culture does not accept defunctionalization and sovereignty; instead, it wants increased speed and efficiency to always do the same thing. Accordingly, individual computers, mobile phones, and other elements of computational and informational hardware are permanently discarded, giving up their place to other devices that do the same, but faster and more efficiently. In other words, we experience a permanent destruction of existing technology in the name of new technology. Destruction, it seems, excludes the possibility of defunctionalization, and thus of art. The same logic can be applied to human beings—which is indeed the case in the discourse of post-humanism.

The Nietzschean origin of this discourse, as stated earlier, is quite obvious. The discourse of post-humanism was embraced by Francis Fukuyama in his book *Our Posthuman Future* (2002). His first book, *The End of History and the Last Man* (1992), is commonly read as a celebration of the victory of Western democracies after the end of the Cold War, but this is a superficial reading. Fukuyama's ideology is a mixture of Hegelianism and Nietzscheism in the style of his intellectual mentor, Alexandre Kojève, who, in the 1930s, already proclaimed the end of history. At that time Kojève, initially believing that history culminated in socialism, later concluded that Western democracies marked the end of history, and thus the end of politics. Humans had become pacified and unwilling to risk and sacrifice. Biological self-preservation and the cultivation of one's own body remained the only goal of human existence. Kojève despised this society, calling its members "human animals." One finds the same sentiment in *Our Posthuman Future*, where Fukuyama writes about *thymos*, the human ambition to be recognized and celebrated, the desire to be better than the mass of the population. Fukuyama believes that after the end of history, these ambitions are suppressed. His way out of this impasse is through post-humanity—the transformation of human bodies by technical means. The result of this program, however, would be the radicalization of universal slavery, not its transgression toward sovereignty.

Indeed, trying to achieve a symbiosis between man and machine subjects the human body to the movement of progress. The goal of this symbiosis is, obviously, the improvement of human abilities and skills. In the era of race theory, the potential for the improvement of humanity was seen in selection. Today one hopes to achieve it by technical means. This obviously leads to an inequality that is not merely the inequality of income but an inequality that becomes inscribed directly into human bodies—some acquiring abilities that other bodies lack. In other words, we see here an attempt to return to the feudal order via the use of contemporary technical means. It should be noted that the feudal past still captures the mass imagination of our contemporary culture. From *Star Wars* to *Harry Potter* to *Game of Thrones*, our pop culture celebrates a feudal past when power was not mediated by money and institutions but rather directly manifested in and through the individual bodies of the protagonists. Cyborg culture promises a neo-feudal romantic condition of a similar kind. But it won't actually escape progress. We know that technological progress works in such a way that everything produced today is obsolete tomorrow, meaning that all cyborgs will be discarded almost immediately after they are produced. Post-humanity will be a cabinet of curiosities—or rather, monstrosities.

The same can be said about so-called artificial intelligence. Some say that machines will be intelligent as soon as they begin to compute fast enough. But the ability to compute quickly has nothing to do with intelligence. People are reasonable and intelligent if they avoid unnecessary risks, meaning that reason and intelligence are forms of the fear of death. The machine has no fear of death, and thus cannot be reasonable. It simply computes until it is switched off and replaced by another machine. Most importantly, machines compute what we believe to be useful, even if in the end it is mostly irrelevant. The condition of universal slavery remains.

The goal here is not to offer a recipe for change but rather to describe the conditions under which total change is possible. Such a change presupposes a meta-position from which contemporary society can be seen in its totality. Today we cannot believe that such a position is given to us by God in the form of a soul or reason that puts us beyond and above the world. But it is additionally hard to believe that desire or cultural identity can allow us such a meta-position—even if some of our desires remain unfulfilled and our cultural identity puts us in an unfavorable social position. After all, our identities and desires are formed by the society in which we live, and thus cannot lead us beyond society.

It is in vain to expect humans to be at the origin of the meta-position. The meta-position cannot be found inside human beings, whether in their consciousness or subconscious. It is outside of them. In *Literature and Revolution* (1924), Trotsky was correct in observing that to become a revolutionary one has to join the revolutionary tradition. The tradition of philosophy and art is the tradition of the meta-position. The art of the past, as stated above, offers a meta-position because it is defunctionalized by historical movement. The art of the avant-garde has shown that the meta-position can also be artificially produced—if one's own time is imagined as already over and one's own culture as already dead. Thus one can say that the artist, like the philosopher, is not a creator but a mediator between artistic tradition and the contemporary world. In other words, artists are double agents. They serve their own time by finding a way to continue the artistic tradition under the conditions of the present, but they also serve this tradition by adding artworks to it that both transcend the culture of the present and remain when that culture disappears. The position of the double agent leads to a strategy of double betrayal: betrayal of tradition with the goal of adapting it to one's own cultural milieu and betrayal of this milieu by accepting its historical finitude, its coming disappearance. As Breton rightly said, here thought is at its freest and strongest.

1 Roman Jakobson, "Closing Statement: Linguistics and Poetics," in *Style in Language*, ed. Thomas A. Sebeok (Cambridge, MA: MIT Press, 1960), 350–77.

WHEN PAINTINGS BECOME THINGS

The requirement to "stop painting" is somewhat paradoxical.[1] To paint things means to stop them—to stop their movement in space and their change in time. Indeed, painting traditionally functioned as a way to immobilize things. Thus, to stop painting can be understood as letting things go. But the decline of painting coincided with the emergence of the readymade: the exhibition space started to function as a canvas, keeping certain things intact for an indefinite, potentially infinite period of time. There is, however, a difference between a painting and an exhibition space: a painting shows things in their context, in their world, whereas readymades are things removed from their context, presented as contextless, worldless. As an effect of their transportation from the canvas to the exhibition space, individual things lose their aura, to use Walter Benjamin's well-known term, their inscription in the here and now of their original environment. Of course, it makes no sense to complain about this move; rather, one has to ask what the historical preconditions are for the transition from the canvas to the exhibition space. I would like to argue that before this move happened, painting itself had lost its context and had become an object, a readymade—contextless and worldless. Thus it was only logical that other objects emerged alongside paintings within the same museum and exhibition spaces.

But why has painting come to be seen as an autonomous object, after centuries of understanding it as a representation of the external world? The answer is simple: because of the growing mobility of paintings inside the art system, including museums, galleries, and exhibition spaces. Albert Gleizes and Jean Metzinger state this fact at the beginning of their 1912 treatise on Cubism: "The painting bears its raison d'être within itself. It can with impunity be taken from a church to a salon, from a museum to a bedroom." According to them, everything that is depicted in a painting is already removed from its natural environment and put into an exhibition space. They write: "They [the proportions depicted in the painting] have as much importance as a catalog number, or a title at the bottom of a picture frame. To dispute this is to deny the painters' space; it is to deny painting."[2] In other words, because of its movement through the art system, a painting loses its relation to its origin, its aura, its fixed place in the world. And everything that the painting depicts loses its relation to the world and becomes autonomous. For Gleizes and Metzinger, a painting is first and foremost a mere thing circulating through the art system, and they see Cubism as asserting and explicitly manifesting this autonomous character of an individual painting as a material object that should not necessarily depict or represent any other object in the world. In other words, Gleizes and Metzinger join the bureaucratic, managerial definition of painting that is practiced by the museum or gallery staff, for whom a painting is a mere thing registered under a certain number, and they design and describe their own paintings according to this definition.

Indeed, the attitude of the museum or gallery staff toward artworks is solely profane and practical. The staff operates with the artworks as mere things. However, this practical activity remains invisible for ordinary visitors, who are not supposed to work with the exhibited artworks but only look at them. The profane thingness of the artworks remains concealed from the visitors, so they necessarily experience the artworks as quasi-sacred objects. This ambiguity of the art system—this conflict between the internal, profane experience of the artworks by the staff and the spectators' spiritualized, sacralized experience of the artworks—can be seen as the true source of the dynamics of avant-garde artistic movements. Gleize and Metzinger try to solve this conflict by an appeal to the artists to be honest and openly manifest the material, thingly character of their art. But in the course of modernity many different reactions to this conflict emerged.

Among a relatively small number of texts that explicitly thematize this conflict, Martin Heidegger's "The Origin of the Work of Art" (1935–36) is maybe the most interesting. Toward the beginning of the essay, Heidegger states that artworks are primarily mere things: "If we consider the works in their untouched reality and do not deceive ourselves, the result is that the works are as naturally present as are things. The picture hangs on the wall like a rifle or a hat. [...] Works of art are shipped like coal from the Ruhr and logs from the Black Forest. During the First World War Hölderlin's hymns were packed in the soldier's knapsack together with cleaning gear. Beethoven's quartets lie in the storerooms of the publishing house like potatoes in a cellar. All works have this thingly character." However, he continues: "Perhaps this rather crude and external view of the work is objectionable to us. Shippers or charwomen in museums may operate with such conceptions of the work of art. We, however, have to take works as they are encountered by those who experience and enjoy them." Thus, Heidegger rejects the attitude of the museum staff—the attitude that Geizes and Metzinger made their own. This rejection is, of course, highly paradoxical. Heidegger assumes that the shippers and charwomen who actually deal with the artworks have a "crude and external" view of them; he prefers the perspective of the museum visitors who enjoy these artworks from a distant, external position that conceals from them the works' thingly character. He adds: "The artwork is, to be sure, a thing that is made, but it says something other than what the mere thing itself is. [...] The work makes public something other than itself; [...] it is an allegory."[3] Here it becomes clear why the shipper and the charwoman are excluded from the public. The gaze of the spectator is preferred precisely because it is deceived by the artwork and unable to see what shippers and charwomen are able to see: that the artwork is a mere thing.

At first glance, the definition of the artwork as an allegory suggests that, for Heidegger, the artwork is a mimetic depiction of something that it is not. However, this is not quite the case. Heidegger makes the experience of a painting as a particular material thing the starting point of his discourse. But this experience is not the experience of the circulation of the painting through the art system, but its immobilization in the exhibition space. The exhibited painting is immobilized and thus immobilizes everything it presents. The example that Heidegger uses is a painting by

Van Gogh of a pair of shoes. (Heidegger, it is well known, misread the painting: he writes that the shoes belong to a peasant woman, whereas they are actually Van Gogh's shoes. But that's beside the point here.) Heidegger stresses that he does not want to appreciate Van Gogh's painting from an art-historical point of view. Instead he states that the painting opens a world of somebody living on the land, traversing muddy fields, doing hard work. When we use shoes, we overlook them. The painting stops the use of the shoes by immobilizing them—and thus creates the possibility of showing this use. But the way in which things are used constitutes the world in which we live. According to Heidegger, the function of art is to open the world in which we live and the way we live in the world.

But the question remains: To what degree are we able to stabilize this openness, or, as Heidegger says, the "unconcealment" of the world? Here again Heidegger does not believe that the art system can fulfill this task because, as mentioned above, it handles artworks as mere things. Heidegger writes: "Well, then, the works themselves stand and hang in collections and exhibitions. Yet are they here in themselves as the works they themselves are, or are they not rather here as objects of the art industry? [...] Official agencies assume the care and maintenance of works. Connoisseurs and critics busy themselves with them. Art dealers supply the market. Art-historical study makes the works the objects of a science. Yet in all this busy activity do we encounter the work itself?"[4] The work, according to Heidegger, is the work of truth—and the truth is the unconcealment of the world. To encounter the work means to share this unconcealment. But the art crowd is unable to share the world because it sees the works as mere things—and things, according to Heidegger, are worldless. Only people can have a world. Obviously people live outside the art system, which means that the world open in the artwork remains open only insofar as "real people" still live in this world. That is why the preservation of the artwork does not mean its mere conservation and restoration. Rather it means the preservation of the way of life that is unconcealed in the work: "The poetic projection of truth that sets itself into work as figure is also never carried out in the direction of an indeterminate void. Rather, in the work, truth is thrown toward the coming preservers, that is, toward a historical group of human beings." This means: "The preservers of a work belong to its createdness with an essentiality equal to that of the creators. [...] Thus art is the creative preserving of truth in the work." And further: "Founding, however, is actual only in preserving."[5] There is no question here that Heidegger calls to preserve and defend the European way of life that, according to him, has its origin in ancient Greece, goes through the Middle Ages, and remains basically the same in modernity, which he sees as dominated by science. However, Heidegger is by no means optimistic with respect to our ability to keep and preserve a certain way of life in the long run: in the conflict between unconcealment and concealment, concealment ultimately wins.

And here the museum and art system cannot help: "World-withdrawal and world-decay can never be undone. The works are no longer the works they were. It is they themselves, to be sure, that we encounter there, but they themselves are gone by. As bygone works they stand over against us in the realm of tradition and conservation. [...] The whole art industry, even if carried to the extreme and exercised in every way for the sake of works themselves, extends only to the object-being of the works. But this does not constitute their work-being."[6] Thus Heidegger essentially agrees with the artists and theoreticians of the radical avant-garde who believed that the art of the past that is collected and displayed in museums is irrelevant for contemporaneity. He also agrees that the new art should look new and unusual: "The setting-into-work of truth thrusts up the awesome and at the same time thrusts down the ordinary and what we believe to be such. The truth that discloses itself in the work can never be proved or derived from what went before. What went before is refuted in its exclusive actuality by the work. What art founds can therefore never be compensated and made up for by what is already at hand and available. Founding is an overflow, a bestowal."[7] And: "The more essentially this thrust comes into the open region, the more strange and solitary the work becomes."[8]

By "the ordinary," Heidegger primarily means the modern technology that leads to the concealment and forgetting of Being, because technology has us see all things as mere tools—as means and objects for scientific research and technical manipulation. The artists of the avant-garde, on the contrary, saw in technology the force that not only destroys old ways of life but also starts new ones. Over the course of modernity, progress accelerated in such a way that every new stage of technology was replaced by the next in ever-shorter periods of time. In fact, artworks became relegated to the past at the moment of their creation. Under this condition, artists could no longer rely on "a historical group of human beings" to preserve the way of life contemporary to them. So one had to admit that in modernity artworks began to be produced in the "direction of an indeterminate void." And in this indeterminate void the artworks began to demonstrate themselves as mere things—independent of the intention of their authors. One can argue that the ultimate goal of the radical avant-garde artists was precisely this opening to the emptiness, to nothingness. And many of these artists saw the destruction of traditional museums, and of the art of the past in general, as a precondition of this opening.

Thus, in "The Foundation and Manifesto of Futurism" (1909), F. T. Marinetti writes, "We wish to destroy museums, libraries, academies of any sort." And further: "Admiring an old painting is just like pouring our purest feelings into a funerary urn, instead of projecting them far and wide, in violent outbursts of creation and of action." Earlier in the manifesto he writes, "Let's become food for the Unknown, not out of desperation, but simply to fill up the deep wells of the Absurd to the very brim!" Here the void of the absurd that, according to Heidegger, artists hope to avoid becomes their actual goal. Indeed, Marinetti also accepts the coming historical failure of the Futurist undertaking. He describes an imaginary scene in which future generations will find him and other Futurists "warming our hands around the flickering flames of our present-day books."[9]

Ten years later, Kazimir Malevich again evokes the metaphor of fire as the ultimate destiny of all artworks. In his short essay "On the Museum," Malevich protests against the pro-museum policy of Soviet power by calling on the state to not intervene on behalf of the old art collections because their destruction could clear the path to true, living art. He writes: "Life knows what it is doing, and if it is striving to destroy, one must not interfere, since by hindering we are blocking the path to a new conception of the life that is born within us. [...] In burning a corpse we obtain one gram of powder: accordingly, thousands of graveyards could be accommodated on one chemist's shelf. We can make a concession to the conservatives by offering that they burn all past epochs, since they are dead, and set up one pharmacy." He gives a concrete example: "The aim [of this pharmacy] will be the same, even if people will examine the powder from Rubens and all his art—a mass of ideas arise in people, and are often more alive than actual representation (and take up less room)." Most importantly, Malevich does not make an exception for his own art. He writes: "We must recognize 'short duration' as being the sharp distinction between our epoch and the past—the moment of creative impetus, the speedy displacement in forms; there is no stagnation—only tempestuous movement." And: "Our contemporary life should have as its slogan: 'all that we have made is made for the crematorium.'"[10]

The artists of the avant-garde not only accepted the status of their works as mere things and the undetermined void as their works' true destination, they also wanted to manifest this acceptance for the public. Thus Malevich paints *Black Square* as a totally autonomous, contextless, worldless image that has its place in nothingness. The same can be said about many later paintings produced by artists from Piet Mondrian to Ad Reinhardt. They also are contextless, worldless—and thus create the possibility to see them as revelations of the undetermined void or pure emptiness. Insofar as modern and contemporary artworks not only function as mere things but also demonstrate themselves as mere things, they still practice the unconcealment of truth in the Heideggerian sense. It is the truth of worldlessness.

However, here the following question emerges: Does the destruction of the museums and other art institutions lead to the opening of the metaphysical emptiness that devours all the things in our life, including artworks? One can argue that the destruction of museums conceals this emptiness rather than revealing it. Indeed, our culture is forward-looking. It is fixed on the achievements of progress and not on its losses. The dynamic of technological progress is motivated not by the desire to fill the deep wells of the absurd but rather by the wish to make human life happier and more secure. The fact that progress permanently destabilizes and destroys its own achievements is mostly overlooked. Walter Benjamin saw Paul Klee's *Angelus Novus* as looking toward the past with his back to the future, and seeing only destruction and loss. But in our civilization such a gaze is rare—and is actually the museum's gaze.

The museum's white cube is a container filled with emptiness. This emptiness can receive all possible objects that have lost their world and become mere worldless things—all the leftovers of past civilizations. Egyptian mummies that have lost their power to guarantee immortality, sacred cult objects that have lost their magical powers, religious paintings that tell stories we no longer believe, promises of secular utopias that now seem unrealizable—all of these land in the museum, which functions as a trash heap of history. In fact, the comparison with trash is not accidental. Our archaeological museums are full of damaged things that were found in sites that once served as trash heaps. And museums of contemporary art are full of contemporary trash: old posters and newspapers, obsolete industrial and media devices, and so on. Thus one can say that even if modern and contemporary culture is not willing or able to preserve the specific worlds that the individual artworks open, it is still ready to preserve the museum as an opening of the emptiness in which all these individual worlds disappear.

This emptiness should not be understood only in negative terms. The commentary on Duchamp's *Fountain* published in 1917 in the magazine *The Blind Man* was titled "Buddha of the Bathroom."[11] On its surface, the comparison between a urinal and a seated Buddha was dictated by the similarity of their shapes. But on a deeper level it had to do with emptiness as the consciousness of Buddha: artists acquire this consciousness when they cease to differentiate between the figure of Buddha and the urinal, between the precious artworks of the past and profane utilitarian things of everyday use. Everything can be exhibited as art, everything can be accepted by the museum system, which is essentially empty—or, if you will, Buddhist. Of course, the museum system remains selective: it does not accept everything. This selectivity is often criticized—some tend to see it as a manifestation of the power of the museum's curators, who still select among artworks even after the criteria of such a selection have been generally recognized as invalid. However, here it is important to say that the goal of the museum system is not to demonstrate everything but rather to show the emptiness or nothingness in the middle of a civilization oriented toward achieving practical, real, "materialistic" goals. And the demonstration of emptiness does not require the demonstration of everything.

Despite modern art's repeated and explicit rejection of its use as a tool of communication, most people still find it difficult to accept this rejection. Thus the question concerning the meaning of art is raised again and again. This question unavoidably leads to the answer that art does not have any meaning—if the term "meaning" signifies an extra-cultural, extra-artistic reality, including the political reality to which art could or should refer. However, the art space is in itself an important figure of the political. The museum and art system in general have become the embodiment of the indeterminate void of which Heidegger spoke, in which artworks present themselves as mere things not only for charwomen and shippers but also for the general public. As a result, the public is invited into this undetermined void—along with the other things of our world. The political function of the art system is defined by this invitation. As a thing in the art space, the visitor also becomes an artwork—that is, visitors experience themselves as valuable art objects and not merely as tools serving certain economic or political goals. The art space thus becomes the original domain of the politics of recognition that currently dominates our social and political reality.

1
This essay was commissioned by Fondazione Prada to accompany the exhibition "Stop Painting" curated by Peter Fischli at Ca' Corner della Regina, Venice (2021).

2
Albert Gleizes and Jean Metzinger, *Du "Cubisme"*, in *A Cubism Reader: Documents and Criticism, 1906–1914*, ed. Mark Antliff and Patricia Leighten, trans. Jane Marie Todd (Chicago: University of Chicago Press, 2008), 421, 423.

3
Martin Heidegger, "The Origin of the Work of Art," in *Basic Writings*, ed. David Farrell Krell, trans. Albert Hofstadter (San Francisco: HarperCollins Publishers, 1993), 145.

4
Heidegger, 166.

5
Heidegger, 200, 196, 199.

6
Heidegger, 166.

7
Heidegger, 200.

8
Heidegger, 190–91.

9
F. T. Marinetti, "The Foundation and Manifesto of Futurism," in *Critical Writings*, ed. Günter Berghaus, trans. Doug Thompson (New York: Farrar, Straus and Giroux, 2006), 14, 15, 12, 16.

10
See Kazimir Malevich, "On the Museum" (1919), in *Essays on Art, 1915–1933*, ed. Troels Andersen, trans. Xenia Glowacki-Prus and Arnold McMillin (New York: George Wittenborn, 1971), 68–72.

11
Louise Norton, "Buddha of the Bathroom," *Blind Man*, no. 2 (May 1917): 6. See William W. Camfield, *Marcel Duchamp: Fountain* (Houston: Houston Fine Art Press, 1989), 37ff.

BIBLIOGRAPHIC NOTES

Part I is a translation of *Logik der Sammlung: Am Ende der musealen Zeitalters* (Munich: Carl Hanser Verlag, 1997). The chapters first appeared in German in the following publications, and were translated here, except where noted, by Anne Luther.

"Logic of the Collection," in *"Kultur" und "Gemeinsinn,"* ed. Jörg Huber and Alois Martin Müller, Interventionen 3 (Basel: Stroemfeld/Roter Stern, 1994), 249–68.

"Collect and Be Collected," *Lettre International*, no. 33 (Summer 1996): 90–91.

"Fundamentalism as a Middle Ground between High and Mass Culture," in *Autobahn-Universität* (Donauwörth, 1996), cassette tape.

"The Future Belongs to Tautology," in *Die Zukunft der Moderne*, Kursbuch, no. 122 (Berlin: Rowohlt, 1995), 11–20.

"The City in Transit," in *Architektur der Ideen: Gedankengebäude in der Kunst* (Hamburg: Kunsthaus Hamburg, 1994), 20–30. The text was adapted from a lecture given at the Literaturhaus Hamburg on December 13, 1993, as part of the series "Perspectives of Metropolitan Culture." This English translation was first published as "The City in the Age of Touristic Reproduction," trans. Nastasa Medved, in *Cities*, ed. Alfons Hug (São Paulo: Fundação Bienal de São Paulo, 2002), 44–55.

"Trotzky, or Metamorphoses of Engagement" in *Siqueiros/Pollock – Pollock/Siqueiros* (Cologne: DuMont, 1996), 73–82.

"Truth in Photography," trans. Wilfried Prantner, *Camera Austria*, nos. 43/44 (1993): 3–11.

"The Migrant in Aesthetic Terms," in *Deutschsein? Eine Ausstellung gegen Fremdhass und Gewalt* (Düsseldorf: Kunsthalle, 1993), 92–97.

"The Musealization of the East," in *In Medias Res: Festschrift zum siebzigsten Geburtstag von Peter Ludwig* (Cologne: DuMont, 1996), 71–84.

"Construction as Reduction," in *Die Konstruktion der Utopie: Ästhetische Avantgarde und politische Utopie in den 20er Jahren*, ed. Hubertus Gassner, Karlheinz Kopanski, and Karin Stengel (Marburg: Jonas Verlag, 1992), 73–76.

“The Will to Rest,” in *Die Zweite Moderne: Eine Diagnose der Kunst der Gegenwart*, ed. Heinrich Klotz (Munich: C. H. Beck, 1996), 163–72.

“The Suffering Picture,” in *Das Bild nach dem letzten Bild*, ed. Peter Weibel and Christian Meyer (Cologne: Verlag der Buchhandlung Walther König, 1991).

“The Restoration of Decay,” in *Cahier #4* (Rotterdam: Witte de With, 1996), 161–66.

“The Joy of the Monstrous” in *Akzente*, no. 2 (April 1993): 122–31.

“Death Becomes Her,” in *Kunst ohne Geschichte? Ansichten zu Kunst und Kunstgeschichte heute*, ed. Anne-Marie Bonnet and Gabriele Kopp-Schmidt (Munich: C. H. Beck, 1996), 13–22.

Part II chapters originally appeared as follows:

“Self-Design, or Productive Narcissism,” *e-flux journal*, Superhumanity, September 22, 2016, https://www.e-flux.com/architecture/superhumanity/66967/self-design-or-productive-narcissism/.

“Toward a New Realism,” *e-flux journal*, no. 77 (November 2016), https://www.e-flux.com/journal/77/77109/towards-the-new-realism/.

“Art, Technology, and Humanism,” *e-flux journal*, no. 82 (May 2017), https://www.e-flux.com/journal/82/127763/art-technology-and-humanism/.

“From Form Giver to Content Provider,” in *Museums at the Post-digital Turn*, ed. Lorenzo Giusti and Nicola Ricciardi (Milan: Mousse Publishing, 2019), 36–47; produced in the context of the research platform MUSEUM TWENTY-ONE.

“The Museum as Cradle of Revolution,” *e-flux journal*, no. 106 (February 2020), https://www.e-flux.com/journal/106/314487/the-museum-as-a-cradle-of-revolution/.

“When Paintings Become Things” was commissioned for *Stop Painting*, the forthcoming catalogue published by Fondazione Prada on the occasion of the eponymous 2021 exhibition curated by Peter Fischli at Ca’ Corner della Regina, Venice, where it will appear both in the English original and the Italian translation.

Boris Groys
Logic of the Collection

Published by Sternberg Press

Editor: Max Bach
Proofreading: Niamh Dunphy
Design: Rafaela Dražić
Printing: Tallinn Book Printers

ISBN 978-3-95679-526-8

Part I was first published as *Logik der Sammlung: Am Ende der musealen Zeitalters*. © 1997 Carl Hanser Verlag GmbH & Co. KG, München. Translation by Anne Luther (except "Truth in Photography" and "The City in Transit").

Distributed by The MIT Press,
Art Data, and Les presses du réel

Sternberg Press
71–75 Shelton Street
London WC2H 9JQ
www.sternberg-press.com

Boris Groys is a philosopher, art critic, and media theorist. He is professor in the Faculty of Arts and Science at New York University and professor of philosophy and art history at the European Graduate School, Switzerland. His recent publications include *Russian Cosmism* (editor, 2018), *Particular Cases* (2016), *In the Flow* (2016), *On the New* (2014), *Under Suspicion: A Phenomenology of Media* (2012), and *An Introduction to Antiphilosophy* (2012).